9A17

6/95

15.00

AF764142

A stagnating metropolis: the economy and demography of Stockholm, 1750–1850

Cambridge Studies in Population, Economy and Society in Past Time 13

Series editors

PETER LASLETT, ROGER SCHOFIELD and
E. A. WRIGLEY

ESRC Cambridge Group for the History of Population and Social Science

and DANIEL SCOTT SMITH

University of Illinois at Chicago

Recent work in social, economic and demographic history has revealed much that was previously obscure about societal stability and change in the past. It has also suggested that crossing the conventional boundaries between these branches of history can be very rewarding.

This series will exemplify the value of interdisciplinary work of this kind, and will include books on topics such as family, kinship and neighbourhood; welfare provision and social control; work and leisure; migration; urban growth; and legal structures and procedures, as well as more familiar matters. It will demonstrate that, for example, anthropology and economics have become as close intellectual neighbours to history as have political philosophy or biography.

For complete list of titles in the series, see end of book

A stagnating metropolis: the economy and demography of Stockholm, 1750–1850

JOHAN SÖDERBERG, ULF JONSSON
AND CHRISTER PERSSON
Department of Economic History, University of Stockholm

The right of the University of Cambridge to print and sell all manner of books was granted by Henry VIII in 1534. The University has printed and published continuously since 1584.

CAMBRIDGE UNIVERSITY PRESS
Cambridge
New York Port Chester
Melbourne Sydney

Published by the Press Syndicate of the University of Cambridge
The Pitt Building, Trumpington Street, Cambridge CB2 1RP
40 West 20th Street, New York, NY 10011, USA
10 Stamford Road, Oakleigh, Melbourne 3166, Australia

© Cambridge University Press 1991

First published 1991

Printed in Great Britain at the University Press, Cambridge

British Library cataloguing in publication data
Söderberg, Johan
A stagnating metropolis: the economy and demography of Stockholm, 1750–1850.
1. Sweden. Economic conditions, history.
I. Title. II. Jonsson, Ulf. III. Persson, Christer. IV. Series
330.9485

Library of Congress cataloguing in publication data
Söderberg, Johan, 1950– .
A stagnating metropolis: the economy and demography of Stockholm, 1750–1850 / Johan Söderberg, Ulf Jonsson, Christer Persson.
p. cm. – (Cambridge studies in population, economy, and society in past time: 13)
Includes bibliographical references.
ISBN 0 521 39046 X.
1. Stockholm (Sweden) – Economic conditions. 2. Stockholm (Sweden) – Population – History.
I. Jonsson, Ulf 1944– . II. Persson, Christer, 1941– . III. Title. IV. Series.
HC378.S8S63 1990
330.9487'303–dc20 90–34061

ISBN 0 521 39046 x hardback

CE

Contents

Figures

Tables

Preface

This volume attempts to fill a gap in the economic history of Stockholm. Most of the recent research has dealt with either earlier or later periods than the long phase of stagnation from the mid eighteenth to the mid nineteenth century which we are dealing with. The great period of industrialization starting between c. 1860 and 1914 has been particularly well covered from economic, social, and demographic aspects.

The book grew out of the project 'Stagnating metropolis: growth problems and economic inequality in Stockholm, 1760–1850', for which financial assistance was provided by the Swedish Research Council in the Humanities and Social Sciences. We wish to thank the participants of the Economic History Seminar, Department of Economic History, Stockholm University, and in particular Rolf Adamson, Sven Fritz, Staffan Högberg, and Sture Martinius, for their comments on earlier versions of several of the chapters included here.

Earlier versions of various portions of the book were presented at the conference 'Living Conditions in the Nordic Countries c. 1700–1945', Sandbjerg, Denmark, 1983, and at the workshop 'Methodological Problems in Urban History', Ninth International Economic History Congress, Berne, 1986. We wish to thank the participants of these symposia for their comments and suggestions. We have had the opportunity to discuss various points with many others, including Gunnar Artéus, Tommy Bengtsson, Christine Bladh, Gunnar Fridlizius, Ingrid Hammarström, Arthur E. Imhof, Hans Chr. Johansen, Konrad H. Jarausch, Hartmut Kaelble, Gerry Kearnes, Paul Laxton, Robert Lee, Peter Lindert, Catharina Lis, Herman Schück, Per Schybergson, Lennart Schön, Hannu Soikkanen, Jeffrey Williamson, and Brita Zacke. We also wish to thank Tony Wrigley for many useful suggestions. Naturally, responsibility for remaining shortcomings rests with us.

Chapter 3 on de-industrialization and the manufactories has been written by Christer Persson and the section dealing with mortality in chapter 8 by Ulf Jonsson. The rest of chapter 8 on the economic-demographic system and chapter 4 on labour markets and the informal sector was written jointly by the three authors. The remaining chapters (1, 2, 5, 6, 7, and 9) have been written by Johan Söderberg.

Chapter 2 on Stockholm's growth problems draws on a version published in Swedish in *Historisk tidskrift*. Portions of chapters 5 and 7 dealing with real wage developments and inequality trends have previously appeared in *Social History* and *Historisch-Sozialwissenschaftliche Forschungen*.

The staff of the Stockholm City Archive has been most helpful; Ulla Johanson and Lars Wikström aided us in several ways. Finally, we wish to thank Ulrika Moberg, who typed several chapters in her usual efficient way.

1

Introduction

The economic history of Stockholm can be divided into five major phases.

1 The medieval town developed from a bastion strategically situated at the point where the lake Mälaren meets the Baltic. Already during medieval times the trade in iron, exported from the Bergslagen iron-producing districts, was important. German merchants had dominated economic life for a long time.

Though Sweden entered a new stage in her history after the establishment of a strong national state during the reign of Gustavus Vasa from the 1520s onwards, Stockholm's economy did not change dramatically during the sixteenth century. The population in 1582 can be estimated at 8,000.[1] The town still was of a largely medieval character.

2 The expansive bureaucratic town of the seventeenth-century Great Power era. The reforms of Gustavus Adolphus, starting in the 1620s, were accompanied by a spectacular strengthening of the central administration and the military. The capital also dominated foreign trade. The population in 1674 has been estimated at between 50,000 and 55,000, a roughly fivefold increase since 1620.[2] Stockholm's development during the seventeenth century was similar to that of Madrid, Vienna, Berlin, and Copenhagen, for example. From a European perspective, Stockholm was a more prominent city then than it was during the eighteenth and early nineteenth centuries. The first decades of the eighteenth century, the final part of the Great

1 B. Lager, *Stockholms befolkning på Johan III:s tid* (Stockholm, 1962).
2 G. Utterström, 'Stockholms folkmängd 1663–1763', in *Historiska studier tillägnade Nils Ahnlund* (Stockholm, 1949).

Power era (the Great Nordic War ending in 1721), was a period of strain. The plague of 1710, the largest demographic disaster in the history of the capital, is estimated to have killed 18,000 people.

3 The stagnation period of the century following 1750 is the subject of this volume. Stockholm encountered serious growth problems, with economic development lagging behind that of the country as a whole.

4 The industrializing city of the latter part of the nineteenth and early twentieth centuries. In connection with strong immigration, population grew rapidly from 93,000 in 1850 to 301,000 in 1900 and 502,000 in 1930. In contrast with the manufactures of the eighteenth and early nineteenth centuries the emergent leading industries, mechanical engineering and the printing industry, were far more intensive in the use of capital and skills. Real wages and standards of living improved much. Within the working class there was a shift from unskilled to more skilled labour.

5 The post-industrial city of today, where employment is to a large extent within the public sector. The service sector has grown, while industrial activities have largely been located outside the administrative boundaries of the city. From about World War I onwards, the proportion of the population in the industrial sector of the capital has steadily declined. Since 1950, more than half of the active population has been working in public services and trade.[3]

This volume deals with the economic history of Stockholm during phase 3 above, the long period of economic and demographic stagnation from the mid eighteenth to the mid nineteenth century.

Several valuable studies of the economic and social history of Stockholm take the mid nineteenth century as their starting point.[4] There are some good reasons for doing so. A new type of census, a major source of Swedish demographic research, began in 1860. Somewhat later an improvement in the registration of the population was

[3] G. Ahlberg, *Stockholms befolkningsutveckling efter 1850* (Stockholm, 1958), 127. For an overview of Stockholm's history see S. Högberg, *Stockholms historia 1–2* (Stockholm, 1981).

[4] Major works on the economy and demography of the industrialization period include: I. Hammarström, *Stockholm i svensk ekonomi 1850–1914* (Stockholm, 1970); U. Gustafson, *Industrialismens storstad* (Stockholm, 1976); W. William-Olsson, *Huvuddragen av Stockholms geografiska utveckling 1850–1930* (Stockholm, 1937); G. Ahlberg, *Stockholms befolkningsutveckling*; J. Cederquist, *Arbetare i strejk* (Stockholm, 1980); M. Matović, *Stockholmsäktenskap; familjebildning och partnerval i Stockholm 1850–1890* (Stockholm, 1984).

carried out with the establishment of *rotemansinstitutionen* (1878). Of course, the period 1860–1914 also deserves special attention as the era of rapid and successful industrial and demographic growth, radically transforming the pre-industrial economy.

The preceding stagnation period, covering almost a century, has been analysed far less extensively. Although valuable monographs exist, many aspects of the stagnation period have not been studied.[5] While it is well known that the quality of that part of population registration, which was administered by the church, was less efficient in Stockholm than in other parts of the country, it has been observed that the capital in other respects exhibits important source materials to which there is no counterpart in most other parts of Sweden. Unlike rural regions there are, for instance, Stockholm registers reporting eighteenth-century real estate valuations. There is also a wealth of information on the wages of labour employed by the municipality. The sources relating to manufacturing are very rich.

There were several aspects to the stagnation period. Economic growth was weak and a process of de-industrialization took place during which much of the largest sector, the textile industry, was closed down. Demographic growth was slow, involving a very high mortality, normally an excess of deaths over births, a declining nuptiality and a rising bastardy rate.

Stockholm was a town where death was never far away. The contrast between love of pleasure and death is a central theme of the greatest Stockholm poet of the time, Carl Michael Bellman (1740–95). Death is always at hand as a liberator from a life which never was worth much. Drinking and gambling in the hectic life of the tavern, his characters are well aware that they are journeying towards the graveyard, 'the best of ports'. We find a typical symbolic combination in Cornelius, a gravedigger of Maria parish in southern Stockholm, and also the keeper of a nearby tavern. One used to find him snoring in the graveyard, leaning over a child's coffin with a dusty beer tumbler in his hand. Bellman himself died from tuberculosis, like Father Movitz, one of his Bacchic heroes whose fate he described and feared:

5 E. F. Heckscher, *Sveriges ekonomiska historia från Gustav Vasa II:1* (Stockholm, 1949) contains an important discussion of the causes of the stagnation. On foreign trade see S. Högberg, *Utrikeshandel och sjöfart på 1700-talet* (Stockholm, 1969), on handicrafts E. Söderlund, *Stockholms hantverkarklass 1720–1772* (Stockholm, 1943), and Söderlund, *Hantverkarna* II (Stockholm, 1949), and on manufacturing P. Nyström, *Stadsindustriens arbetare före 1800* (Stockholm, 1955, reprinted 1983).

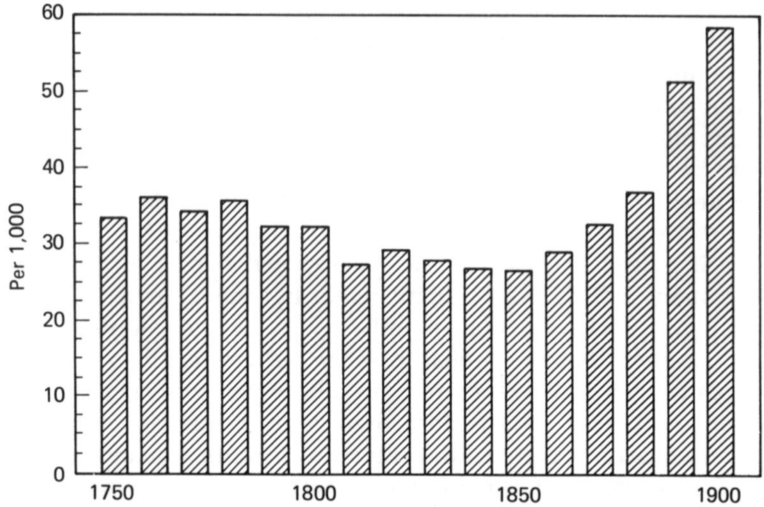

Figure 1.1 Stockholm's population as a proportion of Sweden's, 1750–1900. *Source: Statistisk årsbok för Stockholms stad* 38 (1905); *Historisk statistik för Sverige* 1 (Stockholm, 1955), tables A2, A5.

> Heaven, thou diest! Each cough with fear inspiring
> hollowly grates, and all thy parts repine.
> White is thy tongue, thy frighten'd heart expiring,
> Muscles and flesh, all soft to death incline.
> Breathe! Ah, preserve us! Such fumes from thy throttle!
> 'Cello – Reach me the bottle!
> Movitz, thy health! Skål! Praise the god of wine![6]

An example from the parish of Katarina, the most proletarian one, is illustrative. So many died there that the graveyard was filled to bursting point; a complaint in 1780 describes it as 'at the southern side exhibiting alternating elevations and depressions from which bones and skulls, as it were, are looking up from the ground'.[7]

As a consequence of slow population growth, Stockholm's share of the population of Sweden decreased between about 1760 and 1850 (figure 1.1). The long stagnation contrasts sharply with late nineteenth-century economic growth.

The economic aspect of the stagnation involved the capital's role as a centre of trade, administration, and manufacturing. Eli Heckscher described how a general decentralization of internal trade took place,

[6] Translation by Paul Britten Austin, *The Life and Songs of Carl Michael Bellman* (Malmö, 1967). Austin's book is a fine introduction to the life and works of Bellman. Towards the end of his life, Bellman liked to call himself Movitz.

[7] J. Söderberg, 'Stockholm på 1700-talet: metropol i stagnation', *Folkets Historia* 13 (1985).

in which Gothenburg and the Finnish coastal towns advanced during the second part of the eighteenth century. The secular westward shift in foreign trade, in which the Baltic declined in importance relative to the Atlantic, also was disadvantageous for Stockholm as a port town.

The regional pattern of agricultural growth had decentralizing effects as well. Agricultural economic growth during the first part of the nineteenth century was stronger in western and southern Sweden than in the lake Mälaren region of which Stockholm was part. The export of oats from the western and southern areas grew rapidly around the mid nineteenth century, whereas the east-central part around the capital, dominated by comparatively large landed estates, developed more slowly and did not experience any notable agricultural growth until the last decades of the century.[8]

The outline of this volume is as follows. Chapter 2 analyses Stockholm's growth problems in a wider European perspective. How typical was the long stagnation of the Swedish capital within the pattern of urban European development during the eighteenth and nineteenth centuries? Did long-term demographic stagnation and de-industrialization take place elsewhere? The impact of broader processes – shifts in world trade, administrative and military expansion, and interregional competition – on Stockholm's development are traced. Stockholm is also placed within the larger Swedish regional economic and demographic framework.

Chapter 3 deals with one of the most prominent features of the stagnation, the decline of manufacturing. In 1760, half of Swedish manufacturing workers were found in Stockholm; by 1846, this share had declined to only 12 per cent. While previous research has concentrated on the eighteenth century, this chapter traces the number of enterprises, their composition and employment needs up to the mid nineteenth century.

Chapter 4 discusses the development of the informal sector of the economy and the interplay between long-term economic stagnation, labour markets, and demographic behaviour. The concept of the informal sector as used in Third World studies is discussed. An hypothesis of alternating swings in the informal economy is advanced, arguing that a wide range of informal sector activities grew as employment in the formal sector stagnated or declined.

[8] G. Fridlizius, *Swedish Corn Exports in the Free Trade Era* (Lund, 1957); S. Martinius, *Agrar kapitalbildning och finansiering 1833–1892* (Gothenburg, 1967); S. Martinius, *Jordbruk och ekonomisk tillväxt i Sverige 1830–1870* (Gothenburg, 1970); J. Söderberg, 'A long-term perspective on regional economic growth in Sweden', *Scandinavian Economic History Review* 32 (1984).

In chapter 5, trends in real wages are investigated and compared with those of several other European towns. Did the real wages of the unskilled develop more unfavourably in the stagnating Swedish capital than in other European urban centres during the period 1730–1850? What is the relevance of the international standard of living debate, focussing on the period before the mid nineteenth century, to the interpretation of the Stockholm data?

An analysis of real wages cannot be expected to provide more than a clue as to long-term change in living standards. Other materials are used in chapter 6, charting the spatial patterns of wealth and poverty. What parts of the capital were the richest and poorest, and how stable were these patterns? Can levels of poverty be compared with other European towns or with other parts of Sweden? How was the poorest segment of the population composed?

Chapter 7 discusses the long-term trends in inequality. How unevenly were earnings and real estate distributed? Can any long-term tendency towards levelling or widening be discerned? The chapter draws on the wage data on unskilled labour in chapter 5 but also takes the salaried into account.

Demographic phenomena are the focus of chapter 8, which attempts to analyse demographic patterns in relation to the economy. The chapter covers the relationship between the vital series (mortality, fertility, and nuptiality) and economic and climatic fluctuations. How did short-term economic fluctuations affect the fundamental demographic series? Was the Stockholm economic-demographic system of the same low-pressure type as Sweden as a whole?

During the whole period of investigation Stockholm was characterized by a very high level of mortality. The mortality rate, generally above 35 per thousand, was exceptional not only within Sweden. It also surpassed that of European metropolises such as London, Paris, and Berlin, or even British cities such as Manchester and Liverpool.

Chapter 8 also takes a closer look at this pattern of mortality, its age- and sex-specific structure as well as the causes of death, and compares the results with what we know about mortality in other European cities at the time. The traditional interpretation of Stockholm's high mortality rates, which emphasizes the poor sanitary conditions, is challenged.

The concluding chapter 9 summarizes the previous discussion and points to some unsolved problems.

In summary, chapters 2 and 3 emphasize the causes of stagnation, while the other chapters look more into its effects. However, the distinction between causes and effects is not a simple one. They are inextricably interwoven.

We believe that research on the economic history of Stockholm benefits from a European perspective that attempts to take similarities as well as differences into account. As yet we are far from a general picture of the conditions in which urban Europe was transformed during this period. Such a picture will have to combine the analysis of global or general processes with those of local ones, specific to each town. Most research so far has underestimated the importance of economic processes acting in Europe as a whole during a large part of the eighteenth century, processes tending to produce similar effects in terms of trends in real wages and inequality in many urban centres. This is argued in chapter 5, for instance. On the other hand, Stockholm's situation is also peculiar and unique in many respects. We have tried to point to what we find to be broader features as well as particularities. It will be evident that systematic comparison can often be carried out only with demographic data, and only because of the lively research in historical demography during the last decades, whereas many non-demographic phenomena are still waiting to be explored.[9]

[9] This volume does not aim to provide an introduction to general Swedish economic and social history. One of the best introductions in English remains E. F. Heckscher, *An Economic History of Sweden* (Cambridge, Mass., 1954). The recent Swedish handbook, G. Behre *et al.*, *Sveriges historia 1521–1809* (Stockholm, 1985) is very useful.

2

Stockholm's growth problems, 1760–1850, in a comparative European perspective

A comparative view of European urban history

This chapter discusses the growth problems of Stockholm 1760–1850 in a comparative European perspective. The main questions posed are: How unique is the long-term stagnation of Stockholm? How often do we elsewhere observe a de-industrialization process of the kind that Stockholm experienced?

Within the field of urban history there has been a shift in perspective in recent years. Philip Abrams pleaded for a point of view according to which towns are seen as social forms where social relations are intensified and concentrated. This means a reorientation from the treatment of the town as a sort of independent variable in the analysis of historical change. An earlier line of research is illustrated by the debate of the 1950s on the effects of 'parasitic' or 'regenerative' cities on their environments. Parasitic towns, exemplified by St Petersburg or by rapidly growing Third World centres, were supposed to have had negative development effects while the contrary applied to the external effects of regenerative cities, culturally as well as economically.[1]

The debate around this pair of opposites clarified little. Researchers increasingly seem to have realized the complexity of the phenomena under study. It is true that old differences in opinions still exist; we

[1] P. Abrams, 'Towns and economic growth: some theories and problems', in: *Towns in Societies*, eds. P. Abrams and E. A. Wrigley (Cambridge, 1979). For the discussion of the 1950s see B. Hoselitz, 'Generative and parasitic cities', *Economic Development and Cultural Change* 3 (1954/5). A useful overview of the literature is provided by A. Gilbert and J. Gugler, *Cities, Poverty and Development; Urbanization in the Third World* (Oxford, 1982), chapter 1.

Table 2.1 *Percentage population growth in 61 European towns, 1750–1800 and 1800–1850.*

	Growth 1800–1850		
Growth 1750–1800	<50 %	≥50 %	Total
<30 %	14	15	29
≥30 %	9	23	32
Total	23	38	61

Sources: Data for 1750 mainly from T. Chandler and G. Fox, *3 000 Years of Urban Growth* (New York, 1974), 18, 21, supplemented by C. M. Law, 'Some notes on the urban population of England and Wales in the eighteenth century', *Local Historian* 10 (1972). For 1850 B. R. Mitchell, *European Historical Statistics* (London, 1975), 76–8, supplemented by Mitchell, *Abstract of British Historical Statistics* (Cambridge, 1962), 24–6.

have only to recall Fernand Braudel's reference to the antiurbanism of Rousseau ('it is the big cities that drain the state of its resources and give rise to its weakness') and compare it with the British historian, Martin Daunton's, reference to Adam Smith's opposite view ('through the greater part of Europe the commerce and manufacture of the cities, instead of being the effect, have been the cause and occasion of the improvement and cultivation of the country').[2] Nonetheless there seems to be widespread agreement that straight questions concerning economic growth effects, once prominent in the discussion on the Industrial Revolution and Third World problems, are not necessarily the most relevant to historical analysis, at least not when dealing with units smaller than nations.

An overview of the urban development in the century after 1750 must depart from population trends. The economic series available are far from sufficient. Demographic growth is of course not a perfect indicator of economic development but we should still expect them to be clearly and positively correlated. Weak population growth in general corresponds to weak economic growth.

The 61 European towns in table 2.1 include all with a total population of at least 50,000 in 1750, *or* 70,000 in 1800, *or* 90,000 in 1850.

[2] F. Braudel, *Les structures du quotidien: le possible et l'impossible* (Paris, 1979), chapter 8; the Rousseau quotation from *Emile*. M. J. Daunton, 'Towns and economic growth in eighteenth-century England', in: Abrams and Wrigley, *Towns and Societies*; the Smith quotation from *Wealth of Nations*.

They are divided into four categories with regard to growth during the subperiods 1750–1800 and 1800–50.

Out of the 61 towns, 14 were slow growers during both subperiods. Stockholm belongs to this group as do Copenhagen, Königsberg, and Amsterdam, all of which were part of the Baltic trading area which was declining in importance relative to the Atlantic. Most other towns in the group are Spanish and Italian centres such as Genoa, Venice, Florence, Bologna, Rome, and Granada, affected by the long-term urban stagnation in the Mediterranean region.[3]

A group of nine towns exhibits strong growth during the latter part of the eighteenth century slowing down during the first half of the nineteenth. Like the preceding group it is primarily composed of towns in southern Europe, but here Spain rather than Italy predominates (Barcelona, Seville, Valencia, Cadiz, Oporto, and Naples). Hamburg and two of the most prominent centres of French colonial trade, Bordeaux and Nantes, also belong to this group. Many of the expansive ports of the eighteenth century were to experience difficulties in the next century.

On the other hand 15 towns were moving from weak to strong growth. The two largest metropolises, London and Paris, were quite expansive in the first part of the nineteenth century after having passed through a less dynamic phase during the second half of the eighteenth. A number of emerging centres in the north-west (Lille, Liège, Antwerp, Rotterdam, and Cologne) and further to the south (Milan, Turin, Lyon, and Toulouse) are also part of this group. Finally it includes Marseille, the only Mediterranean port capable of secular expansion.

The fourth and largest group in table 2.1 includes 23 towns characterized by growth throughout. Two main components may be distinguished. More than half are British (Liverpool, Manchester, Glasgow, Edinburgh, Leeds, Sheffield, Plymouth, Birmingham, Bristol, Bradford, Belfast, and Dublin). The extent to which new industrial centres developed into large cities in Britain has no counterpart elsewhere in Europe before the mid nineteenth century.

The other subgroup among the expansive towns, less studied than the preceding one, is primarily composed of little industrialized central and eastern European centres (Moscow, St Petersburg, Budapest, Bucharest, Warsaw, Prague, Berlin, Munich, and Vienna). The

[3] On Italian towns see G. Felloni, 'Italy', in: *Introduction to the Sources of European Economic History 1500–1800*, eds. C. Wilson and G. Parker (London, 1977). Granada and Valencia: J. Harrison, *An Economic History of Modern Spain* (Manchester, 1978), 15. Most of the modern literature in Spanish and Italian economic history in original languages is regrettably missing in Scandinavian research libraries.

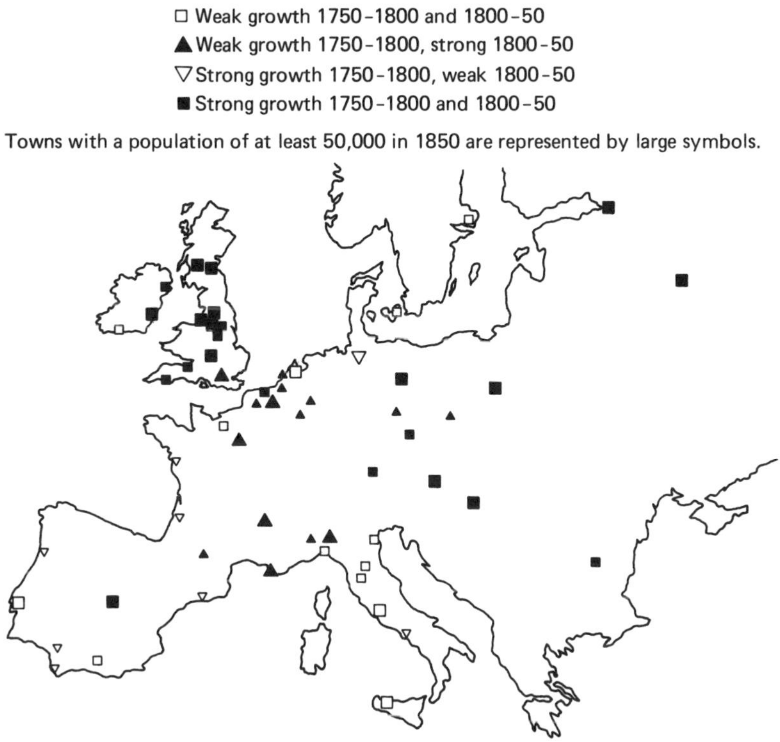

Figure 2.1 Population growth in European towns, 1750–1850.

expansion in some of these is related to a late strengthening, by western standards, of the civil and military state machineries. Only one city in southern Europe, Madrid (which probably resembles some of the central and eastern European ones) and one industrial town in the north-west (Ghent, which rather shares some features of the British growth centres) belong to the expansive catagory. See also figure 2.1.

Stockholm thus is among the towns marked by the weakest growth. Apart from a few others linked to the Baltic economy, most of the cases of such long-term stagnation are found in Italy, Spain, and Portugal. In the literature on Stockholm the difficulties during the second half of the eighteenth century have been stressed. From the European perspective it deserves to be pointed out that during this period so many other towns also exhibited a weak growth in population that Stockholm declined from about rank 30 to just rank 33 with regard to size. The retrogression within the European hierarchy was more evident during the next century: by 1850 Stockholm had dropped to rank 54. Rapid industrialization in the second half of the nineteenth century enabled the capital to advance to rank 43 by 1900.

Aspects of Stockholm's growth problems

Five aspects of the growth problem of Stockholm in the century after 1750 may be separated.

1 Population growth was weak not only by European standards but also when compared with other Swedish towns. One of the underlying factors is the capital's extremely high mortality, which did not decline substantially until after 1860. The long-term drop in nuptiality from the mid eighteenth century onwards probably reflects growing economic barriers to family formation.[4]

2 The relative decline of the capital is most pronounced with regard to manufacturing. Textiles, the dominating sector, was severely affected during the second half of the eighteenth century. Only a few small trades such as sugar and tobacco succeeded in increasing their workforce. In contrast, Norrköping, an emerging factory town, displays larger textile employment even in absolute numbers from about 1825.[5]

One of the processes involved was increasing regional competition, of which ship-building provides an example. During the third and fourth decades of the eighteenth century several new shipyards were established in Stockholm in response to growing demand from the merchant navy after the Great Nordic War. In the second half of the century, however, the trend turned downward. Shipyards in northern Sweden and Finland could deliver at lower prices, and even the shipping firms of the capital increasingly placed their orders there. By 1800, output at the Stockholm shipyards had been reduced to less than a tenth of what it had been fifty years earlier.[6]

Glass manufacturing provides another instance of sharpening interregional competition, where Stockholm firms were largely on the Schumpeterian negative side of development. Until the mid eighteenth century the glasswork of Kungsholmen in Stockholm was practically the only one in the country capable of producing quality

[4] See also chapters 4 and 8 below.

[5] E. F. Heckscher, 'De svenska manufakturerna under 1700–talet', *Ekonomisk Tidskrift* 39 (1937); P. Nyström, *Stadsindustriens arbetare före 1800–talet* (Stockholm, 1955, reprinted 1983).

[6] G. Zethelius, 'Stockholms-varven under 1700–talet', *Sjöhistorisk årsbok* 1955/6.

glass. During the latter part of the century, however, a number of new enterprises were established in various parts of Sweden. The Kungsholmen works declined rapidly and was discontinued in 1814.[7]

3 As a centre of trade Stockholm was on the decline in relative rather than absolute terms. Its share of total Swedish foreign trade was reduced, which was also true of internal trade, when sources permit these flows to be traced. Trade and shipping was in a process of regional decentralization.[8]

4 Within the handicrafts sector of the capital, employing 15–20 per cent of the population in the 1760s, profits were depressed during the latter part of the eighteenth century, according to an analysis by Ernst Söderlund. The number of masters did not change appreciably, however, and unlike manufacturing the handicrafts sector did not deteriorate drastically. Conditions during the first part of the nineteenth century remain to be explored, but no substantial expansion is likely to have taken place.[9]

5 Real wages of unskilled labourers and in some other categories were falling secularly during the eighteenth century, reaching a trough around 1800. After a marked rise in the first quarter of the nineteenth century, the period up to 1850 is distinguished by heavy fluctuations around a somewhat downward-sloping curve. By 1850, the purchasing power of a hodman in terms of rye was approximately the same as in 1760.

The development of nominal as well as real wage rates for unskilled labour in the capital did not deviate much from that of rural Sweden as a whole, as investigated by Jörberg, and divergences were even less significant when Stockholm is compared with nearby counties in the lake Mälaren valley.[10]

The downward pressure on eighteenth century real wages was part of a general European process affecting urban as well as rural areas. Industrializing Lancashire and southern Scotland constitute two major exceptions.

7 Å. Nisbeth, 'Kungsholms glasbruk', *Sankt Eriks årsbok* 1963.

8 E. F. Heckscher, *Sveriges ekonomiska historia från Gustav Vasa* II:1 (Stockholm, 1949), chapter 2; S. Högberg, *Utrikeshandel och sjöfart på 1700–talet* (Stockholm, 1969). For tendencies from the mid nineteenth century see I. Hammarström, *Stockholm i svensk ekonomi 1850–1914* (Stockholm, 1970).

9 E. Söderlund, *Stockholms hantverkarklass 1720–1772* (Stockholm, 1943), chapter 7; E. Söderlund, *Hantverkarna* II (Stockholm, 1949), chapter 2.

10 See also chapter 5 below.

Not until the 1840s were there any marked tendencies towards more favourable economic development. A far-reaching transformation of the economic structure of the capital took place in the second half of the century. More skill-intensive and capital-intensive industries entered, among which engineering and chemicals were the most successful. A strong growth in production and employment gained momentum, in sharp contrast with the previous long stagnation.[11]

Growth problems in urban Europe

The discussion below starts from a simple representation, in figure 2.2, of influences on urban economic development. Two types of influence are distinguished. Flows, on the one hand, are here taken to include three broad processes: shifts in patterns of international trade, the expansion of administrative and military apparatuses, and changing interregional competition. Stocks, on the other hand, refer to secularly fairly stable conditions modifying the impact of changes generated elsewhere. The size of the town is seen as one of those stocks, the demographic and ethnic structure a second, and the position of the town within the regional system a third.

Flows

Shifts in international trade can hardly have contributed decisively to the stagnation of Stockholm. Foreign trade never was central to the economy. It is true that the important iron exports could not expand much as a result of the policy of limiting production with the purpose of raising prices.[12] However, export prices were favourable during the latter half of the eighteenth century. Moreover, year-to-year fluctuations in iron exports were small compared with other commodities.[13] Iron rather formed an element of stability and continuity in the development of the capital.

Neither can the loss of Finland, conquered by Russia in 1808–9, be shown to have caused any retrogression for Stockholm as a trading centre. Finland continued to form an important area for the trade of the capital. From the Finnish point of view the importance of Stockholm was reduced, but this process was well under way already during the eighteenth century with the advance of the Finnish coastal

[11] Hammarström, *Stockholm i svensk ekonomi*.

[12] G. Utterström, 'Befolkningsutveckling och näringsliv efter mitten av 1700–talet', in *En bok om Mälardalen* (Stockholm, 1953).

[13] Högberg, *Utrikeshandel och sjöfart*, 84. On iron exports see *Historisk statistik för Sverige 3. Utrikeshandel 1732–1970* (Stockholm, 1972), 149, 189.

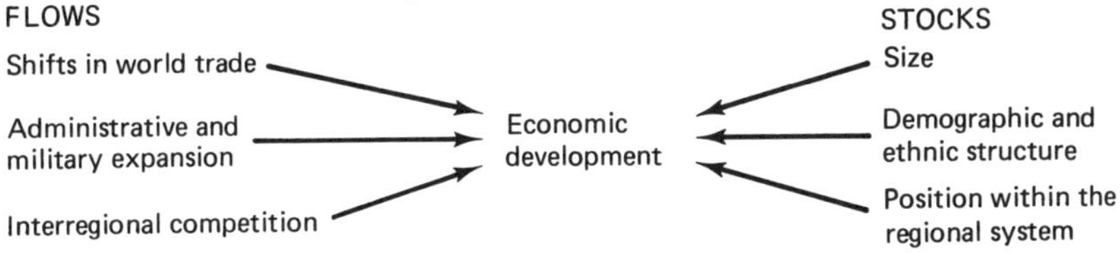

Figure 2.2 Schematic representation of types of influences on urban economic development.

towns. In Finland, too, developments are characterized by continuity rather than by crisis or ruptures.[14]

The foreign trade of many European towns was far more uneven than Stockholm's over time. Centres basing their economies on imports of colonial products frequently experienced dramatic fluctuations in connection with the great sea wars of the eighteenth century. Moreover, a commercial sector relying on imports and re-exports of raw materials often fails to generate growth elsewhere in the urban economy.

The Bordeaux case illustrates the limited spread effects as well as the violent economic swings. As shown above this was a city exhibiting a substantial eighteenth-century population growth, later to slow down. Basing its position on imports of sugar and other colonial products, its development was spasmodic in the eighteenth century, phases of rapid growth alternated with dramatic setbacks during wartime. The Seven Years' War and the American Revolution were severe enough but the catastrophe came in the 1790s with the revolution in Saint-Domingue, the revolutionary wars in Europe, and the growing British hegemony at sea. The commercial wealth of Bordeaux generated high wage levels acting as a barrier to industrial investment. Industrial employment (at shipyards, sugar refineries, and tobacco factories) at least in the 1780s was of a decidedly smaller dimension than in Stockholm. Commercial growth was fragile, with limited secondary effects.[15] Several other major ports of the eighteenth century were declining within the urban hierarchy during the subsequent period. This applies to, e.g., Nantes, Rouen, Amsterdam, Hamburg, and Königsberg, in addition to a number of southern European cities. Inland towns remarkably often were among the most dynamic during the earlier part of the nineteenth century.[16]

14 K. Samuelsson, 'Den ekonomiska betydelsen för Stockholm av Finlands förlust', *Forum navale* 6 (1945).

15 J.-P. Poussou, *Bordeaux et le Sud-Ouest au XVIIIe siècle* (Paris, 1983), 247.

16 On Rouen see P. Dardel, *Navires et marchandises dans les ports de Rouen et du Havre au XVIIIe siècle* (Paris, 1963); Dardel, *Commerce, industrie et navigation à Rouen et au Havre au XVIIIe siècle* (Rouen, 1966), chapter 1.

One of the few centres of colonial trade that continued to expand was Bristol. Even this town, however, points to some of the problems connected with attaining a stable basis for growth. The African trade had generated the economic surplus upon which the town's position as a regional centre of western England relied. While certain sugar and tobacco industries were established, activities demanding more labour and energy could not survive there. The merchant capital of Bristol rather was channelled into financing the emerging industrialization of south Wales, and, after the take-off of growth there, the tendency was towards de-industrialization of Bristol. Notwithstanding expansion in banking and insurance, the town appears as relatively stagnating in the British context in the first half of the nineteenth century. Only against the background of the enormous urban growth in the rest of the country is it, however, reasonable to label the process one of 'decline', as British researchers are inclined to do. Bristol belonged to the most expansive category in table 2.1 above.[17]

It is nonetheless evident that Bristol was outdistanced by Liverpool. The American trade of Bristol never recovered after the Revolution, and Liverpool had a firm grasp of the West Indian trade. Industrializing Wales created ports of its own. The trend towards direct trade at the expense of middlemen of course did not stimulate centres such as Bristol, the French ports on the Atlantic, or Amsterdam. Not even Liverpool with its exceptional population growth could avoid some de-industrialization during the first part of the nineteenth century. Similar to the Bristol case, Liverpool merchants were behind investments in the surrounding regions contributing to a decline in manufacturing industry and to further specialization in trade in Liverpool itself.[18]

Shifts

(a) The diminishing role of central power in urbanization is evident in the Stockholm instance when the century after 1750 is compared with the mid seventeenth-century decades. Similar observations can be made for many other places in western Europe. As noted by de Vries, the large towns were those which expanded most rapidly during the period 1600–1750, while towns numbering less than 40,000 frequently retrogressed. Capitals such as London, Paris, Madrid, Berlin, Copenhagen, and Stockholm were all among the more dynamic. Industrial towns tended to lag behind. The creation of an administrative and

[17] W. E. Minchinton, 'Bristol – metropolis of the West in the eighteenth century', *Transactions of the Royal Historical Society*, Fifth Series, 4 (1954).

[18] F. E. Hyde, *Liverpool and the Mersey* (Newton Abbot, 1971), chapter 2.

military apparatus of new dimensions was strategic to the successful centres.[19]

After 1750 we have to search in central and eastern Europe for decisive contributions on the part of government to the development of major towns. St Petersburg, Moscow, and Berlin provide the clearest examples. A quarter of the population of St Petersburg in 1789 was made up of soldiers and sailors (with families); the corresponding figure for Berlin was just slightly lower. Only heavy government investment made possible the impressive expansion of these cities during the eighteenth century.[20]

The military population of Stockholm comprised about 10 per cent of the total in the middle of the eighteenth century as well as a century later; neither is the proportion of civil servants likely to have changed substantially during this period. Changes in government and municipal employment can hardly have been significant to Stockholm's overall situation.[21]

(b) The third major process mentioned above is the changing patterns of interregional competition. Two aspects may be separated. On one hand, the position of established towns could change relative to industrial growth poles and smaller centres. On the other hand, the balance between urban and agrarian sectors taken as a whole could shift.

Both aspects play a part in explaining Stockholm's stagnation and especially the decline of textile manufacturing. The advance of Norrköping as a specialized industrial town during the former part of the nineteenth century, partly at the expense of Stockholm, exemplifies a type of regional competition that has its clearest European parallel in the relation between Antwerp and Ghent. In much the same way as Stockholm, Antwerp was affected by de-industrialization in textiles, while Ghent, the specialized low-wage town, was gaining a larger share.[22]

The European wave of urbanization from about 1750 (or from about 1800 in the Mediterranean area) primarily fell upon small or middle-

19 J. de Vries, *European Urbanisation 1500–1800* (London, 1984), chapter 4.

20 Braudel, *Les structures du quotidien*.

21 On the military part of the population see Utterström, 'Stockholms folkmängd 1663–1763', in *Historiska studier tillägnade Nils Ahnlund* (Stockholm, 1949), 265; also *Minnesskrift med anledning av den svenska befolkningsstatistikens 200-åriga bestånd* (Stockholm, 1949), tables 1–5. The unreliability of data on Stockholm city in the official population statistics (*Tabellverket*) is stressed by S. Carlsson, *Ståndssamhälle och ståndspersoner 1700–1865* (Lund, 1973), 39, 46.

22 C. Lis and H. Soly, 'Food consumption in Antwerp between 1807 and 1859: a contribution to the standard of living debate', *Economic History Review* 30 (1977).

sized towns. The general pattern thus was the reverse to that of the previous period. When explaining the advance of small towns, de Vries points to the well-known fact that the Industrial Revolution initially was tied to the exploitation of natural resources at some distance from the established centres. He also stresses the growth in agrarian income and agrarian production connected with growing market exchange. After the mid nineteenth century the large towns once more were the most expansive.[23]

For the period from about 1730 to the end of the century there are reasons to emphasize the consequences for urban development of the shifts between the agrarian and the non-agrarian sectors. These shifts are connected with inflation and relative price changes. The secular inflation involved larger price increases for foodstuffs than for textiles, iron, and building materials. The relative price shifts to the disadvantage of industrial products are incompatible with the thesis of an *industrial* profit inflation maintained by Earl J. Hamilton. His view of the inflationary effects of industrial innovation, industrial investments, and income distribution did not rely on any analysis of relative prices.[24] In most of Europe we actually observe a drop in real wages for labourers – urban as well as rural ones – combined with an income redistribution in favour of agrarian producers. This long eighteenth-century trend was not terminated until the post-Napoleonic depression in agricultural prices.[25]

This background is central to an understanding of the difficulties that established urban centres frequently encountered in the course of the eighteenth century. Contrary to the Hamiltonian thesis we should expect growing problems with regard to industrial profits under the double pressure from rising costs of living for labour (although nominal wage rises were usually small) and deteriorating terms of trade against the agrarian sector.

One way of adapting to these circumstances, from the point of view of urban industrial production, was to rely on decentralized forms of production and on a labour force that had only part of its income from industrial employment. It was essential that the labourer and his/her family found part of their income from other sources. Stockholm textile manufacturers generally established a division of labour with a small core of skilled craftsmen and labourers on one hand, and a large

23 de Vries, *European Urbanisation.*

24 E. J. Hamilton, 'Profit inflation and the Industrial Revolution, 1751–1800', *Quarterly Journal of Economics* 56 (1941/2); Hamilton, 'Prices as a factor in business growth', *Journal of Economic History* 12 (1952). L. Jörberg, *A History of Prices in Sweden* II (Lund, 1972) dismisses Hamilton's profit inflation thesis with reference to Swedish data.

25 See chapter 5 below.

number of loosely connected domestic female labourers on the other. The degree of employment varied enormously among the domestic spinners; for many of them spinning cannot have provided more than a subsidiary source of income. For the firm this had the advantages of minimizing investment in fixed assets and enabling some flexibility in adapting to business fluctuations. In difficult years the firms tried to keep the core of skilled workers intact while the volume of domestic labour was reduced.[26]

Domestic textile production in rural Sweden became increasingly competitive during the century after 1750. As a result of agrarian economic growth the textile market was shifted spatially as well as socially, to the disadvantage of Stockholm. Areas in close touch with the growing rural demand were stimulated. Stockholm's position deteriorated not only when compared with factory production in a town like Norrköping but also when compared with domestic rural production, orientated towards coarser and cheaper qualities.[27]

The changes in demand are illustrated by the firm of Bergman & Bohnstedt, the most advanced cotton spinning mill in the country during the time it was operating in Stockholm (1836–41). Modern spinning machines were used for the fine yarn, and weaving was mechanized too. After a fire in 1841 the company left the capital and founded a new mill outside the small town of Nyköping in the county of Södermanland. It is significant that the new establishment was equipped with machines for coarse yarn only, presumably in order to meet demand from domestic industry for this quality.[28]

The tendency towards textile de-industrialization was a common phenomenon among middle-sized and large European towns during this period. The extent of discontinuations varied, however, and so did the extent to which alternative activities emerged. In Vienna, for instance, much of the mechanized textile manufacturing was relocated into rural areas during the second quarter of the nineteenth century as entrepreneurs tried to utilize lower wages, water power, and generally lower costs of production. On the other hand the city was able to keep large parts of its silk industry. Slower technological transformation facilitated this as well as orientation towards a stable upper-class market. From the 1830s factories requiring relatively skilled labour, producing articles such as wagons, gloves, and earthenware, expanded. Vienna succeeded fairly well in adapting to the

[26] Nyström, *Stadsindustriens arbetare*, chapter 8; Heckscher, 'De svenska manufakturerna under 1700–talet'.

[27] L. Schön, *Från hantverk till fabriksindustri* (Lund, 1979), 146.

[28] Schön, ibid., 103; more detailed in N. G. Wollin, *Industrierna vid Hargs ström under fyra sekler* (Stockholm, 1943), 273.

Industrial Revolution, not by transforming itself into an industrial centre but by exploiting those comparative advantages that still existed.[29]

Similarly, London, Paris, and Berlin were all affected by regional competition. London to some extent lagged behind the enormously expansive north-western industrial districts in the century after 1750. It is common opinion that the pre-industrial characteristics of the capital were accentuated by this process. Already during the seventeenth century low-productive activities such as shoemaking and weaving had been relocated and the economy of the capital increasingly directed towards qualified production and services. In Paris, textiles lost in importance during the earlier part of the nineteenth century. The survivors relied on an ethnically heterogeneous labour force; nearly one half of the tailors in 1847 had been recruited from abroad. They were German, Hungarian, and Polish who accepted lower remuneration than did the French. At the same time there were plenty of dynamic elements within the Parisian economy, in the form of quality production in ready-made clothing, and in the chemical and mechanical engineering industries.[30]

(c) Figure 2.2 above indicated some aspects of established urban economic and demographic structures which would serve to modify the effects of the processes discussed so far. Two such properties – size and ethnic heterogeneity – may be discussed with reference to Paris.

The mere size of the metropolitan economy offered a buffer against exogenously generated crises. The Parisian economy was far more diversified than that of other French towns, and the social middle stratum comprised large segments. Seasonal fluctuations in employment were according to Chevalier less pronounced in the first half of the nineteenth century than they were to become later. The crises were also less severe than in the industrial towns of the north.[31]

More generally it seems very likely that the comparatively stable

[29] On Vienna see J. Ehmer, *Familienstruktur und Arbeitsorganisation im frühindustriellen Wien* (Munich, 1980); Ehmer, 'Produktion und Reproduktion in der Wiener Manufakturperiode', in R. Banik-Schweitzer *et al.*, *Wien im Vormärz* (Vienna, 1980), 115–17.

[30] London: F. J. Fisher, 'London as an "Engine of Economic Growth"', in *Britain and the Netherlands*, ed. J. S. Bromley (The Hague, 1971); *Economic History of Britain since 1700*, vol. 1, eds. R. Floud and D. McCloskey (Cambridge, 1981), and literature cited therein. Paris: L. Chevalier, *La formation de la population parisienne au XIXe siècle* (Paris, 1950), 104. Berlin: L. Baar, *Die Berliner Industrie in der Industriellen Revolution* (Berlin, 1966), chapter 2; Baar, 'Probleme der Industriellen Revolution in grosstädtischen Industriezentern: das Berliner Beispiel', in: *Wirtschafts- und Sozialgeschichtliche Probleme der frühen Industrialisierung*, ed. W. Fischer (Berlin, 1968).

[31] Chevalier, *La formation de la population parisienne*, 106.

development path displayed by large metropolises like London, Paris, Berlin, and Vienna was connected with their size, diversified structure, and orientation towards quality production. They could not avoid being affected by macroeconomic processes which could be regarded as exogenous in relation to them. But the problems of adaptation were less acute than is frequently seen among towns lower in the urban hierarchy. With the exception of Amsterdam foreign trade was not central to any of the largest cities, a sector so often characterized by abrupt changes.

Another property found in the Parisian and several other metropolitan economies but not in Stockholm is a considerable degree of ethnic heterogeneity, facilitating a segmentation of the labour force such that certain segments were to work under conditions clearly deviant from those applying to the indigenous population. The survival of low-productive handicrafts in Paris because of ethnic heterogeneity has already been mentioned. Another instance is the migration to Vienna of young and cheap labour from Bohemia and Moravia. Their overrepresentation in unskilled industrial jobs did not stop but probably modified the extent of relocations to rural regions. Among the machine-breakers arrested during the riots of March 1848 a remarkably high share proved to have come from Bohemia.[32] The tension caused by the recruitment of Irish labour to London, where they earned one half to two thirds of the wages of English labour in the building trades, is well-known.[33] In Stockholm Finnish labour to some extent formed a substratum. This component was small, however. According to the 1860 census, the earliest one to report birthplaces, not more than 2 per cent of the capital's population was born outside Sweden.[34]

Segmentation could otherwise be based on immigration from poor regions within the nation. According to Braudel, 'the normal partnership is between a poor region with regular emigration and an active town'. The thesis is exemplified by the relation between Venice and Friuli, the latter furnishing the city with labourers and servants, and similarly between Marseille and Corsica and London and Ireland. To this list could be added the importance to Berlin of lagging Prussian

32 Ehmer, 'Produktion und Reproduktion', 119–20; W. Häusler, 'Von der Manufaktur zum Maschinensturm', in R. Banik-Schweitzer *et al.*, *Wien im Vormärz*, 40–2, 52.

33 Braudel, *Les structures du quotidien*; G. Rudé, *Paris and London in the Eighteenth Century* (London, 1970), 299.

34 F. T. Berg, 'Om folkräkningen i Stockholm vid utgången av året 1860', *Statistisk tidskrift* 1 (1862).

regions; the capital's migration field was overwhelmingly orientated towards the east.[35]

Stockholm departs from this pattern insofar as most of the immigrants came from lake Mälaren valley in the earlier part of the nineteenth century and in all likelihood also previously. Poorer regions like the county of Kalmar did not become prominent as major areas of emigration until the latter part of the nineteenth century. Stockholm's labour force thus to a large extent came from the relatively developed and well-to-do area that the lake Mälaren region traditionally was. Real wage differentials between the capital and the rest of the region were small during the century after 1750.[36] Stockholm employers can hardly have been able to place significant numbers of immigrants in particularly low-paid jobs.

Conditions in Stockholm, associated with its position within a regional system, thus differed from those in, for example, Cologne and Amsterdam. Cologne exemplified a town affected by a large influx of cheap labour attracted by the cotton industry. Even though this industry was under stress from British competition, the population of 50,000 in 1815 had doubled by 1852. The town embraced numerous strata of poor, sensitive to economic swings. The Prussian administration was convinced that industrial growth was necessarily tied to unemployment and misery, and it actually valued the lack of new investment as a positive factor. The textile industry left survived only by relying on child and female labour which was paid extremely low wages. The technological and financial transformation did not get under way until the 1850s when the gaps versus French and Belgian industry were reduced.[37]

In other respects Stockholm's place in the regional system differed from that of Amsterdam. Migration to Amsterdam in the latter half of the eighteenth century has been described as a process of 'internal contraction' in which the metropolis for a long time succeeded in avoiding the unfavourable economic development of the provinces.

35 Braudel, *Les structures du quotidien*; K. Obermann, 'Du rôle et du caractère des migrations internes vers Berlin de 1815 à 1875', *Annales de démographie historique* (1971), 158–9.

36 J. Söderberg, 'A long-term perspective on regional economic development in Sweden, ca. 1550–1914', *Scandinavian Economic History Review* 32 (1984); J. Söderberg and N.-G. Lundgren, *Ekonomisk och geografisk koncentration i Sverige 1850–1914* (Lund, 1982), 7–20. U. Jonsson, *Jordmagnater, landbönder och torpare i sydöstra Södermanland 1800–1880* (Stockholm, 1980), 29, aptly characterizes the development of the lake Mälaren region 1820–60 as a 'stagnation at a relatively high level'.

37 P. Ayçoberry, 'Probleme der Sozialschichtung in Köln im Zeitalter der Frühindustrialisierung', in *Wirtschafts- und Sozialgeschichte der frühen Industrialisierung*; more detailed in Ayçoberry, *L'histoire sociale de la ville de Cologne*, 1 (Lille, 1980), chapter 2.

Table 2.2 *Percentage share of population born within some European towns around the mid nineteenth century.*

Town	Percentage	Year
Paris	36	1861
Stockholm	43	1860
Vienna	44	1856
Marseille	45	1846–51
Berlin	50	1864
Brussels	51	1856
Liège	61	1856
Ghent	63	1856
Antwerp	64	1856
Rotterdam	67	1849
Copenhagen	68	1850
Amsterdam	79	1849

Sources: Paris: L. Chevalier, *La formation de la population parisienne au XIXe siècle* (Paris, 1950), 45 note 2. Stockholm and Vienna: F. T. Berg, 'Om folkräkningen i Stockholm vid utgången av året 1860', *Statistisk tidskrift* 1 (1862), 332–3. Marseille: W. H. Sewell, Jr, *Structure and Mobility. The Men and Women of Marseille, 1820–1870* (Cambridge, 1985), 140. Berlin: K. Obermann, 'Du rôle et du caractère des migrations internes vers Berlin de 1815 à 1875', *Annales de la démographie historique* (1971), 158. Brussels, Liège, Ghent, Antwerp: *Population. Récensement général 1856* (Brussels, 1861). Rotterdam, Amsterdam: *Uitkomsten der derde tienjarige volkstelling in het koningrijk der Nederlanden ... 1849* (The Hague, 1852). Copenhagen: *Befolkningsforholdene i Danmark i det 19. aarhundrede* (Copenhagen, 1905), 39.

Not until the economy of the city had been seriously undermined in the 1780s did the inflow decrease. The retrogression in shipping and trade occurred simultaneously with a crisis for shipyards and sugar refineries, the two major industries. De-industrialization, continuing into the next century, was extensive. Because of emigration, the city even experienced population decrease during certain periods.[38] When compared with Stockholm, we are not only dealing with a more dramatic decline from a better original position in the Amsterdam case but also with heavier fluctuations within a more unstable regional system.

Against this background there are reasons to stress the extent of migratory movements to Stockholm. A minority (43 per cent) of its population in 1860 was born in the capital. From table 2.2 this appears

[38] P. Jansen, 'Poverty in Amsterdam at the close of the eighteenth century', *Acta Historiae Neerlandica* 10 (1978).

as a comparatively low proportion, close to that of Vienna and Marseille. Only Paris gives the impression of higher population turnover.

A few reflections can be made on table 2.2. When Eli F. Heckscher discussed mortality in Stockholm, he not only touched upon the effects of economic conditions on demographic ones but also the reverse causal chain. A short productive age span was linked to high mortality because, he assumed without actually presenting any evidence, a high morbidity reduced the ability to work. Demographic conditions in this perspective gave rise to a vicious circle by counteracting possibilities of economic improvement.[39] His thesis is strengthened if it is taken into account that tuberculosis was a major cause of death in the capital, especially among active age groups, and that the high mortality relative to the national average was particularly noticeable with respect to this disease. The high frequency of a disease with a drawn-out morbid state only serves to support Heckscher's line of reasoning.

Another causal chain can be distinguished. Stockholm's mortality rate at least for tuberculosis is likely to have been connected with the extensive migration, leading to high exposure risks. In her great study of tuberculosis in Sweden from 1750, Puranen has demonstrated that nutrition can hardly have been strategic in explaining mortality from this disease. Tuberculosis proves to have been the most common cause of death among the employees and servants at the court during the latter part of the eighteenth century, despite an ample food supply. Exposure, associated with migration and conditions of habitations, rather appears to have been of vital importance.[40]

We are inclined to stress these relationships to at least the same degree as Puranen. The lake Mälaren valley, the area of the most extensive migration in the county, for a long time was characterized by a tuberculosis mortality rate of such dimensions that it precludes a simple explanation in terms of standards of living. Tuberculosis mortality is clearly positively related to migration intensity.[41] Note

39 Heckscher, *Sveriges ekonomiska historia från Gustav Vasa* II:1, 126.

40 B.-I. Puranen, *Tuberkulos* (Umeå, 1984), 268–9, 339–41.

41 On regional variations in tuberculosis mortality see Puranen, ibid., 160–2. Migration intensity 1816–20 (as defined by the sum of in-migration and out-migration relative to size of population) is described by S. Carlsson, 'Flyttningsintensiteten i det svenska agrarsamhället', *Turun historiallinen arkisto* 28 (1973).

On regional poverty levels see J. Söderberg, 'Causes of poverty in Sweden in the nineteenth century', *Journal of European Economic History* 11 (1982), and literature cited therein. At the county level the correlation coefficients between migration intensity on the one hand (Carlsson, *Ståndssamhälle och ståndspersoner*, 194) and tuberculosis mortality 1811–20 and 1821–30 on the other are as high as 0.75 and 0.79, respectively.

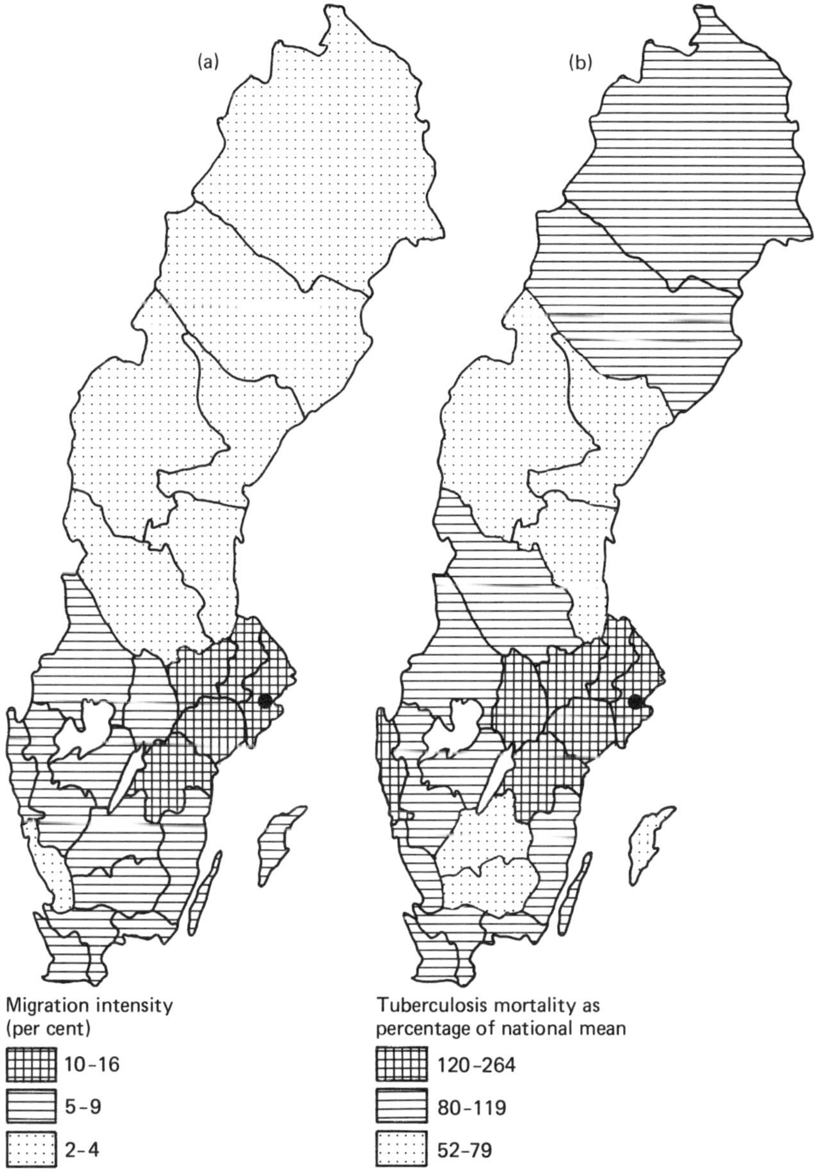

Figure 2.3 (a) Migration intensity, 1816/20 (per cent). Data for Stockholm city not available. (b) Tuberculosis mortality in 1805 as percentage of national average. *Sources*: See note 41.

the similarities between figure 2.3a (migration intensity) and figure 2.3b (tuberculosis mortality).

Stockholm then found itself in another vicious circle. It is well known that excess mortality contributed towards a high level of in-migration; were it not for this a gradual diminution of the population of the capital would have taken place. High mortality made room for heavy in-migration even in the absence of economic growth. Migration, in turn, served to maintain a high mortality level through exposure.

For Paris, table 2.2 suggests an even higher rate of migration. Paris, like Vienna, also exhibits a high tuberculosis mortality. Yet the crude death rate of Paris fell so much below that of Stockholm as to allow a population growth of quite other dimensions. Chevalier, in his analysis of the Parisian economy, regards population growth as a dynamic element through its effects on aggregate demand. Extensive migration thus had clearly different implications depending upon the larger economic and demographic framework within which it was taking place.[42]

Concluding remarks

At the highest level of the European urban hierarchy stability was remarkably high between 1750 and 1850. Large metropolises like London, Paris, Vienna, Berlin, and Madrid succeeded fairly well in adapting to the new conditions of which the eighteenth-century relative price shifts formed one part and the Industrial Revolution another. The mere size of these cities appears to have constituted a resource or buffer against short-term swings. The combination of a wealthy upper-class market, a diversified economy traditionally orientated towards qualified production and, at least in the case of Paris, a lack of export dependence provided conditions for a long-run economic growth that many middle-sized towns lacked.

We often find more development problems among middle-sized

Correlations are however very weak between poverty levels in 1826 and tuberculosis mortality, only −0.10 and −0.22 for the periods 1811–20 and 1821–30, respectively. The relationship between regional tuberculosis mortality and poverty levels is thus negligible. Stockholm city is not included in these calculations since migration and poverty data are missing.

42 On patterns of mortality see chapter 8 below. L. Chevalier, *Laboring Classes and Dangerous Classes in Paris during the First Half of the Nineteenth Century* (Princeton, N.J., 1973) reports respiratory diseases as the most frequent cause of death in Paris around 1830. The level is likely to have been lower than in Stockholm during the first half of the century but to have risen later; see S. H. Preston and E. van de Walle, 'Urban French mortality in the nineteenth century', *Population Studies* 32 (1978), 112–14.

towns. One group of such towns includes centres of foreign trade such as Bordeaux, Nantes, and Rouen. Colonial trade was sensitive to economic fluctuations and above all to international military rivalry, leading to a sort of pulsating growth. In many cases the trading sector was not linked to other sectors of the urban economies. In cases such as Bordeaux and Hamburg the trading activity could even block the establishment of industries.[43]

The ports were often involved in a conscious and fierce struggle among themselves. The rivalry between towns such as Marseille, Genoa, Venice, and Trieste had quite other dimensions than the competition between Stockholm and Gothenburg.[44] The secular advance of Gothenburg as a trading centre was partly based on products such as herring which Stockholm had never exported.[45] The relation between the two largest Swedish towns was to a lesser degree than elsewhere characterized by a zero-sum game in which the profit of one constituted the loss of the other.

De-industrialization tendencies can be traced in a large number of towns because of competition from growing industrial centres as well as from rural small-scale production. The dislocation of relatively low-productive sectors, primarily textiles, affected not only Stockholm but also, for example, Antwerp, Venice, and Granada and even large cities such as Paris, Vienna, and Berlin. Even a specialized textile town like Lyon after 1800 experienced a relocation of silk weaving to neighbouring rural areas, while the town succeeded in keeping those areas using larger proportions of skilled labour.[46] De-industrialization

43 The factory industry of Hamburg was negligible before 1850. Contemporary observers thought that the town could exist only in few numbers since industry wages could not compete with those in the trading sector. Recently migrated labour was recruited to the worst paid jobs, usually in domestic work, but after a while they often found more profitable employment elsewhere in the town. A. Kraus, *Die Unterschichten Hamburgs in der erste Hälfte des 19. Jahrhunderts* (Stuttgart, 1965), 64–5.

44 On the rivalry between Marseille, Genoa, Livorno, Venice, and Trieste see H.-T. Niephaus, *Genaus Seehandel von 1746–1848* (Cologne and Vienna, 1975), 339–41; K. R. Greenfield, 'Commerce and New Enterprise at Venice, 1830–48', *Journal of Modern History* 11 (1939). For a general view of the competition see M. Lévy-Leboyer, *Les banques européennes et l'industrialisation internationale dans la première moitié du XIXe siècle* (Paris, 1964), chapter 5.

45 On exports of herring see Högberg, *Utrikeshandel och sjöfart på 1700-talet*, chapter 6. Grain exports at the middle of the nineteenth century are analysed by G. Fridlizius, *Swedish Corn Export in the Free Trade Era* (Lund, 1957), chapter 3; on the effects on agrarian economic growth in southern and western Sweden see S. Martinius, *Agrar kapitalbildning och finansiering 1833–1892* (Gothenburg, 1970), 139–41.

46 The commercial development of Venice during the second part of the eighteenth century was rather favourable. During the successful neutrality a previous retrogression was transformed into expansion in trade and shipping. Industrial activity in the city declined while exports of textiles and agricultural products from the rest of the state grew. Similarly to many other cases there was a redistribution of textile

in other sectors, ship-building and sugar refineries, hit Amsterdam as well as dynamic centres such as Bristol and Liverpool.

The long-term economic and demographic stagnation of Stockholm was marked by abrupt changes to a lesser degree than was the case in many other towns. Several factors contributed to this relative stability. The volume of foreign trade carried out from Stockholm shifted only gradually. Not even the loss of Finland in 1809 was associated with any abrupt decline in trade. Commercial relations between Stockholm and Finland continued to be important after the Russian conquest. Stockholm's iron exports are characterized by continuity. Neither in handicrafts nor in the civil or military areas of the public sector were there any sudden shifts. De-industrialization also was a drawn-out process which for manufacturing began as early as the 1760s. This undramatic development is in contrast to the experiences of many continental towns during the great sea wars, the French Revolution (Lyon's population diminished by a quarter during the 1793 siege), the Napoleonic Wars, and the partitions of Poland. Towns such as Hamburg, Genoa, Venice, Milan, Turin, and Barcelona could not avoid being devastated by war.

The relative homogeneity of the population made segmentation along ethnic lines impossible in Stockholm. In this the Swedish capital differed from Vienna and several British cities. In the latter extremely low-paid groups co-existed with better paid. In a dual labour market activities could continue to exist which otherwise would have fallen victim to the sharpening interregional competition.

The lack of expansion in mechanized or large-scale production in Stockholm meant that the town did not suffer the adverse affects of the Industrial Revolution in the form of the elimination of handicrafts, a phenomenon that was more important in Berlin, Paris, and Vienna,

production from urban to rural areas. In the case of Venice the Napoleonic Wars rather than any secular economic process produced the collapse. See F. C. Lane, *Venice; a Maritime Republic* (Baltimore and London, 1973), chapters 28–9; more detail in J. Georgelin, *Venise au siècle des lumières* (Paris, 1978), chapters 2, 4. Lyon is dealt with by P. Cayez, 'Une proto-industrialisation decalée: la ruralisation de la soierie lyonnaise dans la première moitié du XIXe siècle', *Revue du Nord* 63 (1981); R. Bezucha, *The Lyon Uprising of 1834* (Cambridge, Mass., 1974), chapter 1. Rouen's textile industry was ruralized in a similar way; J.-P. Bardet, *Rouen aux XVIIe et XVIIIe siècles*, 1 (Paris, 1983), 196–9. The exports of Naples were transformed until the end of the eighteenth century with a diminishing importance of fabricated silk and a greater part for raw silk and in particular olive oil, reflecting de-industrialization. Most of the decline in the processing of silk probably took place during the seventeenth century. P. Chorley, *Oil, Silk and Enlightenment; Economic Problems in Eighteenth Century Naples* (Naples, 1965), 177–80. On the decline of the textile industry in Florence see E. Cochrane, *Florence in the Forgotten Centuries 1527–1800* (Chicago and London, 1973), 350–1, 401.

and which formed part of the background to the 1848 movements in Continental towns. Recent research has increasingly stressed how collective movements were rooted among craftsmen and other middle strata rather than among factory workers or the poorest urban strata.[47]

Stockholm's place in a relatively rich agricultural region gave rise to special conditions of internal migration. In this respect the town deviated from what some researchers have seen as a general European pattern involving a lively interchange between an urban centre and poor regions. Migration to Stockholm was probably conditioned less by real wage differentials than by the more varied labour market of the capital. The continuity within the eastern Swedish regional system could be expected to have contributed towards the rather stable economic-demographic system of the capital, in contrast to, for example, the shifting regional balance in the Netherlands.

On the other hand the mere continuity of the stagnation of Stockholm raises questions concerning entrepreneurial adaptation. In the Berlin case we saw examples of dynamic adaptation where new foreign investment formed a strategic component. The expansion of shipping in Venice during the latter part of the eighteenth century rested with immigrants, while the old families preferred landed property.[48] Barcelona constituted one of the more striking cases of adaptation as capital accumulated in agriculture was channelled into a successful cotton industry under the influence of falling relative prices of wine during the late eighteenth century.[49] In Antwerp the reaction to de-industrialization was increasing activity among merchants directed to the profitable trading and banking business.[50] The textile manufacturers of Ghent during the expansion phase in the first decades of the nineteenth century showed an enthusiasm for technological innovation and an originality in experimenting with new forms of organization with vertical integration, of which there is no counterpart in Stockholm.[51] Here it is rather the lack of initiative before the decline in textiles that is striking. The many failures when trying to establish a

47 For the line of research emphasizing the reactions of craftsmen and other middle strata who perceived small-scale production as a threat, and on the other hand de-emphasizing the role of factory workers and poor strata in the urban movements of 1848 see P. N. Stearns, *The Revolutions of 1848* (London, 1974). The link between collective social protest and economic change undermining traditional modes of living is central in C. Calhoun, *The Question of Class Struggle; Social Foundations of Popular Radicalism during the Industrial Revolution* (Oxford, 1982).

48 Lane, *Venice*, 425.

49 P. Vilar, 'La Catalogne industrielle', in F. Léon *et al.*, *L'industrialisation en Europe au XIXe siècle* (Paris, 1972), 424–6.

50 Lis and Soly, 'Food consumption in Antwerp', 480.

51 J. Dhondt, 'The cotton industry at Ghent during the French régime', in *Essays in European Economic History 1789–1914*, eds. F. Crouzet *et al.* (London, 1969), 48–50.

match industry in Stockholm (about fifteen attempts, all unsuccessful, were made during the 1830s and 1840s in this typical low-wage branch) do not indicate any ability to exploit the comparative advantages of the capital.[52] The comparative analysis of the conditions of urban economic growth provides a framework within which the actual alternatives available to actors can be investigated more intensively. In the Stockholm case the situation of the entrepreneurs, especially during the former part of the nineteenth century, is a field which should bring more fruitful future research.

[52] On the match industry see Hammarström, *Stockholm i svensk ekonomi*, 280 ff.

3

The decline of manufacturing

The purpose of this chapter is to present some structural features of the de-industrialization process that took place in Stockholm from the 1760s until the middle of the nineteenth century.

The current discussion of pre-factory de-industrialization has primarily taken place within the proto-industrialization debate and has so far mostly concerned rural domestic industry within a regional context.[1] This chapter, however, concerns manufactures which were primarily an urban phenomenon existing alongside the proto-industries proper. The competition between them was probably rather limited, as their markets normally separated regionally and socially.[2]

In Sweden, economic policy has been the main focus of the discussion concerning manufacturing. Therefore it will be briefly outlined as a background.[3]

The first Swedish factories were established during the early seventeenth century under royal privileges. Later in the century a governmental factory policy was initiated. In the true spirit of mercantilism the policy contained protective customs duties, subsidies, and tax exemptions. Some attempts were made to centralize the factories in Stockholm under one roof, but this was never realized. The institutional framework was laid down firmly in 1739 with an extensive set of laws regulating manufacturing under the supervision of local courts, *hallrätter*, which exercised immediate jurisdiction over them.

Also in 1739, an extremely mercantilistic group gained power in the Swedish parliament, leading to still more favourable legislation for the

1 See, e.g., S. Pollard, *Peaceful Conquest* (Oxford, 1981), 63ff.
2 There are of course counterinstances to this picture. See, e.g., L. Schön, *Från hantverk till fabriksindustri* (Lund, 1979), who relates the expansion of textile manufacturing in Norrköping to changes in the market structure of the hinterland.
3 Primarily based on P. Nyström, *Stadsindustriens arbetare före 1800–talet* (Stockholm, 1955, reprinted 1983).

manufacturers. Compared with the continental pattern, the Swedish legislation focussed on the relation between manufacturers on the one side and masters and workers on the other, very much favouring the manufacturers, while quality standards and other responsibilities of the manufacturers were more concealed.

The law was written by one of the large manufacturers in Stockholm during the period, Eric Salander, owner of the Barnängen factories. The legislation was supplemented by a law prescribing compulsory labour and maximum wages.[4] Furthermore, a credit institution was established (the *manufakturdiskontfonden*) where low-interest loans could be obtained against security in produced goods, stored in the stamphalls of the local court (*hallrätt*).[5] This policy surely contributed to the substantial expansion of manufacturing in the following decades. However, due to the lack of quality control and the possibility of obtaining credits without actually being forced to sell the goods, the policy led to generally bad quality textiles which is confirmed by an extensive contemporary criticism. Furthermore the import restrictions led to widespread smuggling.[6]

The basic purpose of this policy was of course to support an import substitute industry in Sweden. The main industry was textiles, but important branches were also sugar and tobacco. Other industries, too small to form a guild, were also subordinated to the factory legislation. This meant that the manufacturing sector contained more than 50 diverse industries made up, normally, of small enterprises, averaging not more than three workers. The manufacturing sector thus was, regarding products, production process, mechanization, size of the enterprises, etc., very heterogeneous.

In connection with the international trade crisis of 1763, which had a substantial impact on the Swedish economy, political power was shifted towards a more moderate group. The subsidies, conditions of borrowing working capital, and tax exemptions were substantially modified.[7] Yet, pro-manufacturing policy retained its influence until 1846 with regard to customs and domestic consumption as well as to taxes and other kinds of regulations. At this time the free establishment of private enterprises was allowed and the local courts, *hallrätterna*, were abolished.

[4] Ibid., pp. 105ff.

[5] See, e.g., S. Gerentz, *Kommerskollegium och näringslivet 1651–1951* (Stockholm, 1951), and S. Fritz, *Studier i svenskt bankväsen 1772–1789* (Stockholm, 1967).

[6] E. F. Heckscher, *Sveriges ekonomiska historia från Gustav Vasa II:2* (Stockholm, 1949), 586f, 618ff.

[7] See, e.g., K. Stadin, 'Skattepolitiken och de kapitalistiska företagen 1719–1812', *Historisk tidskrift* 102 (1982), 500.

Eli F. Heckscher, who first studied Swedish manufacturing in detail, saw a close connection between the mercantilist policy of the time and the development of the factories, which he characterized as 'hot house plants' under the cover of this economic policy.[8] No doubt the factories decreased strongly with regard to number of workers and handlooms after the crisis in the 1760s, at least in Stockholm as will be seen later. However an opposite view was put forward in the 1950s by Per Nyström, who ascribed a progressive role to manufacturing in industrial development.[9]

The decline in the number of workers and handlooms was, according to Nyström, a result of the rationalization of the product mix within the textile industries. This conclusion he based on a study of the Stockholm silk industry from 1700 to 1815. Whereas the mercantilist policy made dynamic enterprising impossible in Heckscher's view, to Nyström the merchant capitalists of this era played a progressive role in the industrialization process.[10]

The results from the study of the Stockholm manufacturing will be related to the two approaches referred to above and also to the following discussion of the informal sector in chapter 4.

The Stockholm manufacturing industry, 1750–1850

The statistical sources for Swedish manufacturing are exceptionally comprehensive for this period, thanks to the mercantilistic legislation of the early eighteenth century. As for the reliability of the material, there has been no systematic examination. Heckscher, working with the material on a national level, found that the primary weakness (apart from a number of miscalculations) was its irregularity.[11] There are reasons to believe that such irregularity is less of a problem in the Stockholm material.

The material contains yearly reports from the manufacturers to the *hallrätt* and the statistics compiled there on the basis of these reports. The statistics were sent to Kommerskollegium, the central government commercial authority, where the material was aggregated at a national level. The information mainly used in the following presen-

[8] E. F. Heckscher, 'De svenska manufakturerna under 1700–talet', *Ekonomisk tidskrift* 39 (1937).

[9] The main point in the controversy between Heckscher and Nyström was precisely the impact of the economic policy on the development of manufacturing.

[10] Nyström, *Stadsindustriens arbetare*, 313.

[11] Heckscher, 'De svenska manufakturerna', 157ff. For a comprehensive presentation of the material from Stockholm *hallrätt* see Berg L. O., 'Hall- och manufakturrätten i Stockholm', *Stockholms stads arkivnämnd och stadsarkiv. Årsberättelse*, 1967.

tation refers to (a) the number of workers and (b) the value and volume of production. Some short comments on these variables will be given in advance.

The statistics were reorganized in 1829. Before this year they included workers officially registered as employees, according to the current legislation. From 1829 other workers were included as well. The majority of these other workers were probably female spinners working in their homes.[12] As a consequence, the numbers reported before and after 1829 are not directly comparable. It should also be underlined that the level of employment between different labourers, especially those working in their homes, could fluctuate highly.[13] Therefore the number of workers only approximates the amount of manpower engaged in manufacturing. There is so far no systematic information available to adjust for this anomaly.

In the absence of value-added figures, the value of production must be used as indicating the volume of production, which of course in itself is problematic. There is also a weakness connected with these figures insofar as they report administered prices, at least in textiles, which means that especially in times of inflation they lagged behind market prices. Furthermore, the currency situation in Sweden was very complicated during most of the period, and without the utmost caution these figures may be more confusing than illuminating. Bearing these introductory remarks in mind, we will start with an overall discussion of the development of the Stockholm manufacturing sector, in some cases comparing it with patterns of change in the rest of Sweden.

Employment

The long-term development of the aggregate numbers of factory workers in Stockholm and Sweden as a whole is shown in figure 3.1. The beginning of the period was characterized by expansion, starting in the 1720s and continuing until the beginning of the 1760s. In connection with the national financial crisis of the 1760s the number of workers in Stockholm was halved. Though recoveries took place in the 1770s, 1790s, and 1800s, the number of workers in 1760 was never reached again in the capital.

Table 3.1 records the number of workers in the silk, woollen, and cotton industries as well as the aggregate numbers for Stockholm and

12 Schön, *Från hantverk till fabriksindustri*, 143.

13 Heckscher, *Sveriges ekonomiska historia*, 628–35, especially on the conditions of the unskilled female workers.

Table 3.1 *Number of factory workers by branch in Stockholm (St) and the rest of Sweden (Sw).*

	Silk		Woollen		Cotton		Other branches		Total	
Period	St	Sw	St	Sw	St	Sw	St	Sw	St	Sw
1751/60	1,737	268	4,638	4,016	1,435	815	1,222	1,245	9,032	6,344
1761/70	1,512	219	3,003	3,908	982	975	1,757	1,861	7,254	6,963
1771/80	1,278	148	2,646	2,418	818	1,807	1,477	1,517	6,219	5,890
1781/90	1,165	127	2,510	1,878	593	2,015	1,334	1,782	5,602	5,802
1791/1800	1,097	63	2,364	1,797	359	1,460	1,262	1,510	5,082	4,830
1801/10	1,233	96	1,390	2,078	323	2,360	1,243	1,450	4,189	5,984
1811/20	790	0	848	1,221	356	905	1,251	1,662	3,245	3,788
1821/28	933	0	749	1,174	476	755	1,554	2,229	3,712	4,158
1829/40	784	8	596	2,569	557	966	2,003	5,455	3,940	8,998
1841/50	811	0	365	3,909	330	1,737	2,153	8,314	3,659	13,960

Sources: Hall- och manufakturrättens arkiv, SSA; Kommerskollegii arkiv, RA. Fabriksberättelser; Eli F. Heckscher's collection, RA.

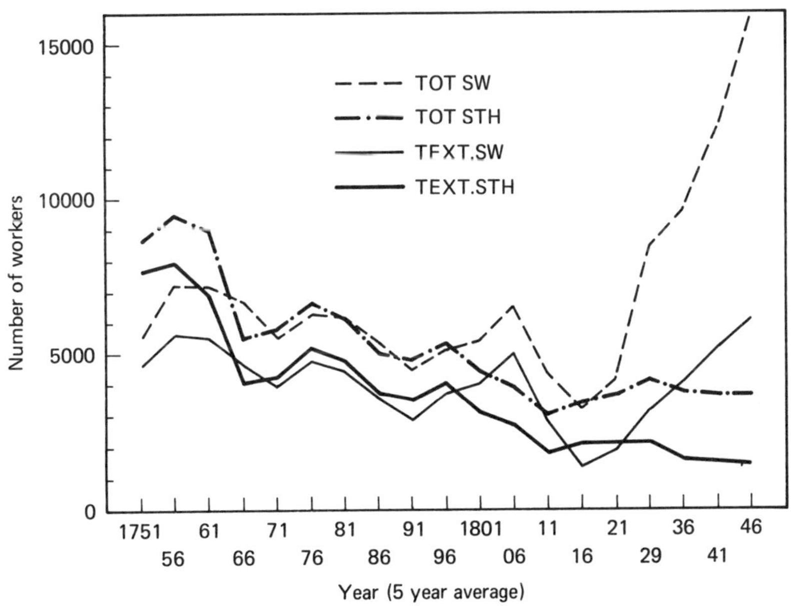

Figure 3.1 Number of manufacturing workers in Stockholm and the rest of Sweden, 1751–1846.

Table 3.2 *Population and number of factory workers in Stockholm, 1751–1846.* (10-year averages)

Period	Population Stockholm	Population Sth/Sw %	Workers/ pop Sth %	Workers Sth/Sw %
1751/60	67,340	3.6	13.4	59
1761/70	70,340	3.5	10.3	50
1771/80	73,070	3.6	8.5	51
1781/90	74,430	3.4	7.5	49
1791/1800	74,220	3.2	6.8	51
1801/10	71,640	3.0	5.8	41
1811/20	71,920	2.9	4.5	47
1821/28	78,475	2.9	4.7	47
1829/40	82,266	2.7	4.9	31
1841/50	88,230	2.7	4.2	21

Sources: See table 3.1 above and *Historisk statistik för Sverige 1* (Stockholm, 1955).

Sweden. In table 3.2 the total number of workers in the factories is related to the population figures.

The relation between Stockholm and the rest of Sweden

Before the 1760s Stockholm dominated the Swedish manufacturing industry with about 60 per cent of the total labour force in the 1750s. After the crisis of the 1760s, the capital held about half the total number of workers until the end of the century. During the first decade of the nineteenth century, Stockholm's share dropped to about 40 per cent, but recovered somewhat in the following two decades. In the 1830s the figure declined again to 30 per cent and further to 21 per cent in the 1840s.

The relative decrease for Stockholm in the 1760s (see table 3.2) may at least partly be explained by the fact that it was the Stockholm factories that most heavily relied upon the subsidiary policy which was substantially reduced in connection with the crisis. Calculations made from the records of official financial support allocated through the *manufakturdiskontfonden* show that for the period 1760–1810 loans were granted for 25–30 per cent of the total production value in the country. The figure for Stockholm in the period 1773–87 amounted to over 40 per cent.[14]

The fall in the first decade of the nineteenth century is primarily due to the war period 1808–9 which also clearly affected the population

[14] Based on Fritz, *Studier i svenskt bankväsen*, 254.

figures for Stockholm. Another explanation for the secular relative decrease in the nineteenth century for Stockholm was the lack of waterpower, important to the mechanization of the textiles. This should also explain why in the same period Norrköping, a provincial town in middle Sweden with access to waterpower, rapidly expanded its textile manufacturing.[15] This explanation has since been questioned,[16] and there is as yet no explicit investigation into the relation between textile manufacturing in the two towns to see whether the divergent trends was an effect of competition.

In a secular perspective, however, de-industrialization before the 1820s was a national phenomenon, though the tendency was stronger in Stockholm. After the 1820s the relative share of manufacturing employment in Stockholm decreased sharply. This was due partly to the fact that homespinners, mostly living in the countryside, were included in the statistics.

There was, however, a real change in the relation between Stockholm and the rest of the country after the 1820s. From that time the textile factories in Stockholm continued to decrease while they began to expand in the rest of the country where also other miscellaneous industries increased.

Population and labour force

The absolute number of factory workers went continuously down throughout the period (table 3.1 above). Though Stockholm was a stagnating town in this period, population rose slowly. Therefore the relative decline in the numbers employed in manufacturing was even greater than the absolute decline. In the 1750s about 13 per cent of the population was employed in manufacturing. By the end of the period this figure was about 4 per cent. This decline was not compensated for by any other known formal labour market. The number of people employed in the guild handicrafts remained fairly stable (ca. 6,000 workers) throughout the period.

The composition of the labour force

For the period 1767–1828 skilled and unskilled workers are separated. The skilled workers are masters, journeymen, and apprentices. That is, the concepts from the guilds were used even though the regulations were less strict in manufacturing. The skilled textile workers were primarily male weavers while the unskilled workers were mostly female spinners and children.

In the silk industry there was a downward tendency in the share of

15 Nyström, *Stadsindustriens arbetare*, 161. 16 Compare note 2 above.

Table 3.3 *Skilled workers as % of the total labour force, 1771–1828.*

Period	Silk	Woollen	Cotton	Textiles total
1771–80	51	24	26	32
1781–90	60	23	36	35
1791–1800	57	19	37	33
1801–10	43	23	23	35
1811–20	32	29	35	34
1821–28	28	29	35	32
1771–1828	46	24	32	33

Sources: See table 3.1.

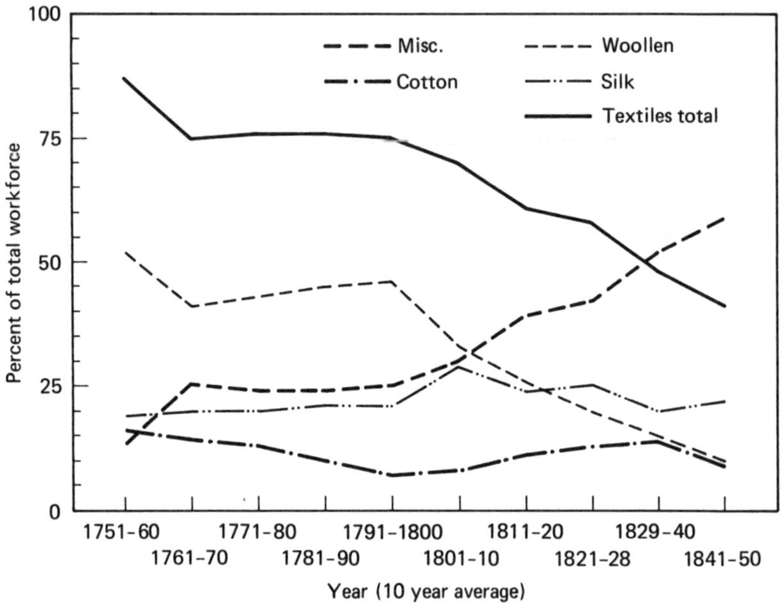

Figure 3.2 The relative size of manufacturing branches measured in number of workers, 1751–1846.

skilled labour, from 51 per cent in the 1770s to 28 per cent in the 1820s. Nyström explains this trend as a tendency from the 1790s onwards to use female unskilled workers as weavers.[17] In the woollen industry, the share of skilled labour went down from 24 to 19 per cent in 1800

[17] Nyström, *Stadsindustriens arbetare*, 180.

and up again to 29 per cent in the 1820s. For the total textile sector, the share of skilled labour amounted to around 35 per cent throughout the period. The figures for the other sectors were higher (about 70 per cent skilled labour), but they are not easily comparable with the textile workers (see table 3.3).

Sector analysis

The recorded percentage of workers in different sectors shows that it was the textile sector that declined, while other sectors (sugar, tobacco, and miscellaneous sectors) were relatively stable at an aggregate level. The woollen industry especially dwindled throughout the period, from about 50 per cent of the total labour force in the 1750s to 20 per cent in the 1820s (see figure 3.2). In absolute figures it lost more than 80 per cent of its workforce. The national figures show much the same development for the woollen industry, so this was not a regional phenomenon before the 1820s. In fact the manufactured goods were, irrespective of fluctuations in demand and extent of smuggling, substituted for by the domestic industry.[18] During the following decades the woollen industry continued to decrease in Stockholm while it increased in the countryside. Since this was a period of increasing demand for textiles throughout the country this is also an indication that it was primarily from the 1820s that the de-industrialization of Stockholm became a regional phenomenon.[19]

The development of the enterprises

Another interesting feature of the de-industrialization pattern is the fact that the average size of the enterprises diminished while the number of enterprises was rising. Most of this development was an effect of the 1760s crisis, when the average size of the textile factories went down from 44 to 19 workers. But the tendency continued at a slower tempo, and by the 1820s the average size of the textile factory was 11 workers. There was also a downward trend in the other sectors which halved their average size during the period from six to three workers. For the total manufacturing industry the average number dropped from 24 to six workers during the period. There are however indications that some factories in Stockholm were putting out jobs to certain parts of the countryside. The extent of this is not known but it

18 There is very little quantitative data underpinning this conclusion. For a general discussion of the domestic industry see G. Utterström, *Jordbrukets arbetare II* (Stockholm, 1957) passim.

19 For the increase in demand from the 1820s see Schön, *Från hantverk till fabriksindustri*, 59ff.

Table 3.4 *Number of enterprises (E) and workers per enterprise (W/E)* (Five-year averages, selected years 1756/1760 – 1821/1825).

	1756/60		1766/70		1796/1800		1821/25	
Branch	E	W/E	E	W/E	E	W/E	E	W/E
Silk	52	39	70	15	93	13	64	15
Woollen	78	58	89	25	98	26	75	11
Cotton	20	63	28	28	23	15	44	11
Textiles, total*	186	44	221	19	243	18	211	11
Others	209	6	248	5	233	5	402	3
Total	395	24	468	12	476	11	614	6

* Including dye works, calico printers, etc.
Sources: See table 3.1.

could if it was an expanding activity partly explain the decreasing number of workers in the Stockholm factories (see table 3.4).

Production

Had there been an expansion in the volume of production notwithstanding the decline in the number of workers, an hypothesis of de-industrialization would be doubtful. It is also in this area that the discussion concerning the character of Swedish manufacturing has taken place. As mentioned before the statistical material concerning production is more difficult to elaborate on. However an attempt shall be made here to outline the general trend in the development of the volume of production in one case, the cloth factories.

Table 3.5 is based on the production of fine, medium, and coarse cloth representing about 70 per cent of the total volume of production in the cloth factories. The miscellaneous products representing the remaining production may have differed throughout the period and therefore the figure should be seen as an approximation of the development.

This type of calculation is possible only where there are figures available on homogeneous products. Therefore, an effort to evaluate the development of the total production must be based on the value of production. As mentioned before there were at times discrepancies between market prices and the tariff values of production and furthermore the currency system went through many changes throughout the period. The studies made in this field have however

Table 3.5 *Volume of production in Stockholm cloth manufacturing, 1767–1846.* (Index 1771/75 = 100. Five-year averages)

Period	Volume	Quality index	Period	Volume	Quality index
1751–5	68	-	1801–5	97	106
1756–60	83	-	1806–10	106	112
1761–5	67	-	1811–15	76	140
1766–70	78	90	1816–20	98	165
1771–5	100	100	1821–5	81	172
1776–80	109	114	1826–30	62	171
1781–5	115	113	1831–5	57	186
1786–90	123	107	1836–40	40	183
1791–5	109	113	1841–6	31	174
1796–1800	126	107			

Sources: See table 3.1.

used the value of production figures in calculating the development of production.[20]

In the column 'Quality index' the actual volume figures for each quality are weighted by current relative prices for the three different qualities in each period. This gives an indication of the relative development between the qualities. No doubt a great deal of the price differential between the qualities is due to the prices of the raw materials used, and they only partly reflect production costs. Therefore, to let the volume figures be fully weighted by the quality index, would be to overestimate the part played by the factories in the quality-specific development of produced goods. However, as the figures stand, they tend to somewhat compound the expansion in the late eighteenth century and weaken the recession in the first half of the nineteenth century.

The figures recorded are in accordance with the results accounted for by Heckscher, Nyström, and others. Combined with a decreasing number of workers they indicate a strong productivity growth in the decades after the crisis. As there are no indications of substantial technological change during the period, this development has led to different types of explanations.

To Heckscher, this development contradicted his general view on manufacturing and he had great difficulty in finding an explanation.

[20] For a more recent study in this field see O. Krantz, 'Production and labour in the Swedish manufactories during the 18th century', *Economy and History* 19 (1976). The Swedish currency system and its changes during the period are described in L. Jörberg, *A History of Prices in Sweden I* (Lund, 1972), 78ff.

Partly, he thought, it could be explained by the possibility that the weakest firms were eliminated through the change in economic policy after the crisis.[21] In Nyström's view it was a development towards more easily produced goods that explained the rise in productivity. This conclusion he based principally on a study of the silk industry.[22] For the cloth industry this would have meant a development towards greater production of coarse cloth in the woollen industry. As we have seen the development was on the contrary.

Discussion

The contemporary interest in manufacturing was very intense in relation to the marginal role it played in total industrial production: the domestic industry was the dominating form of production. This interest, of course, was a consequence of the efforts to substitute for imports, especially of textiles. The great political interest in the manufactures gave us on the one hand comprehensive statistical information that may be unique in international comparison. On the other hand it may have led to an overestimation of the role of politics in the development of manufacturing. For Heckscher, the mercantilistic policy was an effective obstacle to dynamic industrial development, for which a liberal laissez faire policy was required.[23] Nyström saw the manufacturers as a progressive element in the development towards the factory industry, putting less weight on the economic policy of the time. To somewhat simplify their positions, there was according to Heckscher a strong political impact obstructing economic growth, whereas Nyström saw a positive industrial development which was relatively independent of the economic policy pursued. That is, in both cases, the factories per se were (or could be) a progressive form of production.

As we have seen the evidence suggests two contradictory tendencies. There was no doubt a substantial absolute decrease in the number of workers as well as in production volume, but there is also an agreement among authors that there was an obvious rise in productivity within textiles from the late 1760s. This raises the question whether, irrespective of changed economic policy after 1760, one could expect an overall dynamic development of manufacturing. Marx characterizes the manufactures by division and hierarchization of

[21] Heckscher, *Sveriges ekonomiska historia*, 614.
[22] Nyström, *Stadsindustriens arbetare*, chapter 5.
[23] Heckscher, 'De svenska manufakturerna', 220.

labour, promoting the capitalists 'conscious goal' of cheapening production.[24] But

> At the same time, manufacture was unable either to seize upon the production of society to its full extent, or to revolutionize that production to its very core. It towered up as an artificial economic construction, on the broad foundation of the town handicraft and the domestic industries of the countryside. At a certain stage of its development, the narrow technical basis on which manufacture rested came into contradiction with requirements of production which it had itself created.[25]

The economic basis of manufacturing, according to Marx, rather than the economic policy, was the bottleneck.

For a further analysis of development it is of course necessary to supplement the data with information at the micro level. As said before there is very little information saved from the factories except for the official data in the Kommerskollegium, which on the other hand are all the more comprehensive. Apart from this data, it is also possible to obtain information from bankruptcy and estate inventories.

Nyström characterized the factories as normal types of enterprises, expressing the entrepreneurial ambitions and industrial aspirations of the time.[26] This conclusion he based primarily on studies of the largest factories. The impression given by the general development is rather that there must have been certain variations in this respect.

To what extent an accumulation of capital was undertaken on the basis of the manufacturing businesses cannot yet be answered, but anyway the accumulated capital did not have to accrue to the manufacturers. The fixed capital recorded in the bankruptcies was still in this period rather small, about 10–30 per cent of the turnover, and substantially less than the value of the stock of goods and raw materials accounted for. The possible profits made therefore were not primarily invested within the sector. This fact is also indicated by the change in the size of the factories, measured by number of workers.

One possibility of providing capital to the manufacturers was within the framework of a putting-out system between financiers and manufacturers.[27] The law gave the financiers a strong position in case of bankruptcy. It seems, however, that the formal putting-out system did not dominate, at least not in the 1830s. Nevertheless there was a great flow of credit to the manufacturing sector, as well as to merchants, noble persons, etc. The official financial institutions were still an important source of credits, but the legal restrictions made their

24 K. Marx, *Capital*, vol. 1 (Aylesbury 1976), 455ff.
25 *Ibid.*, 490.
26 Nyström, *Stadsindustriens arbetare*, 313.
27 *Ibid.*, 222ff, 309ff.

loans a minor part of the total capital supply. The manufacturers normally needed to obtain loans corresponding to one year's working capital, which had to include the credits that the manufacturer himself had to grant his customers. In the cases studied so far, that of bankruptcy firms, the volume of the loans exceeded that level by several times. The excessive financial transactions recorded in the bankruptcy data may not have been representative for factories in general, but to the extent these loans existed, they may have been profitable for the financiers, as well as necessary for the manufacturers.

Certainly these data are no more than an indication that tends to confirm the impression given by the aggregated statistical data that, notwithstanding the rise in productivity, there was a lack of dynamics in the development of the manufacturing industry. Whether or not this confirms Marx' thesis of inherent contradictions within the manufacturing sector, cannot be answered here.

The labour market of the manufactures and the informal sector

The basic division of the labour force into skilled and unskilled workers also roughly divides the workers with respect to gender. A large proportion of the unskilled workers worked in their homes, sometimes as a form of side occupation. The labour force thus consisted primarily of male skilled workers (and apprentices) and unskilled workers employed on a full-time basis in the factories, and also the homeworkers, mostly female unskilled labourers working on a part-time basis.

If the informal sector of the labour market is taken to be the part characterized primarily by small-scale and irregular self-employment,[28] the relationship between the manufacturers and the informal sector is somewhat complex. As we have seen the relationship between skilled and unskilled workers was on an aggregate level rather stable, and both groups decreased steadily. The degree to which de-industrialization contributed to the growth of the informal sector is however dependent upon how we define the relationship between the informal sector and the homeworkers. Among the homeworkers some should of course belong to the formal sector, but should all of them?

I have calculated two alternatives for the decrease of the formal sector during the de-industrialization process. In the first alternative the whole labour market of the manufacturers belongs to the formal sector, that is, the total decrease in number of workers is also a

[28] No further meaning is ascribed to the concept 'informal sector' in this context.

decrease in the formal sector. In the second alternative all homeworkers are put into the informal sector, which is the minimum alternative with respect to the effect of de-industrialization on the develop ment of the formal sector. In the first alternative about 5,300 jobs disappeared between the 1750s and the 1820s. In the second alternative about 2,000 to 3,000 disappeared in the same period.[29] The latter alternative may in some respects be more realistic, but it does not account for the worsening situation which in that case fell upon the people in the informal sector as jobs disappeared. (In the first alternative disappearing jobs meant a transition from the formal to the informal sector, for the homeworkers also). These calculations do not account for the fact that this decrease in employment could at least partly have been substituted for outside the factories.

[29] The sources do not permit a more precise figure.

4

Labour markets and the informal sector

The concept of the informal sector

A theoretically and methodologically difficult problem concerns the historical study of relationships between the formal and informal sectors of urban economies. This chapter deals with some aspects of the Stockholm experience between the mid eighteenth and the mid nineteenth centuries, exploring the usefulness of the informal sector concept as used in modern research on Third World urbanization.

One of the major mechanisms behind the long-term stagnation of Stockholm seems to have been the competition offered by an expansive rural cottage production. The textile manufacturers of Stockholm had to compete with rural small-scale production, an activity that was successfully combined with peasant farming particularly in western Sweden. Cottage production, culminating during the agricultural off-season, was well adapted to the rural production cycle. Since farming covered much of the subsistence of the labour force, prices could be kept low. The emphasis on coarse and cheap qualities within the cottage industry can be seen as a response to the actual market demand. In terms of comparative advantages, textile production may well have been the industrial activity that the capital was least fit to handle with largely unmechanized technology.

During the century of economic and demographic stagnation following 1750, employment in the regular or formal sector stagnated. Stockholm lost employment in manufacturing while other formal sectors offered little or no growth. A likely consequence is that many people increasingly had to pursue their livelihoods outside the regular economy by combining various odd occupations. What is known as the informal sector in contemporary discussion on Third World cities must have grown in importance for a considerable portion of the working population of Stockholm.

Regardless of how sharply we may try to define economic activities, it will never be possible to produce direct quantitative evidence of the employment shifts. In Stockholm, the formal and informal sectors were so intertwined as to make any attempt at even gauging their relative sizes impossible. In many cases the activities of an individual could be shared between formal and informal ones. This applies, for instance, to large segments of the government and municipal employees during the later eighteenth century. They could not make a living on their salaries alone, but had to find supplementary, more or less legal sources of income.[1] When married, it is probable that the wife performed some work, although we seldom know of what sort or to what extent.

An illustration is provided by the soldier wife Catharina Engdahl, aged 45, applying for poor relief in 1809. According to the investigation carried out by the authorities, she possessed a spinning-wheel and also did some knitting, altogether earning about 2 *skilling* a day (approximately one fifth of the daily wage of an unskilled male labourer). Her 14-year-old son was a tobacco worker, earning 4 *skilling* a day. Catharina's income was 'rather unstable and uncertain' since she was also taking care of two younger sons aged four and two. The family lived in a room with a floor of stamped earth, 'the poorest that has ever been seen', sharing it (and the cost) with 'other tenants'. Part of the explanation for their poverty was reported to be that the husband, while living at home, was constantly doing service. He was thus prevented from supporting his family through earnings other than his meagre salary.[2]

What follows can at best outline some plausible trends in and effects of what may be called the informalization of the economy of the capital. At some points some relatively straightforward indirect evi-

1 For eighteenth-century examples of activity among public employees beside their service see S. Bergh, Svenska Riksarkivet 1618–1837. *Meddelanden från svenska Riksarkivet, N.F., II:5* (Stockholm, 1916), 110. During most of this century, the salaries of officials lagged far behind prices (see chapters 5 and 6 below). While there was a general recognition of the 'well-known distress and poor circumstances' among the officials, little was done to improve the situation. Functionaries repeatedly complained that they simply could not manage on their salary; some stated that they possessed hardly any clothes and no households utensils as they had been pledged. 'Some developed more or less peculiar by-activities', says Bergh, such as taverns of doubtful reputation. Some sold their right to promotion, agreeing to refrain from applying for higher posts against a sum of money. Some even sold archival materials from the National Archive.

2 J. Müller, *Fattigvården i Stockholm från äldre till nyare tid* (Stockholm, 1906), 119–24.

dence from a variety of sources can be presented, but much of the discussion will be speculative.

We will advance the hypothesis that alternating trends of informalization and formalization have occurred depending upon the development of the formal sector of the economy. It is reasonable to expect that people, having the choice, prefer stable incomes and legal jobs before the risks and short planning horizons generally ascribed to informal activities. Informal sector expansion has taken place in periods of over-supply of labour, which in turn may be due to formal sector contraction, growing barriers to entry (for legal or economic reasons), or large-scale in-migration. We expect that the latter part of the eighteenth century was a period of informal sector expansion, possibly continuing during the first decades of the nineteenth. After the mid nineteenth century, however, industrialization generated a strong growth in the formal sector, reducing unemployment and seasonal variations in demand for labour. Then the informal sector declined in importance.

Modern research on Third World urbanization has often separated the urban labour market into a formal and an informal sector, although with varying definitions. In general, the informal sector is taken to comprise a large and varied number of small-scale activities within a self-employment and family employment environment. It is also supposed to involve easier entry and less regulation. Empirically, however, the informal sector is often found to be closely linked to the formal sector from the input as well as from the output side. The notion of informal activities being superfluous or unproductive has increasingly been questioned on the basis of empirical evidence from a number of Third World countries.[3]

When using a concept developed to help explain the reality of present-day Third World urbanization we have to be very careful. In certain respects it is more fruitful to compare contemporary Third World cities with non-industrialized capitalist towns such as Stockholm than with nineteenth-century industrializing cities as is often done.

The informal sector concept was originally formed in close connection with the idea of the presence of a large 'marginal mass' in Third World cities. Dependency writers such as José Nun noted that the gap between the requirements of modern industry and the labour surplus was of such dimensions as to exclude a large part of this 'marginal mass' from any function in the capitalist accumulation

[3] J. F. Linn, *Cities in the Developing World* (New York, 1983).

process.[4] In order to survive they were forced to combine a myriad of scattered economic activities labelled as the informal sector. Its relationship with the regular economy was one of fundamental disarticulation, an urban reproduction of the dualism between urban capitalist and rural subsistence sectors. In this perspective, migration into the cities was not primarily conditioned by pull factors in the urban economy but by push factors in the rural society.

At first sight, the approaches discussed above may seem very relevant for a study of late eighteenth- and early nineteenth-century Stockholm. In spite of a number of obvious differences from contemporary Third World cities, a considerable part of the population was located outside the regular labour market. To a large extent the informal sector in Stockholm must have been recruited from rather recent migrants to the city. Although population stagnated, Stockholm was heavily dependent on in-migration due to a substantial excess mortality not only among infants but also among adult males. The majority of the migrants to Stockholm came from the surrounding lake Mälaren area which was characterized by a comparatively slow growth of employment in agriculture. Consequently, we cannot exclude the existence of strong push factors behind the in-migration to Stockholm.[5]

Even if these early theories of marginalization and the informal sector possess some attractive properties, they have serious weaknesses both in the Third World and the historical context. A considerable number of studies on the informal sector in Third World cities have contributed to a more complex picture of the phenomena. The new literature denies that the informal sector can be interpreted as an urban extension of traditional subsistence activities.

On the contrary the informal sector is regarded as small-scale economic activities outside the state and the state regulated private sector with close but complex connections with the formal economy.[6] Migration to a city, even when confined to employment in the informal sector, often results in a significant improvement in living standards. Thus there are certainly more than simple push factors behind the rural/urban population shift. The new urbanite in the Third World is not necessarily a desperate destitute unwillingly pushed out

4 J. Nun, 'Superpoblación relativa, ejérjito industrial y masa marginal', *Revista Latinoamericana de sociología* 2 (1969).

5 U. Jonsson, 'Godsens förändring under 1800-talet; omvandlingsmönster och effekter på befolkningsutvecklingen', *Bebyggelsehistorisk tidskrift* 9 (1985).

6 C. Moser, 'Informal sector or petty commodity production: dualism or dependence in urban development', *World Development* 6 (1978).

of his rural background as formerly portrayed, but a rather rational economic actor.

The new approaches emphasize the role of the informal sector in reducing the level of subsistence wages and thereby the cost of maintenance of labour employed in the formal capitalist sector. In their discussion on recent research of the articulation of informal and formal economies, Alejandro Portes and John Walton point out three 'income-producing' strategies of the urban lower strata outside the formal economy: (a) subsistence and networking activities, (b) petty commodity production and trade, (c) informal land occupation.[7]

Most of the discussion has focussed on what may be seen as four dimensions of the informal sector concept:

1 It relies on small-scale, family labour.
2 It is largely unregulated by authorities, facilitating ease of entry.
3 It may be composed of legal activities but is more often characterized by quasi-legality, situated on the borderline between legality and criminality.
4 The planning horizons are short, and there is a strong element of instability and discontinuity in the informal activities.

The formal and informal sectors in Stockholm

In Stockholm we can safely disregard informal land occupation; the state and legal machineries were far too strong to make such activities possible. The other areas mentioned are, however, worth considering.

Subsistence activities of different kinds, especially animal rearing, was of fairly great importance in many European eighteenth- and nineteenth-century towns and this also applies to Stockholm. As late as the mid 1850s Stockholm had some 5,000 pigs and 2,000 cows.[8]

In contrast to present-day Third World cities, urban animal rearing was not exclusively an informal occupation.[9] Urban dairies were in general large-scale undertakings. Burgher families frequently raised some pigs on the outskirts of the city. However, we can safely assume that the raising of a pig or two or some hens must have been an

7 A. Portes and J. Walton, *Labor, Class, and the International System* (New York, 1981).

8 *Underdånigt betänkande angående Sveriges ekonomiska och finansiella utveckling under åren 1834–1860* (Stockholm, 1863).

9 See G. Berg, 'Boskapsskötel och jordbruk i det gamla Stockholm', *Sankt Eriks årsbok* 1932. Berg finds some evidence that animal husbandry in the capital, particularly the keeping of cows, was growing during the first half of the nineteenth century, but more as an activity of large burghers on the outskirts of the city proper. The small burghers successively ceased to keep animals. Animal husbandry may then be seen as gradually becoming less of an informal sector activity.

important income supplement for households outside the regular labour market. Regrettably, the sources are rather silent on popular animal husbandry. It is impossible to show, like Brian Roberts and Chris Birbeck for Guatemala City and Cali, that some households not only raised pigs and poultry, using city garbage dumps in a systematic way as a source of fodder, for their consumption but also had enough to sell in the market.[10]

In the Third World housing construction constitutes another important area of subsistence activity. Large segments of the urban population are excluded from even low-cost housing projects in the formal economy. A substantial proportion of the workers in peripheral cities have to build their own houses, often following spontaneous or organized occupation of vacant land. Housing construction as an informal sector activity was of less importance in Stockholm, even though large parts of the outskirts of the capital had a more or less shanty town character. It is difficult to establish any clear cut dividing line between formal and informal building activities. Still, more or less self-constructed low-cost housing was not altogether insignificant as a strategy to keep living costs down for the poor population.

Subsistence activities are not conducted in isolation. Social networks of more or less kinship character are, as shown by Larissa Lomnitz, of extreme importance for survival in Third World cities.[11] The strategic role of social networks for people outside the regular labour market in a European city in decline, eighteenth- and early nineteenth-century Antwerp, has been vividly demonstrated by Catharina Lis.[12] She is inclined to emphasize the relative efficiency of networks, which appear to have been a widespread phenomenon in Antwerp. Social networks were capable of providing aid and support otherwise not available.

It is difficult to believe that social networks in Stockholm were equally important or widespread among the lower strata. The heavy male excess mortality for the age span 20 to 50 years can be taken as an indication that at least for adult men social networks were not well-developed or efficient. Taken together with the high rates of population turnover, this certainly must have made the establishment

10 B. Roberts, *Cities of Peasants; The Political Economy of Urbanization in the Third World* (London, 1978); C. Birbeck, 'Self-employed proletarians in an informal factory: the case of Cali's garbage dump', *World Development* 6 (1978).
11 L. Lomnitz, *Networks and Marginality: Life in a Mexican Shanty Town* (New York, 1982).
12 C. Lis, 'Proletarian Networks in Antwerp during the First Half of the Nineteenth Century.' Paper presented at the conference 'Methodological Problems in Urban History', Stockholm, 1984.

of social networks of kinship character among the lower strata a difficult matter.

Petty commodity production and small-scale trade constitute central parts of the informal sector in contemporary peripheral cities. A large portion of the goods and services consumed by the lower classes, and even by those employed in formal capitalist firms, are provided by informal enterprises. In the same way as for subsistence activities and social networks, informal production serves the purpose of lowering the cost of maintenance of the labour force used in the capitalist sector. Thus, the relationship between the formal and informal sector is one of complementarity rather than competition.

Portes and Walton, for example, are fully aware of the fact that the reliance on family subsistence activities for the maintenance of the labour force is not a new phenomenon in the history of capitalism.[13] In the same way the use of disorganized vulnerable labour is a familiar part of the early history of capitalism in the developed part of the world. 'The new school' on the informal sector strongly maintains that the situation in the Third World is very different from the European experience. The presence of a large informal sector cannot be regarded as a transitional phenomenon in the peripheral societies. Quite on the contrary, the informal sector is a very modern creation and its development is determined by the conditions in which these economies were incorporated into the present-day world system. On the whole it seems reasonable to stress these differences between contemporary Third World and early capitalist Europe although we should not underestimate the reappearance of informal sector activities in developed countries today.

Early non-industrial capitalist cities like Stockholm constitute in certain respects a special case in the relationship between informal and formal sectors of the economy. Still, in the second half of the eighteenth century and up to their abolishment in 1846, the guilds maintained monopoly claims on the production of most goods and services and jealously tried to protect their markets. The lion's share of the informal activities were formally outlawed.

Outlawing informal production and marketing did not stop it, of course. There are constant complaints from artisans and tradesmen of illegal competition from persons outside their organizations, but control never was complete.[14] A wide spectrum of people – unskilled

13 Portes and Walton, *Labor*.

14 In 1772 the guilds asserted that there were 1,115 'known' illegal craftsmen (*bönhasar*, from German *Bohnhasen*) in the capital, whereas the number of masters of legal status numbered about as many, or 1,129. The basis for the calculation is not known, and we

labourers, former soldiers, guards, wives or widows of soldiers, sailors, or other men in low strata – are found among those who got caught for infringing the rights of the guilds. Söderlund, who analysed parts of the judicial material, concludes that 'the prosecuted occupied himself with illegal handicrafts since this has been the only way to keep starvation away'.[15]

From the 1820s it is known that a considerable portion – almost 40 per cent – of the soldiers of the Stockholm garrison were able to perform some sort of handicraft, judging from the occupational titles and the skills they reported themselves to possess at the time of enrolment. As could be expected, many had backgrounds in handicrafts requiring low amounts of capital, usually as shoemakers or tailors. This combination of skills should no doubt be seen against the difficult economic position of the soldiers, necessitating incomes to supplement their pay from the garrison. As employment opportunities expanded with the industrialization from about 1870 onwards, a smaller portion of the soldiers can be assumed to have known any handicraft.[16] The civil side-employments of the soldiers declined in importance with the formal sector expansion in the latter part of the nineteenth century. The burghers naturally regarded the military competition in handicrafts as a threat to the monopoly rights connected with the guild system.

There were members of the urban establishment, for example manufacturers employing much casual labour on a putting-out basis, who showed a more ambiguous attitude towards the informal sector. Mostly, though, informal activities were regarded more as a threat to the established order than as an asset to lower the costs of production. In the aftermath of the severe 1763 crisis some unemployed labourers applied to Kommerskollegium, a government office, for permission to start making their living by brewing and baking in their homes. This proposal met with strong protests from the guilds. The government simply decided to leave it to the workers to find out on their own how to legally earn their living.[17]

A considerable part of the population was thus more or less compelled to make their living on the margin of legality, often crossing

can be sure that the guilds at least did not underrate the extent of illicit competition. B. Boëthius, *Magistraten och borgerskapet i Stockholm 1719–1815* (Stockholm, 1943), 464.

15 E. Söderlund, *Stockholms hantverkarklass 1720–1772* (Stockholm, 1943), 300.

16 Several interesting aspects of the recruitment of the soldiers and the labour market facing them have recently been studied by R. Adolfsson, 'Arbetsmarknad och geografisk rörlighet', 48 and O. Brick, 'Familjebildning och dödlighet', 69, both in *Ett militärt stadsproletariat*, ed. G. Artéus (Stockholm, 1988).

17 See also chapter 3 above.

this borderline. In a stagnating and in certain respects contracting economy like that of Stockholm the conflict between the informal and formal sectors tended to be especially severe.

It is worth noting that female-dominated informal sector activities like laundry work or household services on a casual basis were much less of a threat to established interests. In fact, some important female activities commonly taken to be characteristic of the informal sector were to a certain extent formalized in the Stockholm economy. This applies for instance to street-vending, some of which was legalized. Females could apply for and get permission to sell certain goods, such as trinkets, in the streets (although illegal vending also took place). Another legal female sphere was running public-houses, particularly the cheaper ones (although some doubled as brothels, which was illegal). Some could establish themselves as oarswomen, 'rowing mamsels', transporting people between the islands of the city. Consequently, women could eke out a meagre livelihood somewhat more undisturbed than men.[18]

The main differences between the male and female labour markets are however to be found in the *formal* sector. The dominating occupation among unmarried females was that of being a maid-servant. It was a relatively secure occupation, employment being generally on a one-year basis, protecting the females from seasonal fluctuations in labour demand.

Also, servants could not be fired without legal reason. Police records often report cases of employers trying to get rid of maid-servants, but failing. When a dentist dismissed a maid-servant in 1800, for instance, accusing her of drunkenness and pilfering, she went to the police and was exonerated. The dentist had to pay her a sum corresponding to one fifth of a yearly cash wage. In several similar cases, the arguments of the complaining servant were usually accepted. Although the job as a maid-servant involved much physically demanding manual labour and the cash wage was extremely low (most of the wage being in kind, of course), there was no correspondingly regular and secure sector for

[18] The bakers' guild was one of those affected by informal sector competition from females not belonging to the guild. In an 1839 application the Stockholm guild noted that several permissions had been granted during the last decade to persons outside the guild to conduct bakery in various forms. Moreover, they claimed, 'a lot of old women, partly with a permission and partly without, have started to bake and sell bread'. The bakers regarded the disloyal competition as uncontrollable, and, when the guilds finally were abolished in 1846, the bakers' guild greeted this with satisfaction. Prosecution of these female bakers and vendors does not appear to have been severe. See Å. Campbell, *Det svenska brödet* (Stockholm 1950), 193f., and H. Wallgren, *Sveriges bageriidkarförening och Stockholms bageriidkarförening* (Stockholm, 1924), 50ff.

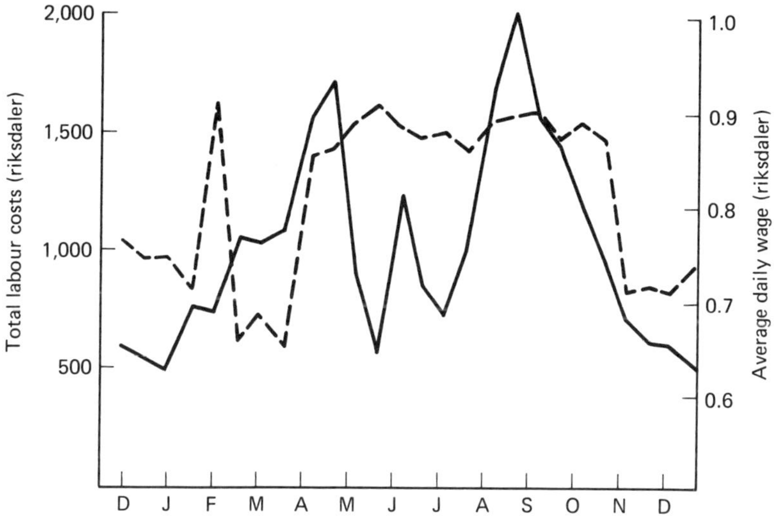

Figure 4.1 Seasonal variation in the daily labour costs in municipal building, 1850 (unbroken line and left-hand scale). Average daily wage cost (dotted line and right-hand scale). *Source*: Byggnadskontorets arkiv, Verifikationer 1850. Stockholm City Archive.

young males. Though not insignificant, the number of male servants was much smaller; out of the number of servants reported in 1769, 74 per cent were females.[19]

A commission on poor relief noted in an 1807 report that the capital suffered from heavy unemployment. 'Work is invariably missing from the large numbers there who need it, particularly those who must make their living with their hands.' Regarding the male labour market, the commission pointed to seasonal migratory labour as a problem. They competed amongst others with the soldiers of the capital who were in need of extra employment. Seasonal migrants did not affect the female labour market. Even without labourers from outside, there was not work enough for all, and those existing workers were very badly paid. In particular, the spinners were described as particularly badly off. A skilled spinner, 'industrious beyond reproach', could make no more than 4½ skilling a day, only half a skilling more than the minimum sum regarded necessary to support a poor person.

The seasonality of labour demand was far more of a problem for males. Many unskilled male jobs were scarce during winter. Seasonal

[19] *Minnesskrift med anledning av den svenska befolkningsstatistikens 200-åriga bestånd* (Stockholm, 1949), 50.

fluctuations are illustrated in figure 4.1 above, presenting the volume of work in municipal building in Stockholm in 1850. The unbroken line refers to total costs of day-labour (unskilled as well as relatively skilled) from December, 1849 to December, 1850. The dotted line describes average daily pay, which was substantially higher in summer.

Employment could obviously be highly fluctuating. Not only was demand for labour far lower during winter, sharp changes also occurred during the summer season (note the decline in May and the peak in August). The differential between summer and winter daily wage rates of course served to further aggravate the income fluctuation problems over the year.

Seasonal unemployment in pre-industrial Stockholm is likely to have been a major social problem, though it probably was reduced during the later decades of the nineteenth century. The capital was increasingly industrialized from about 1860, involving a growth in mechanical engineering and chemical industries. It does not seem possible to estimate the order of magnitude of the change in unemployment.

Mention may be made, however, of the rise in the number of workdays per year among the municipally employed Stockholm labourers. In 1860/4 the unskilled were employed only 166 days a year, a figure which grew to 217 in 1865/70 and then was fairly stable at 250 to 280 days a year up to the turn of the century. Before the 1870s the labourers must have had access to other sources of income during part of the year, about which we know nothing.

In the nineteenth century we have fairly good indications that poverty in active ages did hit males harder than females. Chapter 6 below will report a cross-section study of Stockholm in 1850, involving an analysis of age- and sex-specific poverty using a method based on tax records. Figure 4.2, based on the same material, displays more clearly the differences between males and females by age. Among adults, female ratios are significantly lower up to the age of 50.

Among adults, poverty ratios probably are a rather good estimator of the employment situation. The capitation tax was so low that it was practically impossible to get exempted if not lacking any kind of income for fairly long periods. This, taken together with the large mortality gap between sexes in the age span 25–50, indicates that males in active ages must have faced an unfavourable situation in the stagnating city.

The position of females, on the other hand, was very unfavourable in old age. From the age of 50 upwards, poverty figures suggest that

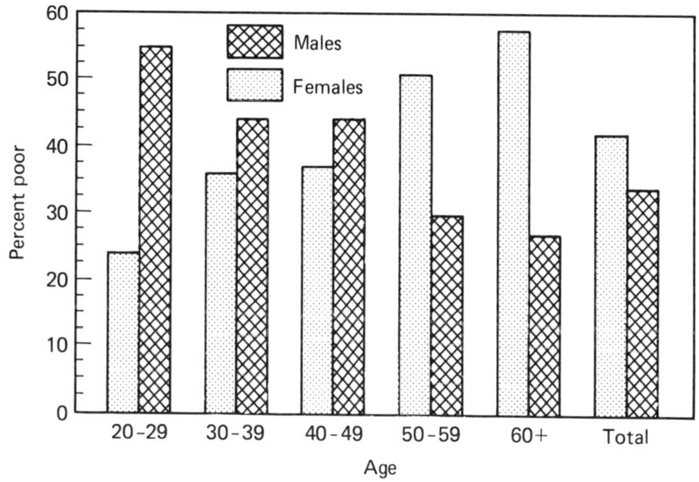

Figure 4.2 Poverty ratios among adults by age group in Stockholm, 1850.
Sources: See chapter 6 below.

females were at a disadvantage. A reasonable interpretation is that females after leaving the comparatively protected household servant sector experienced even greater difficulties than males in providing for themselves in the informal market. The high male mortality also gave rise to many widows who found themselves in a precarious situation. If the man had been a craftsman, the widow could in principle continue to run the shop; otherwise there was a a high likelihood that she would remarry. If the deceased on the other hand was a soldier, civil servant, labourer, or other unpropertied man, the position of the widow was more difficult.

The exposed situation of women in old age is independently indicated by data regarding people labelled as poor or prisoners in the tables produced by the statistical authority (*Tabellverket*). Between 1800 and 1830 the share of females among these fluctuated between 64 and 84 per cent.[20]

The female-dominated part of the informal sector then seems to have functioned similarly to what we observe in the urban Third World today, providing the formal economy with goods and services at low cost. Informal activities of males, on the other hand, met with tougher resistance from important segments of the formal economy. A significant part of the male population was to a certain extent marginal in the original sense of the word.

20 *Ibid.*, 54–66.

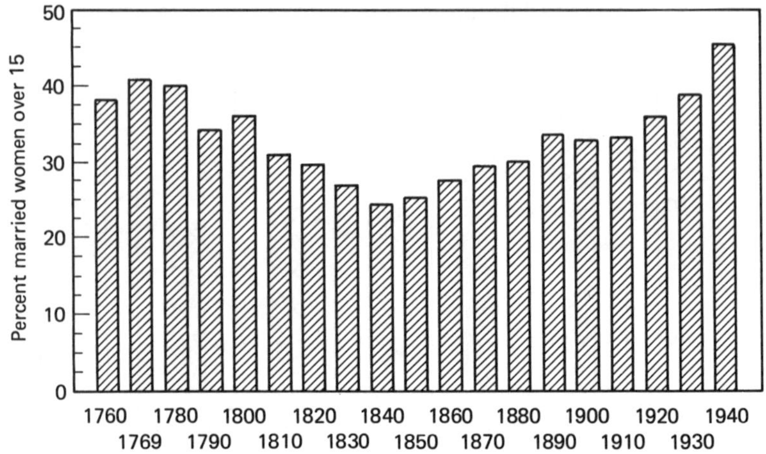

Figure 4.3 Percentage of married females out of the total number of females above 15 years of age in Stockholm, 1760–1940. *Source*: G. Utterström, Stockholms folkmängd 1663–1763 (1760), (1949), 276; Äldre tabellkommissionens arkiv, Folkmängdstabeller, Statistiska Centralbyråns arkiv (1780 and 1790); *Statistisk tidskrift* 1 (1860), 43; *Statistisk årsbok för Stockholms stad* 84 (1953), 5–6.

Several interesting problems relate to the possible demographic consequences of the economic situation of the capital. The changing pattern of nuptiality, with a declining proportion married from the latter part of the eighteenth century to the mid nineteenth, is further described in chapters 6 and 8 (figures 6.7 and 8.2). Focussing on the position of the females and extending the chronological perspective, figure 4.3 describes the U-shaped curve during the nineteenth century of the share of married females (out of the total female population over 15 years of age). After 1780 the proportion married declined substantially, from about 40 per cent to slightly less than 25 per cent in 1840 when the lowest figure was reached. After that date, with industrialization and a greater degree of regularity in economic life, the number of married women grew in the long term. The proportion of married women in 1930 was about the same as it had been in 1760.

The growth in the proportion of unmarried females brings to mind the studies by Oscar Lewis on urban slums in Latin America. Where female involvement in the informal sector was important, the frequency of unmarried females tended to be high and sexual morality to be more open. Extralegal family formation was most common among the poor where females had opportunities to provide for their own livelihood. Moreover, families often were mothercentered where the women had a strong position due to their informal sector activities.[21] The long-term pattern in Stockholm of a declining share of married women during the stagnation phase, to be followed by eroding barriers to marriage during the subsequent economic growth, would by itself suggest a cycle of informal sector expansion and contraction. As we shall see below other indicators point in the same direction.

Associated with the growing barriers to marriage is a rise in bastardy. During the late eighteenth and early nineteenth centuries bastardy was on the rise in many European towns. The rise in bastardy was however steeper in Stockholm than in most other places. Figure 4.4 displays the very long-term evolution of illegitimacy, surging during the late eighteenth century, culminating in the 1840s and then declining with industrialization and improving conditions of marriage and family formation. Not even around 1900, when in-migration of young people was very high, did the proportion of illegitimate children reach the previous high levels of the mid nineteenth century.

The illegitimacy curve of an inverted U may well reflect an underlying expansion and, later, a contraction of the informal sector. One aspect of this is the marriage patterns among the soldiers of the capital. Brick's recent study of family formation among the soldiers of the Stockholm garrison is interesting in this context since it is the only investigation describing trends with reference to a specific occupational category. A long-term decline in nuptiality takes place among the garrison soldiers.[22] Their economic situation probably deteriorated up to the mid nineteenth century. The salary they received was not keeping pace with inflation, and despite side activities in handicraft production the soldiers obviously faced great difficulties in establishing and maintaining a family. The increasingly smaller share of

21 Plenty of examples of such family structures can be found in the works of Lewis on Mexico City and Puerto Rico. See, e.g., O. Lewis, *La Vida* (New York, 1966), and O. Lewis, *A Death in the Sánchez Family* (New York, 1969).

Whether or not the urban poor belonged to a 'culture of poverty' tending to reproduce poverty, as Lewis maintains, is another issue. It is tentatively suggested by C. Winberg, 'Giftas på stockholmska', *Historisk tidskrift* 106 (1986), 95ff., that Stockholm during the stagnation period might be seen as Sweden's only 'culture of poverty' corresponding to the Third World urban slums today. Determining the existence or non-existence of a culture of poverty in Stockholm during this period would however require a study by quite other methods than have been employed here. A minimum requirement would be to analyse such materials (e.g., criminal records) that could elucidate mental outlooks among lower strata. For a thoughtful critical analysis of the 'culture of poverty' concept see C. A. Valentine, *Culture and Poverty* (Chicago, 1968).

22 At the regiment studied 40 per cent of the soldiers were married in 1773 as compared to 35 per cent in 1790 and only 22 per cent in 1800. Brick, 'Familjebildning och dödlighet', *Ett militärt stadsproletariat*, ed. G. Artéus, 68.

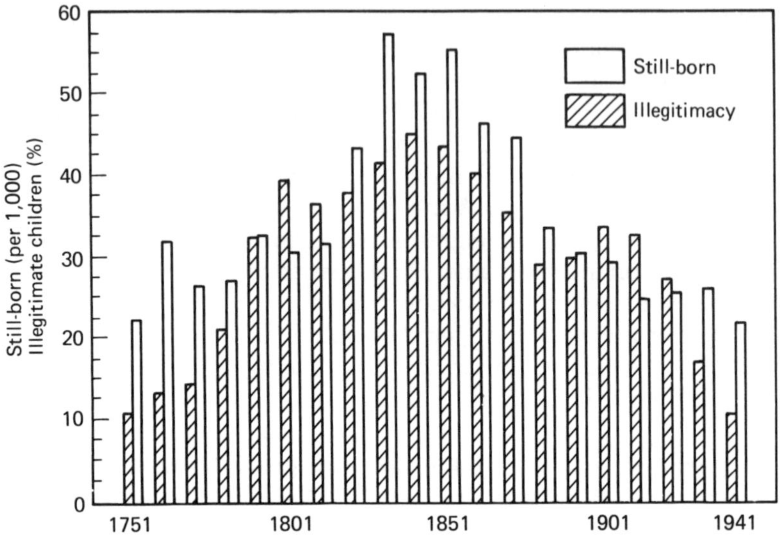

Figure 4.4 Illegitimate children as a percentage of the total number of children born and the proportion of still-born (per 1,000) in Stockholm, 1751/60 to 1941/50. *Source: Statistisk årsbok för Stockholms stad* 84 (1953), 33.

married soldiers no doubt created a demand for extramarital relations of a more or less permanent kind.[23]

The long-term evolution of illegitimacy shows the same pattern as the curve describing the proportion of still-born children, which is also included in figure 4.4. The frequency of still-births is interesting in this context since it is often seen as an indicator of female health. The proportion of still-born, while at the same level in the 1750s as in the 1940s, reaches a peak around the mid nineteenth century.

A tentative but possible explanation of both curves would be that the work-load of females was growing between the mid eighteenth to the mid nineteenth century. If informal sector expansion involved a more extensive utilization of female labour, the joint effect may have been to make women less dependent on formal marriage while at the same time placing greater strain on them, affecting them during pregnancy. In this interpretation female labour market participation

23 Not only were fewer soldiers able to marry, but there are also indications of a drop in marital fertility during the decades preceding 1860 and a subsequent rise as general economic conditions improved thereafter. The proportion of soldier families with children follows a U-shaped curve with a trough around the mid nineteenth century. The share amounted to 59 per cent in 1821–30, dropping to not more than 43 per cent in 1851–60 and then rising substantially to 68 per cent in 1886–95. Brick, 'Familjebildning och dödlighet', 64.

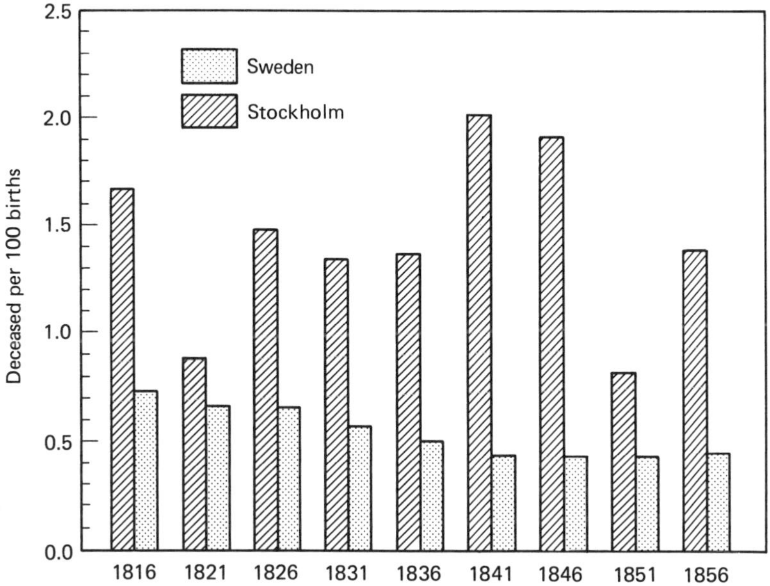

Figure 4.5 Maternal mortality in Stockholm and Sweden. Deceased in childbirth per 100 births. Five-year periods, 1816/20 – 1856/60. *Source:* W. Wretlind, *Undersökningar rörande Stockholms mortalitet* (Stockholm, 1866), 84.

may have given them more of a choice between marriage and extramarital relations, but the additional work pressure also had adverse consequences in terms of the health of the women and their children. The females became more self-supporting, but they achieved this at a cost in terms of their health.[24]

The hypothesis of deteriorating health among pregnant women is not contradicted by data on maternal mortality.[25] Figure 4.5 displays the high rates of maternal mortality in Stockholm as compared with Sweden as a whole 1816–60. Not only did females in the capital face larger dangers in childbirth, but the differential versus the nationwide average was also growing up to the late 1840s. Before mid century there is no trend towards reduced maternal mortality in the capital, in contrast to Sweden as a whole. In this series as well as in the previous

24 See also figure 8.4 below, demonstrating that the difference between infant mortality between legitimate and illegitimate children was not only large during the 1820s but also grew during the 1830s and 1840s.

25 The data on women who died in childbirth were considered by contemporaries to be more reliable than most other statistics on causes of death, since diagnosis was easy. See W. Wretlind, *Undersökningar rörande Stockholms mortalitet* (Stockholm, 1866).

ones the 1840s emerges as a particularly difficult period for the Stockholm women.

The rise in bastardy is clearly linked to the secular decline in nuptiality which is evident during the whole of the second part of the eighteenth century. What lies behind these changes in family formation and reproduction?

Nearly all the prostitutes caught by the police around 1800 were labelled as spinners. When the textile factories were at their height by the mid eighteenth century there were a great number of spinners who were only loosely connected with the enterprises. They usually worked at home, and the production volume varied enormously between spinners. Some spun thirty times as much as others. For many of them, the work for the factories can only have formed a minor part of their means of existence. As manufacturing employment was reduced, it would be reasonable to expect that informal or even illegal activities became increasingly important. Sexual services belonged to these activities. The following examples all stem from police manuscript records for the years 1799–1800 in the City Archive of Stockholm.

Authorities tried to persecute prostitution by severe punishments. A special institution, the spinning house, served as a prison for female prostitutes, vagrants, and beggars. In July 1799 a coachman came to the police claiming that he had been robbed of 4 riksdaler (corresponding to some twenty day-wages of an unskilled labourer) while spending the night at an inn sleeping with a servant-girl. Then the female owner and the girl had started a fight leading to their arrest. Both were sentenced to half a year at the spinning house. The owner lost her public-house rights, and two of her children were taken to the orphanage. After having served the punishment she got work at a brewery as a maid.[26]

It was the duty of the police – certainly not an easy one – to check that those leaving the spinning house immediately got legal work.

26 On prostitution and the brothels during the eighteenth century see P. B. Austin, *The Life and Songs of Carl Michael Bellman* (Malmö, 1967), 27f. Two districts seem to have been more prominent than others in these matters. One was Baggensgatan, a narrow alley in the Old Town, the most well-to-do part of the city. This 'was inhabited during the 1770s, 1780s and 1790s almost by Fröja's practicing priestesses, whose come-hither glances, rouged cheeks, bared breasts and speaking tongues could be seen and felt everywhere at windows and in doorways'.

The other and more disreputable district was the shanty-town of Djurgården, which was officially crown land and not part of the city and its jurisdiction. Among the hazel bushes were 'the small temples of Fröja', reported a contemporary, from which could be heard 'the sighs of lovers and the hiccupping of those who had drunk too much'. Drink was cheaper there, due to smuggling, than in the city proper. See also I. Simonsson, 'Fredmansdiktens verklighet', *Bellmansstudier* 2 (1926).

Those who had run away from factories were to be returned to the same place. Sometimes the females ran into new problems at once. Like many other females of no obvious occupation Anna Maria Ross, a spinner, was sent to the Spinning House on Långholmen Island for one year for vagrancy.[27] Exactly one year and three days later she reappears in the records. A policeman reported that he had observed this spinner at 6 a.m., heavily overloaded and carrying some six *riksdaler* which she claimed to have found in the street. She was arrested but let out after two days. The police kept the money, the rightful owner of which would be advertised for.

More generally, the police records provide an impression of a widespread, economically determined petty criminality. Females in the lower strata often appear in connection with illegal street vending of liquor or other cheap commodities. Two wives of soldiers were arrested for having sold a few yards of linen and a couple of carafes. They were let out with a warning, but the goods were confiscated. A widow of a coachman was sentenced to eight days on bread and water for having roamed about selling corn-brandy by the glass. The overall impression is one of small-scale criminality associated with obvious difficulties in getting a living. Begging seems to have constituted an overwhelmingly female activity; as much as 91 per cent out of 148 persons being kept for begging in April, 1811 were women.[28]

The decline in manufacturing has been described in chapter 3 above. All in all, the facts indicate a trend towards a more unstable industrial structure in Stockholm. A somewhat simplified picture of the development could be one where the privileged textile enterprises run by members of the social establishment were gradually replaced by a lot of small and unstable enterprises working close to the borderline of the formal sector. The manufacturing sector as a whole may be seen as to a certain extent passing from the formal to the informal sector, largely as a reflection of its low profitability.

Concluding comments

Conflicts between the formal and the informal sectors tended to be more severe in stagnating Stockholm than is often the case in the urban Third World today. The traditional guilds jealously tried to protect their monopoly on the production of goods and services within

[27] Convicted prostitutes could be hired by entrepreneurs who forced them to collect sewage cans and row the barges across the Mälaren to the saltpetre works, an idea that the city authorities found charming. See P. B. Austin, *The Life and Songs of Carl Michael Bellman* (Malmö, 1967), 29.

[28] Müller, *Fattigvården i Stockholm*.

their jurisdiction. Their struggle was not entirely successful but it contributed to severe tensions and helped make life more difficult for informal producers.

Among the declining manufactures, on the other hand, the dividing line between formal and informal activities became increasingly blurred. As already mentioned the enterprises tended to be smaller and more unstable. To a certain extent the situation of manufacturing in eighteenth- and early nineteenth-century Stockholm was close to that of some entrepreneurs in highly competitive sectors of present-day advanced capitalist countries, where we notice an increasing use of docile and easily exploitable labour, for example illegal immigrants, and the reappearance of an informal economy.

Thus, Stockholm as well as a number of stagnating cities in the early phase of industrialization shared important features with contemporary Third World cities, in particular the relatively great importance of the informal sector. However, the relationship between the formal and informal parts of the urban economy differed considerably. The dynamics behind the expansion of the informal economy are also in important respects quite different.

The Stockholm informal sector probably was more important relative to the formal sector during the period 1760–1850 than previously or later. This was a period of stagnation or relative decline not only for Stockholm but also for several other European towns that had been expansive during the seventeenth century. The informal sector expansion in Stockholm was followed by a reverse pattern with formal sector growth and informal sector contraction in the great post-1870 industrialization phase.

The period of informal sector expansion in Stockholm between the mid eighteenth and mid nineteenth centuries coincides with what de Vries labels the new urbanization period in European history 1750–1800/50.[29] An urban growth from below took place, stimulated by rapid population growth, changing relative prices to the advantage of agrarian producers, and technological innovation. These factors all encouraged the growth of relatively small cities, often in rural areas.

The capitalist, industrialized city was unable to evolve directly from the bureaucratic, pre-industrial capital that Stockholm constituted by the mid eighteenth century. The slow but persistent and in the long run strategic agrarian economic growth created new pre-conditions for urban capitalism. What we see in Stockholm during the period of stagnation and the peak of the informal sector is the backyard, as it were, of the capitalist development of the era which largely bypassed the European metropolises.

[29] J. de Vries, *European Urbanization* (London, 1984).

5

Real wage trends, 1730–1850: Stockholm in a comparative perspective

When E. J. Hobsbawm published his classic essay on the seventeenth-century European 'general crisis', he emphasized the *rise* in real wages and labour costs occurring over several countries such as England, Germany, Italy, and Spain. The bargaining power of labour was rising, at least in the towns, and effective journeymen's organizations were emerging in several places.[1] Unlike the seventeenth century, however, most of the eighteenth century was characterized by the sustained inflation starting approximately in 1730 and culminating during the Revolutionary and Napoleonic Wars. In this macro-economic setting it would hardly be realistic to expect such a favourable balance between wages and prices as during the preceding 'crisis' century, provided that wages were still, as they had been before, rather inflexible in nominal terms.

It thus appears that real wages should be expected to have dropped in most of urban Europe during the eighteenth century. In very general terms, the historical predictions advanced by Slicher van Bath describe the basic elements of the process.[2] As grain prices were rising relative to other commodities, he argues, the outcome was the typical one during pre-industrial periods of agricultural expansion under population pressure. Real wages decline, poverty increases, and the social structure tends to become more polarized, with widening differential between rich and poor. Land reclamations take place,

1 E. J. Hobsbawm, 'The general crisis of the European economy in the seventeenth century', *Crisis in Europe, 1560–1660*, ed. T. Ashton (London, 1965), 28. A similar view in J. de Vries, *The Economy of Europe in an Age of Crisis* (Cambridge, 1976), chapter 6. Stockholm wages and prices during the seventeenth century are not dealt with in this chapter; see, however, J. Söderberg and A. Jansson, 'Corn-price rises and equalisation: real wages in Stockholm 1650–1719', *Scandinavian Economic History Review* 36, 2 (1988), 42–67.

2 B. H. Slicher van Bath, 'Les problèmes fondamentaux de la société pré-industrielle en Europe occidentale', *A.A.G. Bijdragen* 12 (1965).

accompanied by a growth in agrarian production and marketing, but the surplus will be distributed in a more uneven way than before.

Two empirical questions emerge immediately from the theoretical arguments above. First we must note that Slicher van Bath's model deals with the agrarian economy and not with urban economic trends. Do the trends in real wages in various European towns and cities actually conform to the pessimistic hypothesis of a long-term downward pressure on real wages? Second, how does Stockholm, as a more stagnating town than most, fit into the European pattern? Were the effects of the price shifts in the Swedish capital even more detrimental to the wage labouring population than was normally the case elsewhere?

This chapter will examine the long-term real wage trends in Stockholm 1730–1850 in relation to the broader international background. It is argued that the second half of the eighteenth century exhibited more evident downward real wage trends than did the second quarter of the nineteenth century which has been the subject of most of the standard of living debate. Some hypotheses are advanced as to the links between the real wage decline on the one hand and processes of pauperization and polarization on the other, seen against a background of redistribution of income favouring the agrarian sector during large parts of the eighteenth century. We will compare the empirical evidence on Stockholm wages with some 20 other European towns.

While we do not directly address the problem of the impact of capitalism upon real wages, the general argument would be to play down the importance of this factor and explain the variation between towns in other terms. Emphasis is on trends over periods of at least a few decades, not on short-term fluctuations, and the deep trough in real wages and living standards during the French Wars, which would deserve a separate treatment, will only be touched upon lightly.

The standard work on real wages in Sweden during the eighteenth and first half of the nineteenth century is that of Jörberg's. His data for unskilled agricultural labourers indicate a secular decline in real wages from 1732, when the series begins, to about 1800. Then a substantial improvement occurs until the 1820s. The trend is once more falling during the second quarter of the nineteenth century. A sustained upward trend cannot be seen until the latter half of this century.[3]

For Stockholm, only isolated pre-1850 wage figures can be found in

[3] L. Jörberg, *A History of Prices in Sweden, vol.* 2 (Lund, 1972), 334–49.

the literature, whereas prices are better known.[4] Here we will exploit some of the voluminous wage data kept in the City Archive of Stockholm referring to building labourers employed by the municipality.[5] This type of source is the one most often used in international research, for instance on Copenhagen, London, Paris, and Madrid. The Stockholm material presents wages paid day by day and week by week for several categories of labourer receiving a pure cash wage.[6]

In order to facilitate international comparison only the unskilled, the hodmen, are dealt with. As company or private archives are scarce and uneven, it is not possible to obtain any similar, continuous series referring to industrial labour.

In computing a measure of real wages, money wage rates were simply deflated by the price of rye (see *Appendix 1* on sources, *Appendix 2* on time series of wages and prices). Of course it would be desirable to relate the money wage to a consumption budget representative of the category studied. Lack of data, however, does not permit such an undertaking until the investigations of the social reformers of the 1890s.[7] By then living standards had risen substantially and the consumption pattern can hardly be projected backwards several decades.[8]

Figure 5.1 depicts the real wage for Stockholm hodmen 1730–1850 as well as Jörberg's curve for agricultural labourers, referred to above.

4 On Stockholm prices see S. Högberg, *Utrikeshandel och sjöfart på 1700–talet* (Stockholm, 1969); G. Myrdal, *The Cost of Living in Sweden 1830–1930* (London, 1933).

5 T. Höjer, *Stockholms stads drätselkommission 1814–1864* (Stockholm, 1953), 353ff, describes some of these wage materials.

6 Wage data thus refer to adult male wages only. Next to nothing is known about female, child, or other family labour supplementing the male wage. On the formal and informal labour markets see chapter 4 above. The limitations of data are the same as generally elsewhere; the remarks of, e.g., L. D. Schwarz, 'The standard of living in the long run: London, 1700–1860', *Economic History Review* 38 (1985), 31–3, apply equally well here.

7 On food consumption in Stockholm around the turn of the century see Y. Hirdman, *Magfrågan* (Stockholm, 1983).

8 When calculating a Swedish cost of living index for the eighteenth century, Jörberg assumes that cereals took up 58 per cent of the food budget. Rye was clearly dominant among the grains, and prices of various cereals moved very much in parallel. The weights rely on data from Danviken Hospital in Stockholm. The consumption refers to 'poor charity brothers'. It is not unreasonable to expect it to reflect the diet among lower social strata. Roughly similar assumptions are made by E. H. Phelps Brown and S. V. Hopkins, *A Perspective of Wages and Prices* (London, 1981), 89, putting the share of farinaceous out of total food at 50 per cent and thereby adjusting their earlier estimate upwards. The recent cost-of-living estimates of J. G. Williamson, *Did British Capitalism Breed Inequality?* (Boston, 1985, appendix A) for the period 1781–1850 employs larger weights for bread, flour, oats, and potatoes, which together stand for 68.6 and 70.4 per cent of the southern and northern urban food budgets, respectively. At the same time Williamson notes that the choice between various budget weights matters little to the long-term trends in the cost of living.

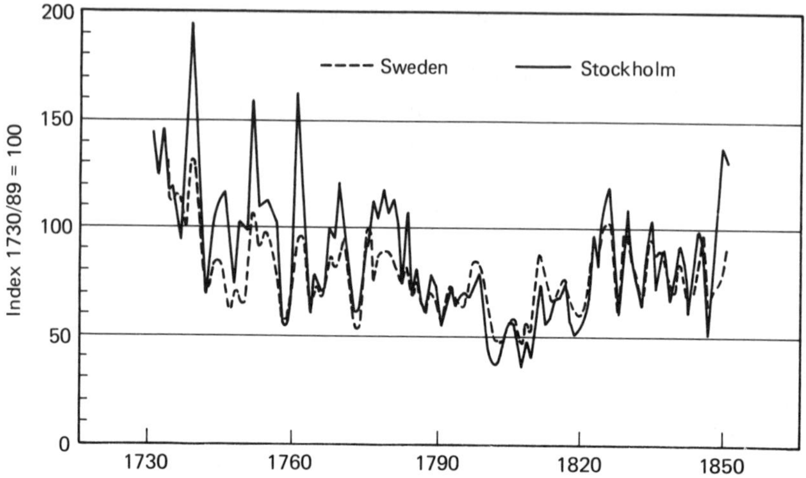

Figure 5.1 Real wage indices for unskilled labourers in Stockholm and rural Sweden, 1730–1850 (Stockholm 1730–89 = 100). *Sources*: Stadskamrerarens arkiv, Stockholms stads verifikationer; Byggnadskontorets arkiv; Börs-, bro- och hamnbyggnadskommitterades arkiv, all in Stockholm City Archive. For prices see *Appendix 1*; for rural Sweden L. Jörberg, *A History of Prices in Sweden, vol. 1* (Lund, 1972), 635–5, 710–3.

Both curves are based on daily wage rates and consequently do not take the degree of employment into account.

By and large, the trends depicted by the Stockholm curve are the same as for agricultural labourers in Sweden as a whole. The most striking feature in both cases is the marked secular downward trend during the eighteenth century and the steep rise in the first quarter of the nineteenth. Common to Stockholm and rural Sweden is also the declining tendency during the second quarter of the nineteenth century. In Stockholm this drop was less pronounced than that of the last decades of the preceding century.

The reduction in real wages in the capital during the eighteenth century exceeded that of rural Sweden. This difference in trends seems plausible in the light of the long-term growth problems that Stockholm experienced (de-industrialization combined with a decline in foreign trade compared with the rest of the country).[9] While Stockholm real wages ordinarily surpassed those of rural Sweden until about 1790, the opposite is true during the French Wars. Rural real wages then were usually higher than in Stockholm. The first decade of

[9] On the growth problems of Stockholm against the European background see chapter 2 above.

the nineteenth century especially is known as a period of economic difficulties in the capital. The number of workers in manufacturing was reduced by almost one quarter, and a large part of the silk industry had to close down. Mortality rose to exceptionally high levels even before the war with Russia in 1808–9 which led to the loss of Finland.[10] After about 1820 the pattern was reversed once more as Stockholm real wages now tended to exceed rural ones.

Both curves display strong short-term fluctuations in the eighteenth century; the variance later declines substantially. The pronounced fluctuations in the Stockholm curve during the eighteenth century are mainly due to the fact that price reductions evidently were larger here than in rural Sweden in good harvest years, resulting in sharp but short-lived upward turns in real wages in the capital. The Stockholm price series is likely to be more sensitive to actual market price changes than the rural Sweden series, the latter being based on yearly official price scales (*markegångstaxor*). If actual market prices were available for rural Sweden, this real wage curve would probably oscillate more.

There is some evidence to suggest that Stockholm by the mid nineteenth century probably was a relatively poor town by European standards. In 1850, one third (34 per cent) of Stockholm's population above 17 years of age was not liable to tax on account of poverty.[11] This method of measuring poverty cannot be employed for the eighteenth century because of differing tax systems. Real wage data offer prospects not only of more long-term analyses but also of a more reasonable basis for international comparison.

What were the differences between European cities in the purchasing power of an unskilled labourer? Figure 5.2 reporting the amount of bread corresponding to a daily wage, represents an attempt to describe the variation. In this context bread is to be preferred to grain as a deflator, partly because workers probably were buying bread rather than grain, and partly because real wages in published research are more often expressed in bread than in any other commodity. Apart from Stockholm, all calculations draw on published research which of course restricts the number of points in time for which comparisons can be made. Rye bread was the most commonly consumed in all cities except Paris and London, where white bread predominated.

10 P. Nyström, *Stadsindustriens arbetare före 1800–talet* (Stockholm, 1955), 184; E. F. Heckscher, 'De svenska manufakturerna under 1700–talet', *Ekonomisk Tidskrift* 39 (1937), 191. See also chapter 8 below.

11 See chapter 6 below.

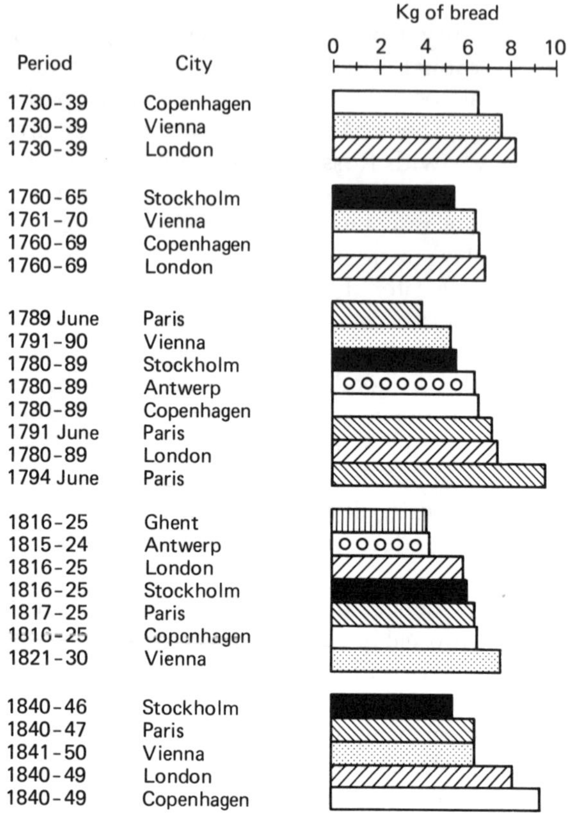

Figure 5.2 Amount of bread corresponding to a daily wage of an unskilled labourer in selected towns.

Sources:
Stockholm: See *figure 5.1*.
Copenhagen: P. Thestrup, *The Standard of Living in Copenhagen 1730–1800* (Copenhagen, 1971), 80–2; V. Falbe Hansen, *Hvilke forandringer er der siden Amerikas opdagelse foregaaet i priserna paa Danmarks væsentligste frembringelser* (Copenhagen, 1869), 92; A. Friis and K. Glamann, *A History of Prices and Wages in Denmark, vol. 1* (Copenhagen, 1958), 157–8; S. A. Hansen, *Økonomisk vækst i Danmark, vol. 2* (Copenhagen, 1974), table 15.
Vienna: A. Pribram, *Materialien zur Geschichte der Preise und Löhne in Österreich* (Vienna, 1938), 608; R. Sandgruber, *Die Anfänge der Konsumgesellschaft* (Munich, 1982), 115.
London: E. Gilboy, *Wages in Eighteenth Century England* (Cambridge, Mass., 1934), 258; A. L. Bowley, 'The statistics of wages in the United Kingdom during the last hundred years, Part VIII. Wages in the building trades – London', *Journal of the Royal Statistical Society* 64 (1901), 103–4; B. R. Mitchell and P. Deane, *Abstract of British Historical Statistics* (Cambridge, 1962), 497–8.
Antwerp and Ghent: E. Scholliers, 'De materiele verschijningsvormen van der armoede voor de industriele revolutie', *Tijdschrift voor geschiedenis* 88 (1975).

Some tentative conclusions may be drawn from the figure. Stockholm is characterized by relatively low real wages, not only by the middle of the nineteenth century but also in the 1760s and 1780s. Around 1820, however, the purchasing power of an unskilled labourer in terms of rye bread was lower in Ghent and Antwerp than in Stockholm. Ghent with its dominating low-wage textile industry is usually described as the poorest of the larger Belgian towns, and strong pauperization tendencies were operating in the first half of the nineteenth century.[12] Like Ghent, Antwerp is often cited in the standard of living debate as a pronounced example of disadvantageous development. Antwerp experienced de-industrialization and rising unemployment during the first half of the nineteenth century, partly as a result of the growing importance of Ghent in textiles. Real wages and consumption declined markedly.[13]

Apart from Ghent and Antwerp, only Paris during the famous food crisis immediately preceding the Revolution of 1789 exhibits a purchasing power per unskilled labourer which falls substantially below that of Stockholm. The much higher figures for Paris in 1791 and 1794 indicate that labourers in this city normally enjoyed a better position than their Stockholm colleagues.

Copenhagen is the only city in figure 5.2 which in the long run improves its relative position. As will be seen below, secular real wage trends were unusually favourable in Copenhagen. London emerges as the normally most well-to-do city, while the position of Vienna is rather unstable.[14]

Figure 5.2, being based solely on data for unskilled labourers, is

[12] J. Kruithof, 'De sociale samenstelling van de bevolking te Antwerpen, Brussel, Gent en Luik in 1846–1847', *Handelingen der Maatschappij voor Geschiedenis en Oudheidkunde te Gent* 11 (1957); C. Vandenbroeke, 'L'alimentation à Gand pendant la première moitié du XIXe siècle', *Annales E.S.C.* 30 (1975).

[13] C. Lis and H. Soly, 'Food consumption in Antwerp between 1807 and 1859: a contribution to the standard of living debate', *Economic History Review* 30 (1977); Lis and Soly, *Poverty and Capitalism in Pre-Industrial Europe* (Hassocks, 1979), chapter 5.

[14] The favourable position of London as compared with the Continent is in line with the results of P. Uselding, 'Wage and Consumptions Levels in England and on the Continent in the 1830s', *Journal of European Economic History* 4 (1975), and W. Abel, *Agricultural Fluctuations in Europe from the Thirteenth to the Twentieth Century*, 3rd edn (London, 1980), 252. Their efforts are, however, directed towards comparison across nations rather than towns.

Paris: G. Rudé, 'Prices, wages, and popular movements in Paris during the French Revolution', *Economic History Review* 6 (1954); J. Rougerie, 'Remarques sur l'histoire des salaires à Paris au XIXe siècle', *Mouvement social* 1968; *Recherches statistiques sur la ville de Paris*, II (1823), table 73; III (1826), table 86; IV (1829), table 104; J. Singer-Kérel, *Le coût de la vie à Paris de 1840 à 1954* (Paris, 1961), 298f., 462f.

Table 5.1 *Main trends in real wages 1730–1850 in 23 European towns.*

Town	Real wage trend 1730–89	1790–1819	1820–50
Stockholm	*Falling*	*No trend*	*No trend*
Gdansk	*Falling*		
Krakow	*No trend*		
Warsaw		*Falling*	*No trend*
Copenhagen	*No trend*		*Rising*
London	*Falling*	*No trend*	*Rising*
Amsterdam	*Falling*	*Falling*	*Falling*
Antwerp	*Falling*	Falling	
Ghent	*Falling*		
Paris	*No trend*		*No trend*
Caen	*Falling*		
Marseille			Falling
Bremen	*Falling*		
Leipzig	*No trend*	*Falling*	
Geneva	Falling		
Vienna	*Falling*	Rising	Falling
Genoa	Falling		
Milan	*Falling*	*No trend*	*Falling*
Naples	*Falling*		
Madrid	*Falling*		
Barcelona	*Falling*		
Seville	*Falling*		
Valencia	Falling		

Sources: As for table 5.2.

directed towards providing a rough picture of real wage disparities between towns during certain rather short periods. We can obtain a more reliable view of secular real wage trends if we are willing to accept series that do not always refer to identical occupational categories and real wage calculations based on somewhat differing deflators (see *Appendix 3*).

Table 5.1, presenting main trends in real wages for 23 European towns during three periods between 1730 and 1850, broadens the perspective. These cases, obviously representing many different types of towns, were those with a population of at least ca. 50,000 and on which we could find a sufficient amount of information, but industrial centres are regrettably underrepresented. Wherever possible, the time trend in the simple regression equation,

$$\text{REAL WAGE} = a + b^{*}\text{TIME}$$

was tested for significance at the 5 per cent level; such cases are italicized. For Geneva, Genoa, Marseille, Valencia, Antwerp (1790–1820), and Vienna (after 1790) the time trend could not be tested as we had access only to results in tabular or graphic form, not to annual time series. Wages mostly refer to unskilled labour (*Appendix 3*). As is immediately clear from the table, far more work by price and wage historians has been carried out on the eighteenth than on the nineteenth century. The standard of living debate, focussed on the second quarter of the nineteenth century, has produced a disappointingly small amount of systematic empirical information on these matters.

The choice of periods in table 5.1 was determined by the wish to explore long-term trends while not entering into a discussion about the effects of the Napoleonic era. Because of the problems associated with the war it is hardly illuminating to see the years, say, 1750 and 1800, or 1800 and 1850, compared. This is sometimes done in the literature although it is practically inevitable that the result will be a declining real wage trend in the former case and a rising trend in the latter. Instead, the periods 1730–89, 1790–1819, and 1820–50 were selected.

The most striking pattern in table 5.1 is the generally downward trend during the period 1730–89. The slope of the curve is clearly negative for no less than 17 out of the 21 towns.

Where was this downward trend particularly strong? Supplementing the qualitative information in table 5.1, table 5.2 ranks towns by the size of the regression coefficient of the time trend. In order to make this comparison possible, all real wage series were calculated as index numbers (base 1730–89 = 100).

As table 5.2 indicates, the secular decline in real wages was most marked in Gdansk and Caen, followed by Milan and Naples. Four towns – Amsterdam, Stockholm, London, and Ghent – exhibit practically the same coefficients indicating average real wage reductions of about 0.8 per cent per annum over the period. Another group with similar trends but with somewhat lower coefficients comprises Madrid, Antwerp, Barcelona, and Vienna.[15]

[15] Some other towns also seem to display a secular real wage drop although detailed information is not available in the literature: for Berlin see H. Krüger, *Zur Geschichte der Manufakturen und der Manufakturarbeiter in Preussen* (Berlin, 1958), 351–61; Brussels: A. Verhaegen, 'Note sur le travail et les salaires en Belgique au XVIIIe siècle', *Bulletin de l'Institut de recherches économiques et sociales* 19 (1953); Liège: A. Dupuis, 'Bâtiments construits par les Etats', *Cahiers d'histoire des prix* 3 (1958); Bordeaux: J.-P. Poussou, *Bordeaux et le Sud-Ouest au XVIIIe siècle* (Paris, 1983), 334–41.
The case of Barcelona requires a comment since it is sometimes stated in the literature

Table 5.2 *Regression coefficients for the trend of real wages against time, 1730–1789.*

Town	Coefficient	Number of observations
Gdansk	−1.25	57
Caen	−1.15	60
Milan	−0.91	60
Naples	−0.89	56
Amsterdam	−0.84	57
Stockholm	−0.78	60
London	−0.77	60
Ghent	−0.76	60
Madrid	−0.66	53
Antwerp	−0.65	60
Barcelona	−0.63	60
Vienna	−0.62	49
Seville	−0.56	60
Bremen	−0.49	60
Paris	−0.26	50
Krakow	−0.17	48
Leipzig	−0.02	60
Copenhagen	+0.05	58

Sources:

Gdansk: T. Furtak, *Ceny w Gdansku w latach 1701–1815* (Lwow, 1935), 122–3, 198–9.

Krakow: E. Tomaszewski, *Ceny w Krakowie w latach 1601–1795* (Lwow, 1934), 29–30, 184–5 (1730–89); M. Gorkiewicz, *Ceny w Krakowie w latach 1976–1914* (Poznan, 1950), 238, 257 (1820–50).

Warsaw: S. Siegel, *Ceny w Warszawie w latach 1816–1914* (Poznan, 1949), 175, 268.

Copenhagen: See *figure 5.2*.

London: L. D. Schwarz, 'The standard of living in the long run: London, 1700–1860', *Economic History Review* 38 (1985).

Amsterdam: P. Jansen, 'Poverty in Amsterdam at the close of the eighteenth century', *Acta historiae Neerlandica* 10 (1978), 112; N. W. Posthumus, *Nederlandische prijsgeschiedenis, vol. 1 (Leiden, 1943), table 7.*

Antwerp: C. Lis and H. Soly, *Poverty and Capitalism in Pre-Industrial Europe* (Hassocks, 1979), 169.

Ghent: *Dokumenten voor de geschiedenis van prijzen en lonen in Vlaanderen*, ed. C. Verlinden, vol. 1 (Brugge, 1959), 520; vol. 2 (Brugge, 1965), 434.

Paris: Y. Durand, 'Recherches sur les salaires des maçons à Paris au XVIIIe siècle', *Revue d'histoire économique et sociale* 44 (1966); Rougerie, 'Remarques sur l'histoire des salaires à Paris au XIXe siècle'; M. Baulant, 'Le prix des grains à Paris de 1431 à 1788', *Annales E.S.C* 23 (1968); *Prix de froment en France au temps de la monnaie stable (1726–1913)*, ed. E. Labrousse (Paris, 1970), 190–1 (the latter series referring to the département of Seine).

Caen: J.-C. Perrot, *Genèse d'une ville moderne: Caen au XVIIIe siècle, vol. 2* (Paris, 1975), 1029, 1040–1.

Table 5.2 (*cont.*)
Bremen: K. Schwarz, *Die Lage der Handwerksgesellen in Bremen während des 18. Jahrhunderts* (Bremen, 1975), 54–9, 83.
Leipzig: M. J. Elsas, *Umriss einer Geschichte der Preise und Löhne in Deutschland, vol. 2A* (Leiden, 1940), 519, 600; see also W. Abel, *Massenarmut und Hungerkrisen im vorindustriellen Europa* (Hamburg, 1974), 350.
Geneva: A. Perrenoud, *La population de Genève du seizième au début du dix-neuvième siècle* (Geneva, 1977), 359.
Vienna: See *figure* 5.2.
Genoa: G. Vigo, 'Real wages of the working class in Italy: building workers' wages (14th to 18th century)', *Journal of European Economic History* 3 (1974).
Milan: A. de Maddalena, *Prezzi e mercedi a Milan dal 1701 al 1860* (Milan, 1974), 379, 420; see also Vigo, 'Real wages'.
Naples: R. Romano, *Prezzi, salari e servizi a Napoli nel secolo XVIII* (Milan, 1965); see also Vigo, 'Real wages'.
Madrid, Seville, Valencia: E. J. Hamilton, *War and Prices in Spain, 1651–1800* (Cambridge, Mass., 1947), 139, 155, 183, 208–15, 268–71; on Madrid during the second half of the eighteenth century see also J. Soubeyroux, *Paupérisme et rapports sociaux à Madrid au XVIII*ᵉ *siècle, vol. 1* (Paris, 1978), 78–87.
Barcelona: P. Vilar, 'Elan urbain et mouvement des salaires dans le bâtiment: le cas de Barcelone au XVIIIᵉ siècle', *Revue d'histoire économique et sociale* 28 (1950).
Marseille: W. H. Sewell, Jr., 'Social change and the rise of working-class politics in nineteenth-century Marseille', *Past and Present* 65 (1974), 85–7.

Only four cities – Copenhagen, Leipzig, Krakow, and Paris – display trends which are not significantly negative during the period. No case has been found of significant real wage improvements. What was special about these cases? Copenhagen experienced a fairly advantageous economic growth based on maritime commerce. Foreign trade was stimulated by the great sea wars after the middle of the century and by the resulting increase for grain and ship's provisions which could be obtained from the Baltic area via Copenhagen.[16] However, it should also be noted that not all categories of labour managed to avoid long-term real wage deterioration. Although data are not sufficiently precise to permit a detailed analysis, there is strong evidence to suggest that real wages of journeymen carpenters and journeymen

that this city as well as the surrounding region registered a secular rise in real wages during the eighteenth century; see, e.g., E. Le Roy Ladurie and J. Goy, *Tithe and Agrarian History from the Fourteenth to the Nineteenth Centuries* (Cambridge, 1982), 171. When Vilar discussed the data he had produced he, however, rather stressed the growing disparity between Barcelona and Madrid, the former's money wage trend rising much more sharply. Barcelona inflation, however, also exceeded that of Madrid, and the conclusion of falling real wages does not depend on the period chosen here; it holds even if the period of analysis is taken to be, say, 1730–1800.

16 S. A. Hansen, *Økonomisk vækst i Danmark, vol. 1* (Copenhagen, 1974), chapter 2.

masons declined. As a consequence, pay differentials between skilled and unskilled labour were reduced.[17]

The rise in Copenhagen foodstuff prices, though far smaller than the rise in Stockholm rye prices (53 as compared with 257 per cent between 1730/9 and 1780/8; for Stockholm data see *Appendix* 2) still exceeded that of several other urban centres such as London, Antwerp, Milan, and Naples. The reasons for the comparative flexibility of the nominal wage rates of Copenhagen unskilled labourers are not clear.

The comparatively favourable trend obtained for Leipzig, Krakow, and Paris is probably related to the fact that price increases for grain were smaller there. Leipzig wheat prices increased by not more than 30 per cent from 1730/9 to 1780/8 as compared with 76 per cent for Barcelona and 96 per cent for Caen. The corresponding Paris figure was 39 per cent. Inflation in Paris was more modest than in other French towns such as Bordeaux and Toulouse. Given that money wages were sluggish for institutional reasons, real wage trends almost wholly depended on price trends. A likely explanation for the modest price rise in Leipzig and Krakow should be their vicinity to the Eastern European grain producing areas.[18]

After about 1790 a further but expected real wage decline took place during the war period. Because of the dramatic price rise many towns reached their lowest real wage level at about the turn of the century. One would expect that the standard of living around 1800 fell below that at any other point between 1730 and 1850.

The immediate post-war years are generally characterized by rapid improvement. It is more interesting to discuss the period 1820–50, exhibiting quite varying patterns. Out of the towns in table 5.1, only Copenhagen and London register a marked rise in real wages, while the opposite is true for Milan, Amsterdam, and to a lesser extent Marseille and Vienna. London, Paris, and Stockholm display no clear trend.

As is well known, the lively standard of living debate on this period has produced few general conclusions. Rather, the main tendency has been to emphasize regional diversity. This seems reasonable also in the light of the evidence presented here. The most plausible conclusion to be drawn from the available data is that this period was characterized by relatively stable or declining real wages rather than

[17] P. Thestrup, *The Standard of Living in Copenhagen 1730–1800* (Copenhagen, 1971), 88ff.

[18] W. Abel, *Geschichte der deutschen Landwirtschaft vom frühen Mittelalter bis zum 19. Jahrhundert* (Stuttgart, 1962), 247, notes a weaker upward grain price trend in inland Germany than in the ports during the eighteenth century.

by improvements. The changes taking place were certainly less continuous and dramatic than those of most of the eighteenth century.

What conditions produced the secular decline in real wages from about 1730? The tendency is so similar in many cities that it does not seem fruitful to explain the phenomenon by reference to local circumstances. It is immediately clear that prices, not money wage changes, are strategic.

From the 1720s a secular inflation commenced in large parts of Europe, accelerating in the last decades of the century. Attempts at explaining the inflation have focussed on four factors. First, there is the monetarist approach, advancing rising production of precious metals and of circulating money as the primary causes. A growing number of researchers stress population growth, leading to increased demand for agricultural products, as decisive. The inflationary effects of the wars of the period may be seen as a third type of explanation and reference to the many harvest failures of the latter part of the eighteenth century as a fourth.[19]

For the purposes of this chapter, inflation may be taken as given and we will direct our attention towards its effects, not its background. However, there is little doubt that agrarian production in many regions of Europe had great difficulty in keeping pace with the substantial growth in population. In a survey of research on the eighteenth century, Le Roy Ladurie argues that the growth in population tended to surpass that of agrarian production in England, France, and Spain (although there are regional exceptions).[20] Such a decline in per capita agrarian production should have been sufficient to produce an upward price trend. The major problem with the monetary hypothesis, as Maynard observes, is that it does not explain the relative price shifts, in this context the well-known fact that relative prices of agricultural and industrial products were changing in favour of the former during the eighteenth century.[21] It may well be argued that monetary factors modified the general inflationary process induced by population growth rather than determining it. The patterns of variations in grain price trends over and above the

19 For general accounts of European price trends see, e.g., E. Labrousse, 'Les bons prix agricoles du XVIIIe siècle', *Histoire économique et sociale de la France*, dir. F. Braudel and E. Labrousse (Paris, 1970); B. H. Slicher van Bath, *The Agrarian History of Western Europe A.D. 500–1850* (London, 1963), 221–39; Högberg, *Utrikeshandel och sjöfart på 1700-talet*, chapter 7.

20 E. Le Roy Ladurie and J. Goy, *Tithe and Agrarian History*, 168ff., 174ff., 190ff.

21 G. Maynard, *Economic Development and the Price Level* (London, 1962), 161ff.

European average must, for instance, have been heavily influenced by monetary phenomena specific to this country.[22]

The relative price shift implies an increase in agricultural incomes relative to non-agricultural. Ever since the pioneering work of Labrousse in the 1930s, French historians have done much valuable work on prices, rents, and wages. Several regional studies support Labrousse's contention that agricultural wages lagged behind prices of agricultural products and rents. The rise in rents reflects the increased profitability of agriculture.[23]

This pattern of relative price shifts does not support the well-known thesis of Hamilton that 'profit inflation, through a lag of wages behind prices . . . implemented the Industrial Revolution'. In his discussion of the long-term effects of the drop in real wages, Hamilton exclusively directed his attention towards the industrial sector, especially the upsurge of technical invention and the growth of the factory system made possible by increased profits and savings. He even believed that incomes of large landowners were reduced as agricultural incomes supposedly lagged behind prices.[24]

Thanks to the research on tithes, production, and rents carried out since the 1970s and covering many regions of Europe, there is by now a fair amount of literature indicating that there was no fall in rents during the eighteenth century. On the contrary, rapid increases are often observed, for instance in Ireland and many French regions such as those surrounding Paris and Toulouse. Very often land prices, too, outstripped the rise in agricultural prices. Prices of small farming units especially surged upwards, stimulating the division of holdings. In relatively expansive regions agricultural production could be increased to such an extent that profits could rise, for instance in parts of southern Italy and in Normandy. In other and less dynamic areas like Brittany and some Italian regions, rents increased more than did agricultural output, resulting in a squeeze on producers.[25]

The interesting question of how income was redistributed between large and small landowners and farmers cannot be answered in a simple way, although we have many indications of growing inequality between better-off rural groups on the one hand and lower strata on

22 On Swedish inflation see Jörberg, *A History of Prices in Sweden, vol.* 2, 75–90, 127–36, 173–7.

23 Labrousse, 'Les bons prix agricoles'.

24 E. J. Hamilton, 'Profit inflation and the Industrial Revolution, 1751–1800', *Quarterly Journal of Economics* 56 (1941/42); quotation from 272–3. See also Hamilton, 'Prices as a factor in business growth', *Journal of Economic History* 12 (1952).

25 For a good overview of recent research see Le Roy Ladurie and Goy, *Tithe and Agrarian History*, chapter 8.

the other. Even if rents generally tended to rise faster than prices of agricultural products, part of this increase in production costs from the point of view of the farmer was offset by the drop in labour costs. The evidence that real wages of labourers in agriculture generally declined in the second half of the eighteenth century is so overwhelming that it seems superflous to describe the pattern in such a detailed way as was done above for urban centres.[26] Abel's contention that 'the purchasing power of wages sank all over Europe' is however a slight overstatement since some regions in England and southern Scotland did not register such a drop, as distinct from the ordinary outcome in Sweden, Holland, Belgium, France, Germany, Austria, and several regions of Italy and Spain. However agricultural income increments were distributed among rural strata, they did not benefit landless workers.[27]

26 Works indicating a long-term real wage decline for agricultural labourers include Abel, *Agricultural Fluctuations*, 199ff. (several German regions); G. Frêche, *Toulouse et la région Midi-Pyrenées au siècle des lumières (vers 1670–1789)* (Paris, 1974), 560ff. (Toulouse region and Languedoc); A. Poitrineau, *La vie rurale en Basse-Auvergne au XVIIIe siècle (1726–1789)* (Paris, 1965), 541–47; R. Baehrel, *Une croissance: La Basse-Provence rurale (fin du XVIe siècle – 1789)* (Paris, 1961), 554, 608; J. Nicolas, *La Savoie au XVIIIe siècle* (Paris, 1978), 714; R. Forster, 'The noble wine producers of the Bordelais in the eighteenth century', *Economic History Review* 14 (1961), 26; E. Le Roy Ladurie, 'Pour un modèle de l'économie rurale française au XVIIIe siècle', *Cahiers d'histoire* 19 (1974), 23; C. Vandenbroeke, 'Mutations économiques et sociales en Flandre au cours de la phase proto-industrielle, 1650–1850', *Revue du Nord* 63 (1981), 88; B. H. Slicher van Bath, *The Agrarian History of Western Europe*, 226 (Overijssel); C. Baars, 'Boukhoudingen van landbouwbedrijven in de Koeksewaard mit de zeventidende en achttiende eeuw', *A.A.G. Bijdragen* 19 (1975); A. Pribram, *Materiallen zur Geschichte der Preise und Löhne in Österreich* (Vienna, 1983), 602 (Vienna region); R. Romano, *Prezzi, salari e servizi a Napoli nel secolo XVIII (1734–1806)* (Milan, 1965), 21–32 (Naples region); E. J. Hamilton, *War and Prices in Spain, 1651–1800* (Cambridge, Mass., 1947), 210 (Andalusia); V. Morgan, 'Agricultural wage rates in the late eighteenth-century Scotland', *Economic History Review* 24 (1971), 181 (north and west Highlands and Islands).

27 Quotation from Abel, *Agricultural Fluctuations*, 198. Morgan, 'Agricultural wage rates', observes steep rises after 1770 in southern Scotland related to the competition in the labour market caused by the growth of the manufacturing industry; for regional prices see *Scottish Population History*, ed. M. Flinn (Cambridge, 1977), 489–98. A similar pattern for Lancashire was described by E. W. Gilboy in her classic *Wages in Eighteenth Century England* (Cambridge, Mass., 1934), 191–215. The analysis of E. W. Hunt and F. W. Botham, 'Wages in Britain during the industrial revolution', *Economic History Review* 40 (1987), 380–99, largely supports Gilboy's view of the regional differences during the second half of the eighteenth century. In particular, they emphasize that the closer workers were to the industrial revolution, geographically as well as occupationally, the greater were their chances of avoiding declining real wages.

An empirical investigation of the distributional implications of inflation and relative price shifts in eighteenth-century agrarian society would be a very demanding task involving several complex problems. One well-known effect is that inflation redistributes real purchasing power from creditors to debtors, provided that debts are stated in fixed money terms (see, e.g., J. L. Palmer, *Inflation, Unemployment, and*

The central features of the actual process – rising prices, rising profits or rents, and falling real wages – were reflected in the Physiocratic programme. When Quesnay in 1757 argued in favour of 'une cherté et un abondance permanentes' he was already in the midst of a process creating exactly these effects.

We are thus dealing with a triple process, involving redistribution of income towards the agrarian sector, pauperization, and polarization.

As peasant farmers or owners often belonged to those gaining from this process, it is quite conceivable that a majority of agrarian producers in countries like France, the Netherlands, and Sweden obtained a share in the real income growth caused by the relative price shifts. While stressing the diverse regional experience, Goubert is inclined to believe that the material conditions among peasants, as judged by probate inventories, were improving in most provinces during the eighteenth century. Very similar views have been expressed by researchers dealing with rural Sweden after 1720.[28]

Such an optimism is not warranted for the urban centres, where those gaining from the redistribution process should have been fewer, relatively. Apart from certain limited categories – e.g., urban landowners, grain merchants, and perhaps foodstuff producers – not many members of the urban community can be expected to have benefited from the changes in terms of trade implied by the price shifts. A hypothesis of widening urban economic inequality between a rather small successful group and a larger unsuccessful one seems reasonable.

Although it should be possible to investigate secular trends in wealth distribution for a considerable number of European cities, exploiting sources such as marriage contracts, probate inventories, and tax assessments, few diachronic studies have been carried out.

Poverty, Lexington, Mass., 1973, p. 47). It is clear that such a mechanism was at work in Sweden, although it has been discussed only in fairly general terms; see E. F. Heckscher, *Sveriges ekonomiska historia från Gustav Vasa II:1* (Stockholm, 1949), 237, and K.-G. Hildebrand, *Fagerstabrukens historia, vol. 1* (Uppsala, 1957), 355–8. More is known about the tax burden of landowning peasants, which was reduced in the course of the eighteenth century as some taxes were fixed in money terms. An important regional study is L. Herlitz, *Jordegendom och ränta* (Gothenburg, 1974). Even more difficult to handle are the inflationary consequences in terms of employment.

28 P. Goubert, 'Sociétés rurales françaises du XVIIIe siècle: vingt paysanneries contrastées', in *Conjoncture économique, structure sociale. Hommage à Ernest Labrousse* (Paris, 1974), 384.

Regarding Sweden see C.-J. Gadd, *Järn och potatis; jordbruk, teknik och social omvandling i Skaraborgs län 1750–1860* (Gothenburg, 1983), 42. E. Söderlund, *Hantverkarna*, II (Stockholm, 1949), 56ff, 74ff, when discussing the changing distribution of handicraft production during the eighteenth century, interpreted the growing importance of country towns as an indication of growing demand especially from the more well-to-do segments of the peasantry.

Most of these concern France. The general trend in urban wealth distribution seems to have been toward growing inequality. In Geneva, for instance, most of the growth in total wealth between 1741–5 and 1770–4 fell on the upper strata, on people engaged in commerce and liberal professions. 'Victimes de la prospérité, les travailleurs auront contribué à l'enrichissement des négociants et des maîtres les plus entreprenants', concludes Perrenoud.[29]

The details of the redistribution process of course vary, but basically similar patterns are found in Toulouse, Lyon, Amiens, Antwerp, Bruges, and some other centres. Toulouse, for instance, was characterized by its powerful rich landowners, successfully expanding their landed property in the surrounding region as well as their rents from it. In Lyon, however, a large share of the results of the economic growth passed into the hands of the upper stratum of merchants (négociants as distinct from marchands). Masters outside textiles, for instance butchers, also advanced in relative terms, whereas the opposite is true of workers and masters in the dominating silk industry. Garden points to a pattern very similar to that observed by Perrenoud: 'La seconde moitié du XVIIIe siècle reste une période de prospérité pour la Fabrique de soierie Lyonnaise, qui accroît le nombre de ses métiers et sa production, mais cette progression se fait en grande partie au détriment des travailleurs de la Fabrique.'[30]

For Stockholm we have indications that far larger groups than the unskilled labourers were adversely affected by eighteenth-century economic processes. First, data on artisans presented by Heckscher reveal a long-term decline in their incomes, as measured by the prices of products sold by them to the municipality of Stockholm.[31]

29 A. Perrenoud, *La population de Genève du seizième au début du dix-neuvième siècle* (Geneva, 1977), 367.

30 M. Garden, *Lyon et les lyonnais au XVIIIe siècle* (Paris, 1970), 295. On Toulouse see Frêche, *Toulouse et la région Midi-Pyrenées* (Maynenne, 1974), 464–76; R. Forster, *The Nobility of Toulouse in the Eighteenth Century* (Baltimore, 1960), chapter 2; J. Godechot and S. Moncassin, 'Structures et rélations sociales à Toulouse en 1749 et en 1785', *Annales historiques de la Révolution française* 1965. See also P. Deyon, 'Les registres de capitation d'Amiens au XVIIIe siècle', *Revue du Nord* (1960); Lis and Soly, *Poverty and Capitalism* (Hassocks, 1979), 167–70 (on Bruges and Antwerp).

On indications of growing British wealth inequality 1740–1810 see P. Lindert, 'Unequal English Wealth since 1670', *Journal of Political Economy* 94 (1986), and the more detailed data in Lindert, *Lucrens Angliae: The Distribution of English Private Wealth since 1670*. Working Paper Series, No. 18–19 (February, 1985). Agricultural History Center, University of California, Davis. It is interesting to note that the polarization tendency 1740–1810 was substantially stronger in the London/Middlesex region than in any other region. During the preceding period 1700–40, urban inequality changed comparatively little.

31 E. F. Heckscher, *Sveriges ekonomiska historia från Gustav Vasa II:1* (Stockholm, 1949), 240. Oddly enough, Heckscher preferred not to make use of his own results in this

In addition Söderlund, the major researcher on Stockholm handicrafts, has demonstrated that the total number of artisans was reduced during the second half of the eighteenth century, as low profits forced many into bankruptcy. Towards the end of the century he discovered 'in many occupations almost as many masters gone bankrupt as entrepreneurs still keeping their workshops'. Relying on tax records and to some extent on inventories, he depicts a situation in which merchants and a limited segment of artisans were economically more successful than most masters. Masters in a few handicrafts employing comparatively capital intensive technology or working primarily for upper-class markets advanced relative to the poor masters. Brewers, millers, hat-manufacturers, and goldsmiths, belonging to the former category, thus improved their position relative to, for example shoemakers, tailors, and coopers. A small minority of masters were beginning to develop capitalist forms of enterprises, sometimes employing dozens of journeymen and apprentices within a large unchanged technological framework.[32]

Second, all available information on wages and salaries of groups other than unskilled labour indicates a decline in real terms. This applies to journeymen, at least in the decades following the war of 1741–3, as well as to two occupations studied by Heckscher, municipal watchmen and boatswains, from 1749 when the series begins and throughout the rest of the century.[33]

Third, the real income of a considerable number of urban civilian and military functionaries declined during the eighteenth-century inflation. Artéus emphasizes the distinction between the *money-salaried* military and civil servants on the one hand and, on the other

respect; he had a strong preconceived opinion that the standard of living did not deteriorate for any substantial segment of the population during the eighteenth century.

In contrast to Heckscher's view, a more pessimistic chord was struck by Bertil Boëthius. He was 'by no means convinced that all social groups were able to maintain their standard of living during the eighteenth century'. He suggested that population growth led to a lowering of the standard of living of the working classes although his reasoning was not underpinned by systematic data. B. Boëthius, 'New light on eighteenth century Sweden', *Scandinavian Economic History Review* 1 (1953), 154, 168, 173.

32 E. Söderlund, *Stockholms hantverkarklass 1720–1772* (Stockholm, 1943), 160–9, 334ff.

33 Söderlund, *Stockholms hantverkarklass*, 271ff; unpublished data on municipal watchmen and boatswains in Riksarkivet; Eli F. Heckscher's collection. Wage differentials between carpenters and unskilled labourers in Stockholm were largely constant during the latter half of the eighteenth century. Since money wage trends were approximately equal between skilled and unskilled labour, it follows that real wage deterioration also affected the skilled. Skill rewards grew, however, during the first half of the nineteenth century. There is as yet no study attempting to estimate changes in the overall distribution of income.

hand, those functionaries who had their pay from *rents or tithes* through a system regulated by the government (*indelningsverket*).[34] The latter category, primarily composed of officers of the county regiments and the clergy, actually gained from the rising grain prices, while the money-salaried suffered from a marked deterioration in real income. This also meant that urban functionaries became increasingly more disadvantaged compared with their colleagues in rural regions. The changes imply a redistribution of income from the urban to the rural sector.

No research has dealt with the overall distribution of wealth in Stockholm. One of the most conspicuous features of the history of the capital towards the end of the eighteenth century is, however, the economic expansion of certain merchant groups. The top stratum (the *Skeppsbroadel*), never comprising more than twenty families, accumulated some of the greatest fortunes in the country although stability across generations was often low at the family level.[35] On the other hand, the declining role of the nobility should have counteracted tendencies towards growing inequality. The questions regarding inequality trends will be pursued in chapter 6 below, focussing on the distribution of real property.

One intriguing task would be to link the intertwined processes of pauperization, polarization, and income redistribution between agrarian and non-agrarian sectors to demographic change. Some interesting problems in this field are discussed by Derouet in his study on Thimerais near Paris.[36] In this region, where population growth outstripped the increase in cereal production between 1720 and 1790, new mechanisms regulating the demographic system developed. The age at marriage was raised and fertility declined, especially among agricultural labourers, the category primarily affected by real income decline. Mortality among the lower social strata rose compared with that of yeomen farmers. The result was thus widening

34 G. Artéus, *Krigsmakt och samhälle i frihetstidens Sverige* (Stockholm, 1982), chapter 5. See also R. Adolfsson, O. Brick, and J. Dahlström, 'Garnisonen, staden och källmaterialet'. *Ett militärt stadsproletariat*, ed. G. Artéus (Stockholm, 1988), 17. It appears that the remuneration of the soldiers of the Stockholm garrison was largely unchanged during the first half of the nineteenth century. This produced a situation in which it was practically impossible for a soldier to maintain a family without side-employment, usually in the form of handicraft work. No major improvements in salaries took place until 1874. By then the process of industrialization was under way, and as other opportunities opened up it became necessary to raise salaries in order to recruit soldiers.

35 S. Carlsson, *Ståndssamhälle och ståndspersoner 1700–1865* (Lund, 1973), 149; T. Söderberg, *Den namnlösa medelklassen* (Stockholm, 1956), 205.

36 B. Derouet, 'Clés pour un système auto-régulateur des populations d'Ancien Régime', *Annales E.S.C.* 35 (1980).

sociodemographic disparities, an increasing inequality before family formation and death. Much research remains to be done on corresponding urban processes; as is well known, most of the voluminous work in historical demography has centred on rural areas. For Stockholm, it is interesting to note the secular drop in crude marriage rates during the latter part of the eighteenth century, from 14.1 per thousand in 1751–5 to only 8.7 in 1786–90. This undoubtedly suggests that barriers to family formation were growing.[37] The birth rate declined too, though not as markedly as bastardy increased towards the close of the century. None of these rates are social-specific, of course, and micro-studies on the changing conditions of family formation would certainly be worthwhile.

Another field emerging as a fruitful one concerns the consequences in terms of changes in the interregional and inter-urban balance in eighteenth-century Europe. From what has been said above, one would expect metropolitan regions to have faced stiffening competition from other areas. Agricultural regions possessing a potential for increasing their marketable surplus should have been at an advantage relative to poor rural regions as well as to the most urbanized ones. Urban growth in better-off agricultural regions also should have been more rapid than metropolitan growth. This conforms well to the findings of de Vries, describing a pattern of European population growth 1750–1800 in which smaller cities grew distinctly faster than the large ones. De Vries notes this as a fundamental change in the basic pattern since the previous century, when growth was dominated by the metropolises, and he relates it to the expansion of agricultural production and regional marketing as well as to the more obvious fact that the Industrial Revolution at this stage encouraged exploitation of resources outside metropolitan regions.[38]

To sum up, we argue that a triple process of pauperization, polarization, and income redistribution towards the agrarian sector was taking place in Europe during most of the eighteenth century. Population growth appears to be a sufficient explanation for the relative price shift between agricultural and non-agricultural products to the advantage of the former. One of the consequences was the secular fall in real wages typical of European cities from about 1730 and throughout the century. Only a small number of urban centres were found (Copenhagen, Paris, Krakow, and Leipzig) *not* exhibiting a marked downward trend in this respect, and no case of sustained improvements 1730–89 was discovered. Gdansk, Caen, Milan,

[37] See further chapter 8 below.

[38] J. de Vries, *European Urbanization 1500–1800* (London, 1984).

Naples, Amsterdam, Stockholm, and Ghent stand out as cities where the downward pressure was particularly strong. A long-term deterioration in real wages usually is characteristic of rural regions, too, although there are some British exceptions (e.g., Lancashire and southern Scotland). Not all social strata were equally affected; urban economic inequality often was on the rise as merchants and urban landowners tended to be more economically successful than others. In rural society the income growth fell on landowners and farmers rather than on the rural strata, implying polarization tendencies there as well.

Like this chapter, Lis and Soly, argue that pauperization and polarization tendencies are characteristic of the eighteenth century. Their views differ from mine, however, on some issues. First, the argument here is limited to a specific period, the inflationary phase from the 1720s continuing throughout the century. The first half of the nineteenth century can hardly be analysed in the same terms, and we find little to support the contention of Lis and Soly that a massive impoverishment was taking place in this period. Second, the Lis and Soly thesis of an 'advancing impoverishment of the peasantry'[39] as a general phenomenon of the eighteenth century is not plausible for the reasons stressed above. Third, we do not think that their pessimistic view of proto-industrialization as necessarily leading to impoverishment can be maintained in the light of much recent research in the field.

Fourth, and perhaps most fundamentally, Lis and Soly attribute the impoverishment process to the 'growth of capitalism', the latter concept, it seems, being defined as a system of surplus extraction based on wage labour. This would presumably imply that the level of poverty would be inversely correlated with the extent to which capitalist relationships had penetrated national or regional economies. Then, however, the thesis is difficult to reconcile with the contention that levels of poverty or destitution were about the same everywhere: 'the number of those living at subsistence minima can almost always be estimated at 40 or 50 per cent of local, regional, or national population',[40] in itself a remarkable hypothesis. There is a not inconsiderable amount of evidence suggesting that poverty and growth problems tended to be most serious in backward areas comparatively unaffected by capitalist development in industry or agriculture.[41]

39 Lis and Soly, *Poverty and Capitalism*, 217.

40 Lis and Soly, *ibid.*, 219.

41 See J. Söderberg, 'Causes of poverty in Sweden in the nineteenth century', *Journal of European Economic History* 11 (1982); Abel, *Agricultural Fluctuations*, 242ff.; J. Mokyr, 'The Industrial Revolution and the New Economic History', in Mokyr, ed., *The Economics of the Industrial Revolution* (London, 1985), 43f.

Table 5.2 above, including towns of many types, did not suggest any marked differences with respect to real wage deterioration between towns of more and less capitalistic character (say, between Barcelona and Madrid).

Notwithstanding the standard of living debate, a surprisingly small amount of systematic data was found regarding the first half of the nineteenth century. Available information suggests that real wage deterioration was less drastic and widespread than during the preceding century. In this perspective, the argument of Lindert and Williamson that the pessimist viewpoint in the standard of living debate must be shifted backwards to the period 1750–1820 in order to maintain its relevance is very convincing.[42] A related point is made by Crafts when demonstrating that the British national product grew less during the latter part of the eighteenth century than has generally been thought. Crafts also thinks that the standard of living, measured by personal per capita consumption, was practically unchanged 1760–1801 and even was reduced to some extent 1760–80.[43] When discussing long-term change in living conditions, poverty, and social inequality we need more work focussing on agrarian processes, urban/rural economic relationships, and the implications of relative price shifts, rather than simple hypotheses of the effects of the 'Industrial Revolution' or the 'factory system'.

Appendix 1 Sources of Stockholm prices, 1730–1850

Several sources can provide reasonably long-term information on Stockholm prices. The most important are:

1 Market place prices of a range of foodstuffs recorded monthly by a municipal clerk. From 1768 onwards they were published in newspapers such as *Dagligt Allehanda,* though not always regularly; see Högberg, *Utrikeshandel och sjöfart på 1700-talet,* 208–12. For certain periods this series can be supplemented by two manuscript series in Riksarkivet: Överståthållarens skrivelser till Kungl. Maj:t, and Kommerskollegii arkiv, Städernas priskuranter.

42 P. H. Lindert and J. G. Williamson, 'English workers' living standards during the Industrial Revolution: a new look', *Economic History Review* 36 (1983).

43 N. F. R. Crafts, 'British economic growth, 1700–1831: a review of the evidence', *Economic History Review* 36 (1983).

2 Wholesale grain prices reported monthly by merchants to the municipal authorities. One series of this type was published in *Stockholms stads pris-courant* 1740–76; we wish to thank Staffan Högberg for permission to use his excerpts from this source. Some wholesale prices are also found in H. Lindgren, *Spannmålshandel and spannmålspriser vid Uppsala akademi 1720–1789* (Uppsala, 1971), 316ff., referring to grain prices charged by the Academy of Uppsala when selling to Stockholm. For the period 1838–63 a convenient summary of monthly prices is available in an official report, *Underdånigt betänkande afgifvet af de för uppgörande af förslag till ny tulltaxa . . . komiterade* (Stockholm, 1863).

For most years, however, wholesale grain prices have to be located in archival sources. We have used the following series: Handelskollegiets arkiv, Protokoll; Grosshandelssocietetens arkiv, Handlingar rörande spannmålspriser 1784–96; Ämbets- och byggningskollegii arkiv, Taxor m fl handlingar rörande prissättning (1814–20); Politi-, ämbets- och byggningskollegii arkiv, Protokoll angående hyrkusk- och åkaretaxor samt taxor å bröd, kött mm (1821–34), all in Stockholm City Archive, and the two series in Riksarkivet mentioned above.

During most of the years 1786–7, weekly current prices were published in Dagligt Allehanda. A comparison between this series and the monthly unpublished quotations in Grosshandelssocietetens arkiv reveals a very close agreement. It is likely that the grain prices in the price current rely on materials provided by Grosshandelssocieteten or by individual merchants. In order to obtain a continuous wholesale price series, we have joined the published price current quotations with the unprinted series listed above.

3 Institutional prices paid by, e.g., hospitals and almshouses. A cost of living index based on this type of material covering the period 1750–72 has been compiled by P.-E. Brolin, *Hattar och mössor i borgarståndet 1760–1766* (Uppsala, 1953), 122ff. The basic material is available for a far longer period.

4 Official price scales. Two types exist. One is the well-known markegångstaxan, on which Jörberg's *A History of Prices in Sweden* relies. He does not report any data for Stockholm City. Such scales were printed, however, during the periods 1705–49 and 1757–72. Some unpublished supplementary material can be found in Stockholm City Archive (Brolin, *Hattar och mössor i borgarståndet*). The other type is the official monthly assessment of various kinds of bread, beer, and meat, published in newspapers such as *Stockholms weckoblad* or *Dagligt Allehanda*.

We have used the wholesale price of rye (type 2 above) as the deflator of the money wage rate over the period 1730–1850, since this source offers the most uniform and accessible series. January quotations were excerpted (or nearest month). The 1779 wholesale prices could not be located, for which reason the market price quotation (type 1) was used for this year; for other years, these series are very close to each other.

When calculating the purchasing power of an unskilled labourer in terms of bread for shorter periods (figure 5.2 above), however, the official price scales (type 4) were used.

Appendix 2 Daily wage rates of unskilled labourers (kronor), rye price (kronor/hl), and real wage index (1730–89 = 100): Stockholm, 1730–1850

Year	Nominal wage	Rye price	Real wage
1730	0.076	0.44	145
31	0.076	0.51	125
32	0.076	0.44	145
33	0.076	0.54	118
34	0.080	0.57	118
35	0.080	0.64	105
36	0.080	0.71	95
37	0.080	0.51	132
38	0.102	0.44	195
39	0.102	0.61	141
1740	0.102	0.69	124
41	0.102	1.23	70
42	0.102	1.01	85
43	0.107	0.85	106
44	0.111	0.83	112
45	0.102	0.74	116
46	0.102	0.98	87
47	0.102	1.14	75
48	0.102	0.84	102
49	0.102	0.85	101
1750	0.102	0.87	99
51	0.102	0.54	159
52	0.102	0.78	110
53	0.102	0.77	111
54	0.102	0.76	113
55	0.102	0.81	106
56	0.102	0.84	102

Appendix 2 (cont.)

Year	Nominal wage	Rye price	Real wage
57	0.102	1.52	56
58	0.102	1.62	54
59	0.106	1.25	71
1760	0.120	0.62	163
61	0.120	0.81	131
62	0.154	1.48	87
63	0.147	2.02	61
64	0.153	1.65	78
65	0.160	1.89	71
66	0.185	2.12	73
67	0.185	1.55	100
68	0.153	1.35	95
69	0.144	1.01	120
1770	0.144	1.28	95
71	0.144	1.55	78
72	0.185	2.56	61
73	0.185	2.56	61
74	0.185	1.82	85
75	0.167	1.55	91
76	0.185	1.38	113
77	0.185	1.50	104
78	0.185	1.32	118
79	0.185	1.45	107
1780	0.185	1.38	113
81	0.185	1.54	101
82	0.185	2.07	75
83	0.185	1.45	107
84	0.185	2.18	71
85	0.185	1.92	81
86	0.185	2.42	64
87	0.185	2.47	63
88	0.185	1.97	79
89	0.185	2.07	75
1790	0.185	2.88	54
91	0.185	2.47	63
92	0.185	2.10	74
93	0.185	2.42	64
94	0.204	2.47	69
95	0.213	2.53	71
96	0.213	2.63	68
97	0.213	2.42	74
98	0.213	2.27	79
99	0.213	3.03	59
1800	0.213	4.14	43
01	0.213	5.00	36
02	0.213	4.75	38

Appendix 2 (cont.)

Year	Nominal wage	Rye price	Real wage
03	0.241	4.34	47
04	0.302	4.55	56
05	0.319	4.60	58
06	0.305	5.10	50
07	0.305	7.17	36
08	0.361	6.21	49
09	0.389	8.11	40
1810	0.389	6.21	53
11	0.444	4.95	75
12	0.472	7.17	55
13	0.636	9.24	58
14	0.657	8.18	68
15	0.657	8.18	68
16	0.657	7.58	73
17	0.657	9.85	56
18	0.657	10.91	51
19	0.657	10.71	52
1820	0.599	8.94	56
21	0.560	6.67	71
22	0.560	4.85	97
23	0.560	5.76	82
24	0.708	5.45	109
25	0.708	5.00	119
26	0.708	5.96	100
27	0.708	10.00	60
28	0.708	5.88	84
29	0.708	5.45	109
1830	0.708	7.37	81
31	0.708	8.03	74
32	0.708	9.04	66
33	0.708	6.21	96
34	0.708	5.76	103
35	0.708	8.33	71
36	0.708	6.82	87
37	0.708	6.59	90
38	0.708	8.87	67
39	0.792	8.87	75
1840	0.792	7.20	92
41	0.792	7.96	84
42	0.792	10.99	61
43	0.792	7.96	84
44	0.792	6.82	98
45	0.792	7.13	93
46	0.792	5.96	51
47	0.896	9.70	78
48	1.021	7.81	110

Appendix 2 (cont.)

Year	Nominal wage	Rye price	Real wage
49	1.021	6.21	138
1850	1.083	7.02	130

Note: Money and weight conversions follow Jörberg, *A History of Prices in Sweden*. During the dual currency period 1789–1803 the sources do not state whether prices are in riksdaler riksgälds or riksdaler banco. We assume that wholesale prices during this period are in riksdaler riksgälds; Högberg, *Utrikeshandel och sjöfart på 1700-talet*, 212ff., makes the same assumption regarding the Stockholm market price scales of the 1790s.

For the years 1731, 1740–41, 1743, 1751, and 1758, the relevant wage records have been lost. Figures reported here are straight-line interpolations from nearest neighbouring years.

The reason why a long period was chosen as the base for the index is that short periods of say half a decade sometimes can produce results that change perceptibly with the location of the base period; for a Swedish example see the criticism of Heckscher in B. Boëthius, 'New light on eighteenth century Sweden', *Scandinavian Economic History Review* 1 (1953).

Appendix 3 Occupations for which real wage trends are reported in tables 5.1 and 5.2, and deflators used

Stockholm, Gdansk, Krakow, Warsaw, Copenhagen, London, Antwerp (1730–89), Ghent, Paris, Vienna, Milan, Barcelona: unskilled labourers in the building trades.

Amsterdam: Ship carpenters.
Antwerp (1790–1819): Laceworkers.
Caen: Qualified services.
Marseille: Several categories, primarily artisan trades.
Bremen: Journeymen carpenters.
Leipzig: Women cooks.
Geneva: Carpenters.
Genoa: Masons.
Naples: Garden labourers.
Madrid: Average of several categories of building artisans and labourers as reported by Hamilton.
Seville: Unspecified labour in building trades.
Valencia: Journeymen painters.

Deflators employed in tables 5.1 and 5.2:

Stockholm, Gdansk, Krakow, Warsaw, Ghent, Bremen: Rye.
Amsterdam, Paris, Caen, Leipzig, Genoa, Milan, Naples, Barcelona: Wheat.
Antwerp (1730–89): Unspecified grain.
Antwerp (1790–1820), Vienna, Marseille, Genoa: Bread.
Copenhagen, London, Madrid, Seville, Valencia: Price indices based on several commodities.

6

Spatial patterns of wealth and poverty

Introduction

This chapter charts patterns of wealth and poverty in Stockholm in the late eighteenth and at the middle of the nineteenth century. The spatial dimension will be central. Against the background of long-term economic stagnation outlined above it is interesting to examine its spatial impact on rich and poor districts as well as on levels and patterns of poverty. Was, for instance, stagnation accompanied by the growth of poor strata and/or the formation of distinct slum districts inhabited by them?

Due to source considerations, not quite the same problems can be attacked throughout the century after 1750. The following section deals with the spatial distribution of wealth towards the end of the eighteenth century, while a subsequent section emphasizes the distribution of poverty rather than that of wealth, concentrating on the mid nineteenth century.

In addition to examining the distribution of poverty across various districts, the composition of the poor segment of the population and the determinants of poverty at the individual level are discussed. The definition of poverty used for the mid nineteenth century cannot be applied to the eighteenth century, when the analysis of poverty must be less detailed.[1] The discussion of long-term change in living stan-

[1] An alternative to relying on tax records for the analysis of distribution of resources would be exploiting the probate records and the lists of deceased, the latter aiming to report on those who were not in possession of sufficient property to make it meaningful to draw up an inventory. In 1790 it can be estimated that approximately one third of the deceased over 20 years of age left an inventory. Compared to Toulouse, Lyon, Paris, or Geneva at about the same time, the Stockholm source situation is better (French studies more often rely on marriage contracts, for which there is no counterpart in Stockholm). Still, such an analysis still presents many methodological problems, especially when it comes to comparison over time. The

dards, while less elaborate than in the previous chapter, supplements it from a somewhat different angle. The real wage data by definition refer only to those capable of work, while the poorest segments among the population may be expected to have comprised many people unable to work because of old age, handicaps, bad health, or other reasons. While poorly paid, the unskilled male labourers dealt with in chapter 5 still were probably at some distance from the very low end of the social scale.

The main source is tax records.[2] These are of three kinds:

1 Nominal population registers (*mantalslängder*). They enumerate the total population liable to taxes. The information given includes the individual's name, occupation, and age. In addition several columns refer to the various taxes that were paid, reporting whether or not the taxes had actually been paid.

Unlike many other European tax records, these registers report not only the heads of households but also wives, children, and other household members including servants. The names of wives and children are usually not given, and ordinarily only the first name of servants.

The population registers are sorted by tax district, and within districts by block and real property numbers. There are often but not always summaries by block. The registers were drawn up yearly, but due to unfortunate archival decisions in the mid nineteenth century they are only preserved every tenth year from 1760 to 1830. From 1830 onwards the yearly volumes have been kept.

In most other parts of Sweden, the parish population registers are a basic demographic source. This applies only to some extent to Stockholm. In rural areas, the catechetical examination records are often extremely informative, reporting total population, demographic events, and population mobility. The examination records are seldom useful for Stockholm. The priests were simply unable to keep track of the highly mobile population in the capital, and the examination

inventories are no doubt better suited to describing wealth than poverty. The lists of deceased are utilized by Zacke, who finds that 56 per cent of the deceased in the parish of Adolf Fredrik during the cholera epidemic of 1834 were classified as poor. See B. Zacke, *Koleraepidemin i Stockholm 1834* (Stockholm, 1971), 141ff., for a brief description of this source. This material is not as completely preserved as the tax materials, nor is the quality always high.

2 Overviews of archival materials are given in N. Staf, 'Mantals- och taxeringslängder i Stadsarkivet', *Stockholms stads arkivnämnd och stadsarkiv. Årsberättelse*, 1932, and B. Broomé, 'Om register och andra hjälpmedel för forskare i Stockholms stadsarkiv', *Stockholms stads arkivnämnd och stadsarkiv. Årsberättelse*, 1942. Generally, this series contains a wealth of valuable information on archives.

records consequently cover only small parts of the population. While other parish registers (birth, burial, and marriage records) are of much better quality, any attempt to examine the total population must start not with church materials but with the nominal population registers.

A few general remarks on the source situation of Stockholm are appropriate here. Nominal tax registers of other European towns often have not aimed at covering total population. The poor or the children, for example, may have been left out. In Liège in 1791 hundreds of houses, whose inhabitants were too poor to pay taxes, were bypassed. This sort of material is also usually more unevenly preserved than for Stockholm.[3]

Stockholm's population registers are a remarkable source. They contain most of the information that is normally given in censuses (individuals by name, occupation, address, age, and civil status) but in addition, since they are tax registers, also economic information not ordinarily provided by censuses. The favourable source situation of Stockholm may be compared with the London case, where the distribution of population by occupation during the late eighteenth and early nineteenth centuries is largely unknown.[4] The information available for Stockholm is also far more comprehensive than for Paris. The first modern census of Paris was not carried out until 1817, for which reason there are great uncertainties in the estimates of the total population during the latter part of the eighteenth century.[5]

Even where primary census records have been preserved (and this does not appear to have been the rule before the mid nineteenth century), they are better suited to answering demographic than economic questions. It is for instance difficult to describe the economic variation *within* occupations without taking other sources into account. This applies for instance to the censuses of Zürich in 1780, of Brussels in 1796, and of Oslo (Christiania) in 1801.[6]

2 Crown tax registers (*kronotaxeringslängder*). Since only a part of total

[3] E. Hélin, 'Les capitations liègoises', *Anciens pays et assemblées d'états* 21 (1961), 282. On early English manuscript census records see, e.g., P. Laxton, 'Liverpool in 1801: a manuscript return for the First National Census of Population', *Transactions of the Historical Society of Lancashire and Cheshire* 130 (1981). These manuscript records have survived only sporadically for the first four censuses (1801–31).

[4] L. D. Schwarz, 'Income distribution and social structure in London in the late eighteenth century', *Economic History Review* 32 (1979).

[5] J. Kaplow, *The Names of Kings; the Parisian Laboring Poor in the Eighteenth Century* (New York, 1972), 18ff.

[6] W. Schellenberg, *Die Bevölkerung der Stadt Zürich um 1780* (Affoltern am Albis, 1951); A. Cosemans, *Bijdrage tot de demografische en sociale geschiedenis van de stad Brussel 1796–1846* (Liège, 1966), chapter 1; G. Johnsen, *Folket i Oslo 1801* (Oslo, 1950).

population actually was liable to pay taxes, it is for many purposes more convenient to work with the crown tax registers than with the population registers. The crown tax registers in principle include only heads of households, not wives, children, or servants. A great variety of taxes were paid, some of which are described in the subsequent section.

3 Registers of the fire brigade tax (*brandvaktsavgiften*). This tax was paid by owners of real property. Before 1810, this is the only source reporting values of real property for Stockholm as a whole. The fire brigade tax was a municipal tax. Starting in 1810, owners of real property were liable to pay taxes to the crown as well, resulting in annual valuations which are part of the crown tax registers (see above).

This study exploits the 1787 registers. A revaluation was carried out this year, which approximately doubled the previous values (dating from 1737). Values were supposed to be estimated market values of properties, land as well as buildings.

Rich and poor districts in the late eighteenth century

The tax system of the latter part of the eighteenth and earlier part of the nineteenth centuries involved a large number of taxes. Some were municipal taxes, some were paid to the crown. Some were based on occupation, some were luxury taxes on, e.g., wagons and watches; as was said above, one tax was based on possession of real property. The most interesting ones for the purpose of describing variations in economic position are dealt with below.

Large amounts of taxes paid will of course reflect a more favourable economic situation in a district. Various taxes, however, describe somewhat different aspects of the social structure and the level of material resources.

The *personal tax* (*personella avgiften*) was based on occupational title alone, although some occupations were divided into more or less wealthy subcategories. There were wide variations in the amount of tax paid. The tax scale from 1789 gives an impression of the differentials.[7] (See table 6.1.)

This tax reflects the formal social structure better than the real one, since it provides no information on variation within occupations (apart from the subcategories among dealers and craftsmen).

[7] R. G. Modée, *Utdrag utur alla ifrån år 1718 utkomne publique handlingar*, 14 (Stockholm, 1804).

Table 6.1 *Personal tax rates by occupation in 1789.*

Occupation	Original currency rdr	sk	Decimal conversion
Government chancellors (*riksråd*)	30	0	30.00
Colonels	16	0	16.00
Wholesale dealers or merchants, most wealthy	20	0	20.00
Wholesale dealers or merchants, less wealthy	12	0	12.00
Wholesale dealers or merchants, least wealthy	10	0	10.00
Craftsmen, wealthy	2	32	2.67
Craftsmen, less wealthy	1	16	1.33
Law-court clerks	2	0	2.00
Journeymen	1	16	1.33
Porters, clerks	1	0	1.00
Male servants	0	32	0.67
Female servants	0	8	0.17
Male labourers	0	32	0.67
Female labourers	0	16	0.33

Note: 1 rdr (riksdaler) corresponds to 48 sk (skilling).

The *window tax* amounted to 8 sk a piece for 'large or double' windows, 5 sk for 'simple or average' ones and 2 sk for 'small' ones. The tax did not apply to rooms that could not be inhabited, such as shops or attics. Differences between districts are likely to roughly reflect variations in habitation standards.

Furthermore, the *average value of real property per capita* is given, based on the ratio of the valuations in the fire brigade tax registers to total population according to the population registers.

Possession of *pocket watches* was considered a luxury and was taxed. Owners of gold watches were to pay 4 sk, those owning other pocket watches 2 sk for each watch.[8]

In addition to these four kinds of tax information, the *share of servants and other employees* in the households is given as a percentage of total population. This is taken from the population registers. It includes not only female and male servants but also journeymen, apprentices, labourers, and other employees, such as bookkeepers in the household of the employer. The share thus does not reflect the frequency of servants in a restricted sense, but rather the trade activity and degree of proletarianization more generally.

[8] This column in the tax records also includes small amounts for possession of furniture covered with silk.

Table 6.2 *Taxes paid (1790) and real property value (1787) per capita in tax districts as per cent of the average Stockholm value, and percentage share of servants and other employees.* (District numbers refer to figure 6.2)

	Tax			Property	% servants
District	Personal	Window	Watches	value	& others
1 Nikolai south/west	183	189	240	209	38
2 Nikolai inner/east	159	157	159	151	33
3 Jakob	144	146	183	153	36
4 Klara upper	128	135	127	139	36
5 Klara lower	133	152	221	157	25
6 Kungsholmen	81	82	61	84	24
7 Adolf Fredrik	52	50	22	53	13
8 Johannes	48	44	18	39	12
9 Ladugårdslandet upper	83	85	99	39	14
10 Ladugårdslandet lower	58	65	42	89	21
11 Maria west	90	84	63	86	19
12 Maria inner	116	111	110	108	25
13 Katarina north	77	78	39	62	20
14 Katarina east/inner	67	63	35	50	21
15 Katarina south	46	33	24	48	20

Note: Figures on total population are drawn from the 1780 registers except for Ladugårdslandet upper, Maria, and Johannes, for which the 1790 records were used. For practical reasons registers reporting summaries of population by block, when existing, have been used.
Sources: Kronotaxeringslängder och mantalslängder, ÖÄ för uppbördsärenden; Trakt- och kvarterslistor 1787, Brandvaktskasseadministrationens arkiv. Stockholm City Archive.

Table 6.2 reports these measures by tax district. The 15 districts that existed in 1787 are mapped in figure 6.2.

The spatial distribution of taxes on luxury consumption should be more unequal than the distribution of real property. The real property values by district should be fairly close to those of the window tax. From table 6.1 this appears to be true. The tax on watches is the one exhibiting the largest variation across districts. Moreover, the distribution of the personal tax is very similar to the window tax, implying a close but hardly unexpected relationship between the occupational and real property structures.

The richest part of Stockholm was the central one, Nikolai (then labelled The City and nowadays called The Old Town), particularly its southern and western parts. Also Jakob and Klara were in all respects above the average. More than one third of the inhabitants in these

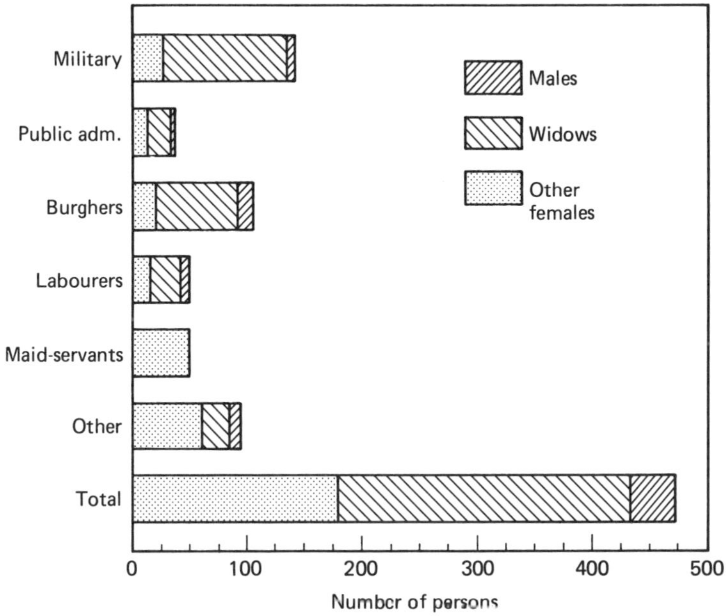

Figure 6.1 Paupers by social category and civil status in 1733. *Source*: U. Johanson, *Fattiga och tiggare i Stockholms stad och län under 1700-talet* (Stockholm, 1984).

well-to-do districts consisted of servants and other employees living in the household of their master.

Johannes and Katarina south were the poorest districts, with Adolf Fredrik only slightly better off. These poor districts are not homogeneous in socioeconomic terms. Katarina was the most proletarianized part of the capital; the textile factories were largely situated here. The window tax values for the Katarina districts may well indicate that habitation standards were particularly low there. Industrial properties were more numerous than in Johannes, accounting for the higher real property per capita values in Katarina.

The share of servants and other employees however was lower in Johannes, Adolf Fredrik, and some other districts, reflecting their less industrialized and proletarianized character. The social structure of Johannes and Adolf Fredrik may be depicted as comprising a substantial segment of marginalized rather than proletarianized people. Large numbers of persons in the lowest positions of the public sector were living there, as well as people whose means of existence are not easily determined (e.g., various widows or former soldiers). However, also the middle stratum of craftsmen was fairly numerous,

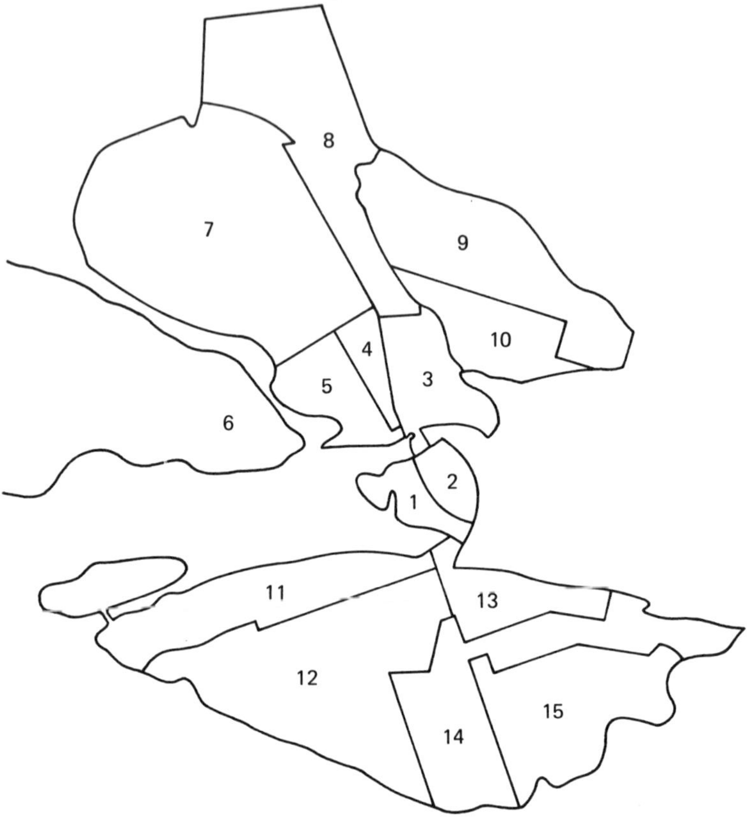

Figure 6.2 Tax districts in 1787: 1 Nikolai south/west, 2 Nikolai inner/east, 3 Jakob, 4 Klara upper, 5 Klara lower, 6 Kungsholmen, 7 Adolf Fredrik, 8 Johannes, 9 Ladugårdslandet upper, 10 Ladugårdslandet lower, 11 Maria west, 12 Maria inner, 13 Katarina north, 14 Katarina east/inner, 15 Katarina south.

and they dominated among the owners of real property. The frequency of pocket watches in these two districts, which is lower than in any other part of the town, suggest that margins for consumption over and above the bare necessities may well have been lower than in Katarina.

Ladugårdslandet, Kungsholmen, and the other districts of Katarina, while not as poor as Katarina south and Johannes in all respects, were below the average. Ladugårdslandet occupied a special position due to the importance of military employment there. Most of the active soldiers and officers were found there as well as retired ones and widows of military personnel. Many craftsmen and workers such as carpenters or shipwrights, who had ties to the military sector, also lived there. The two Maria districts are the ones most closely corresponding to average Stockholm conditions.

At the very periphery of the town, per capita property values tend to rise in some areas which are sparsely populated and more or less constitute a transition to rural settlements.

To sum up, two rather distinct types of poor districts are found. They are either of two types. One is the capitalistic type, with a relative predominance of manufacturing, a proletarianized labour force, a more unequal income distribution, and low habitation standards. The other is the marginalized type, with few industrial establishments, a low share of servants, and a more heterogeneous population often with ties to the public sector. The rich districts are more homogeneous, simply showing high values along all socioeconomic indicators.[9]

[9] These observations have some relevance when discussing the coverage of the population registers. The extent of underregistration cannot be gauged until the census of 1860 (see chapter 8 below). Söderlund, who has worked extensively with the eighteenth-century materials, states that the 1770 registers have been drawn up with great care and that their quality is higher than around 1740. Utterström is of the opinion that the registers from the period 1720–72 are far more complete than the best one of the preceding century (the 1676 register, which probably registers close to 80 per cent of total population). See E. Söderlund, *Stockholms hantverkarklass 1720–1772* (Stockholm, 1943), 122ff.; G. Utterström, 'Stockholms folkmängd 1663–1763', in *Historiska studier tillägnade Nils Ahnlund* (Stockholm, 1949).

A few examples from the 1790 register can illustrate what may be a more general pattern in terms of underregistration. Two poor blocks (each with a per capita property value of less than 50 rdr, that is belonging to the lowest category in figures 6.3 to 6.5) were chosen randomly and studied in detail. One, Beijers trädgård, is in the proletarian district of Katarina south, the other, Väderkvarn, in Johannes.

When the tax authorities were unable to trace a person liable to pay taxes, they made a note of this. These notes indicate that the authorities lost contact with a larger number of persons in the more marginalized Väderkvarn block (nine persons out of 385, or 2.3 per cent) than in the relatively proletarian Beijers trädgård (only one person out of 246, or 0.4 per cent). In Väderkvarn it is recorded for instance that a soldier's widow, Anna Stina Brasell, 33 years old with a four-year-old daughter, together with a foster-daughter aged 22 and a maid-servant aged 40, 'all in a very poor state have left for the countryside, but the place unknown'. The groom Simon Liljegren, 30, had disappeared with his wife and two children after living in with soldiers, leaving without paying the rent. The single case in Beijers trädgård refers to a sailor running away from wife and children.

While these examples are few, they may suggest that areas with a more numerous segment of marginal individuals were more affected by population turnover, which the authorities were unable to control, than was the case with more proletarian areas where people were more strictly tied to specific employments and employers. This also suggests that the problems of underregistration may have been greater in ages above, or at least in the higher end, of the most mobile groups. A large majority of those registered as having moved to Stockholm were under 35 years old (74 per cent in 1815, for instance), and they were overwhelmingly described as female or male

Approximately 2 per cent of the population received public assistance by the mid eighteenth century. Thanks to a detailed study by Ulla Johanson, the composition of this small segment of the very poorest can be described. Figure 6.2 displays the distribution by social category and civil status of 473 paupers reported in 1733. Females of ages over 60 dominated among the paupers. The most interesting feature is the prominent role of persons connected with the military sector, primarily widows of soldiers. The soldiers themselves could often avoid pauperism (after active service they received a small pension). One factor contributing to the contrast between males and females in this category is that the soldiers in many cases had been working in handicrafts (a legal by-employment of garrison soldiers) without formally belonging to any guild. This helped in managing the family economy as long as the man was alive. When the husband died, however, the widow was not entitled to any kind of aid from the guilds.

Among the unmarried females, older maid-servants appear to have been a relatively exposed category. According to the descriptions of the paupers, these females often had been working as servants for a long time in the city. The labourer category was on the other hand rather small, in fact smaller than the number of persons with a burgher background.[10] The composition of the paupers is illustrative of a pre-industrial town with a substantial segment of military and civil employment in positions where salaries were very low.

A more detailed picture of spatial variation not only between but also within districts is given in figures 6.3 to 6.5. They refer to the average real property value per capita at the block level.[11]

Within the richest parish, Nikolai, some of the properties in the eastern blocks were owned by the *Skeppsbroadel*, the upper merchant stratum involved in the export trade with iron and other commodities. The largest owners, such as the wholesale trader Niclas Pauli, Jr., possessed properties valued at about 25,000 rdr altogether. Even the blocks at the lower end in Nikolai were valued highly compared with what is normally found in poorer districts.

servants. These young people, to the extent that they actually became employed as servants in the capital, should have been easier to keep in sight than were persons lacking any stable employment. For some migration data see T. Höjer, *Sockenstämmor och kommunalförvaltning i Stockholm fram till 1864*, 12.

10 The term burgher refers to those endowed with the formal right to exercise a trade as a craftsman or merchant. In socioeconomic terms the category was of course quite heterogeneous, including people ranging from tailors and shoemakers to wealthy merchants.

11 Ladugårdslandet upper has been excluded since it is not comparable with the rest of Stockholm. This is probably due to the large number of properties owned by the crown, and hence untaxed, in this district.

Figure 6.3 Real property values per capita in northern Stockholm in 1787.

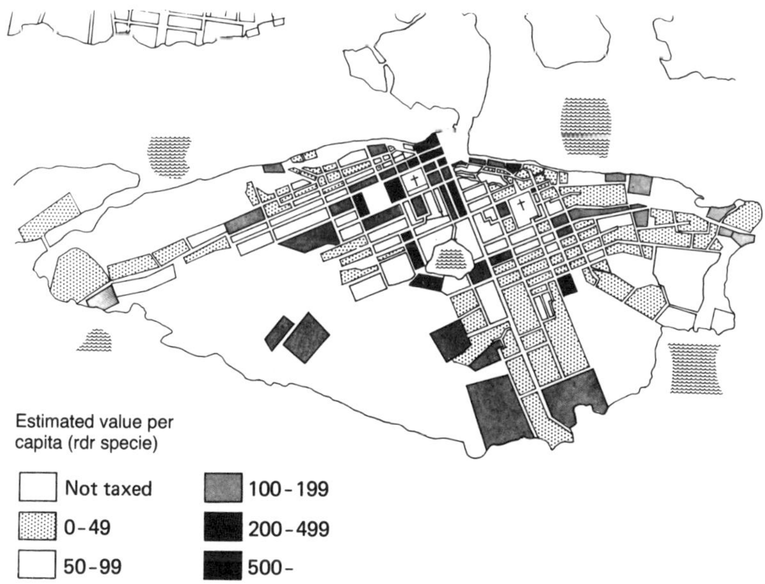

Figure 6.4 Real property values per capita in southern Stockholm in 1787.

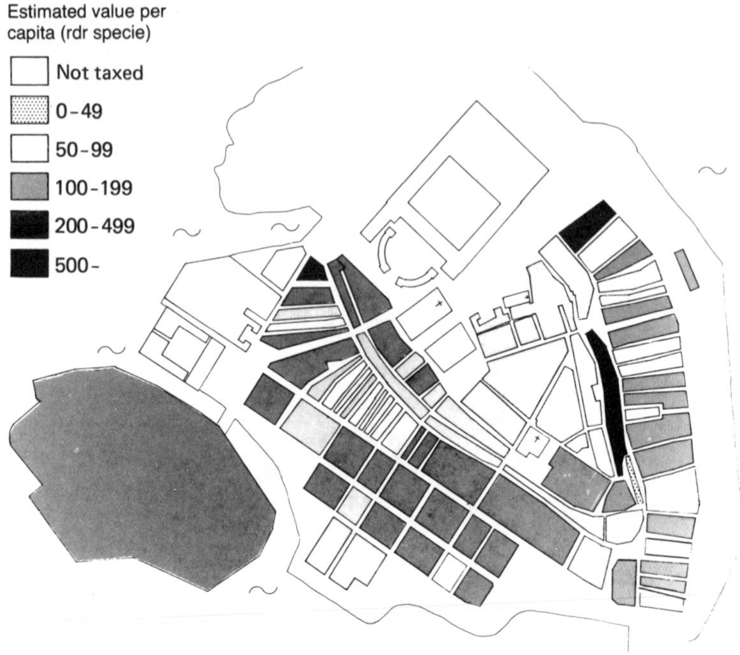

Figure 6.5 Real property values per capita in central Stockholm in 1787.

If we turn to the poor blocks in Katarina south, we find a large number of properties with very low values. In the block of Barnängen the highest taxed property (owned by the widow of a wholesale dealer) reached not more than 400 rdr, and the majority were below 50 rdr. For example the property of Petter Lagerberg, a wool washer, was valued at 17 rdr; that of Stina Lindman, a carpenter's widow, at only 10 rdr. These were simple wooden houses which are often stated to have been in a bad condition. Such properties were often owned by craftsmen, journeymen, labourers, or widows. In this block they often had some relation to the textile factory of Barnängen.[12]

The social geography of Stockholm, with diminishing wealth as we move from the central areas out towards the periphery, corresponds

[12] Even very small properties were often rented to tenants, while the owner occupied only part of it. This probably constituted a not unimportant source of income among small owners, e.g. widows. In Katarina we find for example, Christina Crom, a sailor's widow and the owner of a wooden house valued at 56 rdr. The house was reported to be in a bad condition but yet habitable. She had two tenants. One was the wife of a valet and her daughter (the man was said to be travelling), the other a married paver. The latter in turn had a widow of a boatswain living in (possibly a case of 'Stockholm marriage'; see below). Christina's total rent from her tenants was 10 rdr; we know this income because it was taxable at the time.

well with the classic model of the pre-industrial city. The same pattern is seen, for instance, in London, Lyon, Koblenz, Boston, Philadelphia, and New York. Although differentials between districts appear to be very large in table 6.2, they were probably at least as prominent, and probably larger, between central and peripheral districts of Boston at the same time. Boston was during the later eighteenth century a less industrialized town than was Stockholm. Also in the far more industrialized Lyon spatial inequality was as least as marked as in Stockholm. Mainz during the late eighteenth century, as described by Dreyfus, probably represents an exception rather than the rule. He points to the lack of spatial differentials in a town where few streets lacked a proletariat but few areas also lacked members of the upper class. Inequality was more marked *within* buildings. The owner or higher social strata often lived on the first floor and the lower strata on the higher floors.[13]

Poverty in 1850

This section reports results from a cross-section study of the incidence and structure of poverty in 1850.

The method of measuring poverty employed here is based on tax records. The method has earlier been used to analyse rural poverty and is described in detail in previous publications.[14] In short, an individual is considered poor if unable to pay even the lowest capitation tax, the hospital tax (*kurhusavgiften*). The capacity of each individual to pay taxes was evaluated each year by the tax authorities. The hospital tax was introduced in 1821, which thus constitutes the earliest year that poverty can be studied by this method.

This poverty definition should be regarded as *broader* than one referring to recipients of poor relief only. Those unable to pay any tax were not in possession of an economic surplus but they may or may not have received financial support from outside. On the other hand,

13 J. K. Alexander, 'The city of brotherly fear; the poor in late eighteenth-century Philadelphia', in *Cities in American History*, eds. K. T. Jackson and S. K. Schultz (New York, 1972), 93; R. A. Mohl, *Poverty in New York, 1783–1825* (New York, 1971), chapter 2; A. Kulikoff, 'The progress of inequality in Revolutionary Boston', *William and Mary Quarterly* 28 (1971); E. François, 'Unterschichten und Armut in rheinischen Residenzstädten des 18. Jahrhunderts', *Vierteljahrschrift für Sozial- und Wirtschaftsgeschichte* 62 (1975); F. G. Dreyfus, *La société en Rhénanie et particulièrement à Mayence dans la seconde moitié du XVIIIe siècle 1740–1792* (Paris, 1968), 360ff.

14 O. Lundsjö, *Fattigdomen på den svenska landsbygden under 1800–talet* (Stockholm, 1975); J. Söderberg, *Agrar fattigdom i Sydsverige under 1800–talet* (Stockholm, 1978). See also Söderberg, 'Causes of poverty in Sweden during the nineteenth century', *Journal of European Economic History* 11 (1982).

Table 6.3 *Poverty ratios and per capita values of real property, income tax, and commercial tax in 1850* (Stockholm = 100).

District	Poverty ratio, %	Real property	Income tax	Commercial tax
Nikolai south/west	19	191	147	275
Nikolai inner/east	32	126	96	181
Klara/Kungsholmen	25	142	178	105
Jakob/Adolf Fredrik	32	119	128	97
Maria	31	83	74	94
Johannes/Ladugårdslandet	41	48	55	33
Katarina	42	62	46	77
Stockholm	34	100	100	100

Sources: Huvudböcker, mantalslängder, verifikationer, 1851. ÖÄ för uppbördsärenden, Stockholm City Archive.

the concept is more *narrow* than one taking into account all the propertyless or proletarians whom according to an occupational classification, some of whom fell below the poverty line as defined here while others did not, as will be seen below.

Tax records make it possible to directly estimate the incidence of poverty in seven districts of Stockholm in 1850 (table 6.3 and figure 6.6). They also provide data on three aspects of wealth and income: (1) assessed values of real property, (2) amount of income tax paid, and (3) amount of taxes paid for commercial activity.

The income tax mainly affected public or municipal employees who earned at least 201 rdr a year, an income exceeding that which most labourers are likely to have enjoyed. This tax thus provides an indicator of the importance of public employment in a district. The three aspects of wealth and income are reported per capita in table 6.3 as percentages of the Stockholm average.

The poverty ratio reported is defined as the percentage share of poor among total population above 17 years of age. As children below 17 were not liable to pay taxes, the incidence of poverty among them cannot be estimated from summary tax reports. Below, however, a stratified random sample across districts is used to describe far more closely the risk of being poor according to several individual and household characteristics such as age, sex, occupation, and family size.

From table 6.3 it is clear that there were considerable differences between districts in the incidence of poverty. Levels in the poorest

Figure 6.6 Tax districts and sub-districts in 1850 mentioned in the text.

districts of Katarina and Johannes/Ladugårdslandet were about twice as high as that of the richest part of the capital, Nikolai south and west. There is not surprisingly an evident negative association between poverty ratios on one hand and levels of real property values, income tax, and commercial tax on the other. The division into tax districts regrettably is another one than during the late eighteenth century as described in the previous section, but it is nevertheless clear that the central areas still were those best off, while Katarina, Johannes and Ladugårdslandet were among the poorest.[15]

Compared with Swedish rural society at the same time, studied by the same method, the extent of poverty in Stockholm at 34 per cent of

[15] The division into tax districts by 1850 is rather crude, joining areas of different character. Thus most of Kungsholmen was far less well off than Klara, and the same applies to Adolf Fredrik and as compared with Jakob.

the population is high. The county mean poverty ratio, excluding urban areas, was 22 per cent. Only the level of the northernmost county, Norrbotten, reaching 37 per cent, exceeded that of Stockholm. No other county displayed ratios above 30 per cent, although figures not far from Stockholm's sometimes are registered in pronounced woodland districts with their characteristically small farming units. Urban mid nineteenth-century ratios have been calculated only for some twenty towns apart from Stockholm. None of them outstripped the capital, Gothenburg and several others exhibiting ratios around 20 per cent. In a national perspective, then, Stockholm stands out as a place where the poverty-generating mechanisms appear to have been unusually strong.[16]

The high level of poverty may seem strange, taking into account that the lake Mälaren valley was a relatively rich agricultural region. The high economic level of that region was however to a considerable extent a consequence of the high rates of out-migration. The labour force of Stockholm was to a large extent recruited from the neighbouring counties. The general situation is to some extent similar to what de Vries labels the specialization model of agricultural economic development. According to this model, a subdivision of holdings is prevented by proletarianization of considerable segments of the population, who are forced to migrate to urban areas. This crowding-out of the population surplus permits the agricultural region to experience an economic growth and a rising standard of living.[17]

International comparison is of course far more difficult because of differing ways of defining and measuring poverty. The most common way of judging the extent of poverty is based on measuring the proportion of paupers. Another method relies on estimating family incomes, defining a subsistence line, and calculating the proportion falling below this line. A third approach makes more indirect inferences from variables assumed to be related to poverty, e.g., mortality or heights.

The first method can be illustrated by Mokyr's work on Flanders. He reports proportions of paupers ranging from 17 to 25 per cent in urban areas of East Flanders, and from 30 to 37 per cent in urban areas of West Flanders in the 1840s. This definition should tend to lead to lower estimates than the one employed here, since many of those

[16] On poverty in Gothenburg see A.-M. Fällström, 'Befolkningens sociala och ekonomiska struktur i Göteborg 1800–1840', *Historisk tidskrift* 94 (1974), and Fällström, 'Göteborgs fattigvård från 1800 till 1840', *Göteborg förr och nu* 9 (1974).

[17] J. de Vries, *The Dutch Rural Economy in the Golden Age* (New Haven and London, 1974). See also chapter 2 above on Stockholm's position within the regional system of the lake Mälaren valley.

regarded as poor by the Stockholm tax authorities were not recipients of poor relief. In the 1830s only about 2 per cent of Stockholm's population were indoor paupers.[18] Poor relief expenditure being determined not only by the extent of poverty but also very much by attitudes to the poor and by the financial capacity of the community, it is obviously not possible to base comparisons across cities on this type of data. Still, the very high share of paupers in urban West Flanders is a strong indication of more widespread poverty than in Stockholm at about the same time. The situation of Flanders was, however, exceptional at the time. The decline of the Flemish linen industry combined with the harvest failures of 1845–6 produced one of the most prominent crisis areas of Western Europe of the period.[19]

In British research, John Foster and Michael Anderson employ the second method. They gauge the incidence of poverty by establishing subsistence levels to which family incomes are related.[20] Their conception of the poor consisting of those being on or below the subsistence line is in principle similar to the one employed in the present study. Foster's estimate for Oldham is close to Anderson's for Preston by mid century, or about 20 per cent (of families, not individuals). It may well be that these English industrial towns were not characterized by such widespread poverty as was the less industrialized Stockholm, but no precise comparison can be made. We do not have sufficient information on family incomes in Stockholm to be able to replicate this type of measurement.

The third method, indirect inferences from mortality data, is the basis of Chevalier's estimate of the poor comprising one third of the population of Paris by the mid nineteenth century. This result must be regarded as more uncertain, being based not on any actual count of the poor but solely on mortality data from hospitals.[21] Chevalier assumes that all those who died in hospitals were recruited from the poor and, more critically, that the death rate in hospitals fell somewhat below that of the poorest districts of the capital. No arguments in favour of the latter assumption are presented, and it seems very unlikely that hospital death rates should not have been substantially higher than

18 The study by U. Johanson, *Fattiga och tiggare i Stockholms stad och län under 1700–talet* (Stockholm, 1984), focusses on paupers and particularly the organization of poor relief around the mid eighteenth century.

19 J. Mokyr, *Industrialization in the Low Countries, 1795–1850* (New Haven, 1976), chapter 7.

20 J. Foster, *Class Struggle and the Industrial Revolution* (London, 1974), chapter 4; M. Anderson, *Family Structure in Nineteenth-Century Lancashire* (Cambridge, 1971), chapter 4.

21 L. Chevalier, *Laboring Classes and Dangerous Classes in Paris during the First Half of the Nineteenth Century* (Princeton, N.J., 1973), 329, 353.

elsewhere in the city, which would lead to a lower estimate of the proportion of poor. It seems impossible to compare the extent of poverty in Paris with that of other cities on the basis of this method.

A type of measurement more similar to the one of the present study is that employed for Berlin in the first half of the nineteenth century by Günter Liebchen. He calculates some interesting figures based on the municipal house and rent tax, affecting houses and apartments according to rental value. It was necessary to exempt large numbers of households from this tax because of poverty, even if they did not receive poor relief. In 1850, these households represented 20 per cent of the total. As several poor families could share one apartment, this figure probably underestimates the overall proportion of poor families, which Liebchen believes to have been around 25 per cent. As this method does not seem to differ much from the one employed in this study, it is not unlikely that the extent of poverty in Stockholm exceeded that of Berlin at the same time.[22]

Chevalier also reports the share of rented accommodation not liable to tax on account of poverty, a measure of the same type as employed by Liebchen for Berlin. This share was 21 per cent in 1827, varying from only 7 per cent in the affluent third arrondissement to 38 in the poorest, the twelfth. The overall level thus is close to that of Berlin.

Within-city differences in the incidence of poverty and wealth in Stockholm may seem substantial but were probably rather low by international standards. In Berlin, spatial inequality was clearly greater, the three poorest districts (Rosenthaler Vorstadt, Königsstadt, and Stralauer Viertel) displaying a proportion of poor households more than five times as high as that of the richest district (Dorotheenstadt). The pattern was similar in Paris. Dispersion between districts in per capita real property values, as measured by the coefficient of variation, was about the same in Stockholm as in the industrially backward York of the early 1840s, which was probably less spatially segregated than many industrial urban centres at the time. American cities like New York, Philadelphia, and Boston also typically exhibit far greater internal variation than did Stockholm. This is also true of Vienna with its very large differences between the City (innere Stadt) and poor suburbs like Josephstadt.[23]

[22] G. Liebchen, 'Zu den Lebensbedingungen der unteren Schichten im Berlin des Vormärz', in *Untersuchungen zur Geschichte der frühen Industrialisierung vornehmlich im Wirtschaftsraum Berlin/Brandenburg*, hrsg. O. Büsch (Berlin, 1971).

[23] A. Armstrong, *Stability and Change in an English County Town; A Social Study of York, 1801–51* (Cambridge, 1974), 76, 211ff.; S. Blumin, 'Mobility and change in antebellum Philadelphia', in *Nineteenth-century cities*, eds. S. Thernstrom and R. Sennett (New

To sum up, Stockholm appears to have been poorer than most other Swedish towns and rural areas. International comparison of the incidence of poverty presents far greater problems. Still, the overall impression is that Stockholm by the mid nineteenth century was a relatively poor city when compared with Berlin and Paris, and perhaps also when compared with English industrial towns such as Preston and Oldham. The spatial distribution of poverty, on the other hand, probably was relatively equal by international standards, the proportion of poor in the poorest district not being more than twice that of the richest part of the capital.

The method used here to measure poverty has its strengths as well as its weaknesses. It has the advantages of allowing measurement of the overall incidence of poverty and of the composition of the poor segment of the population. Several determinants of poverty at the individual level can be described well. It is nevertheless evident that no precise measurement of poverty trends in the longer term can be made employing the present method. Because of differences in the tax system, comparison with eighteenth-century conditions is not possible. Another method, the analysis of long-term trends in real wages, was employed in the previous chapter. Analysis of real wages of unskilled labour will facilitate international comparison.

Demographic and social characteristics of Stockholm: a brief comparative view

This section and the following one draw on information obtained from a stratified random sample across tax districts of one per cent of the households (excluding institutions) in 1850, yielding 337 households and a total of 836 individuals. The population registers (*mantalslängd*) at this time provide information on occupation, sex, marital status, and age. In addition, they report assessed values of real property, income tax, and commercial tax. Though some important aspects of the demographic structure are available from published official statistics or fairly easily accessible unpublished tables (the *Tabellverk*), some other aspects such as household size can only be computed on the basis of individual data.

Like many other Swedish and foreign mid nineteenth-century towns, Stockholm had a considerable female surplus (57 per cent in

Haven and London, 1969), 187; E. Pessen, *Riches, Class, and Power before the Civil War* (Lexington, Mass., 1973), 197; W. Hugins, *Jacksonian Democracy and the Working Class; a Study of the New York Workingmen's Movement 1829–1837* (Stanford, 1960), 206; data on the house tax in *Statistik der Stadt Wien*, 2 (Vienna, 1861), table 3.

the sample). Because of the high infant mortality combined with not a particularly high birth rate, the share of the population below 15 years of age was substantially lower than in the rest of urban Sweden (21 and 27 per cent, respectively). Age groups between 15 and 60 however were correspondingly overrepresented in the capital. Stockholm also exhibits a low proportion of married, 25 per cent in the sample as compared with 27 per cent in other towns and 33 per cent in rural Sweden by mid century.[24]

The Stockholm mean household size of 2.5 in the sample is the same as that of Gothenburg in 1840 but is certainly extremely low when compared with a number of towns in other countries. Among other European cities, the smallest household sizes that we observed are those of Paris and Lyon in 1851 (2.7 and 2.9, respectively). The generally small size of French urban households is connected with low fertility rather than with high mortality as in the Stockholm case. Mean household sizes in other Western and Central European cities usually fall between 4 and 5 (for instance, Brussels and Rotterdam, 4.1; Edinburgh, 4.3; London and Amsterdam, 4.4; Vienna and Düsseldorf, 4.6; Glasgow and Graz, 4.7; Antwerp and Copenhagen, 4.9). American households often were even larger – somewhat over 5 in New York City, Boston, and Detroit by mid century, for example.[25]

The exceptionally small size of households in Stockholm must be partly a result of heavy in-migration by young and single persons, but may also point to serious obstacles to family formation. Another unusual feature expressing the same underlying processes is the extremely high share of households headed by females, 40 per cent, to be compared with only 5 per cent in Milwaukee, 12 per cent in Birmingham, about 20 per cent in Preston, Leeds, York, and Los

[24] See *Bidrag till Sveriges officiella statistik A) Befolkningsstatistik 1851–1855, andra afdelningen* (Stockholm, 1859), lxxv ff., for basic demographic data on Stockholm and the rest of Sweden by mid century.

[25] Gothenburg: calculated from data in Fällström, Befolkningens sociala och ekonomiska struktur, 165. See also *Population. Récensement général 1846* (Brussels, 1849); H. van Dijk, *Rotterdam 1810–1880* (Schiedam, 1976), 263; *Census of Scotland, 1861, vol 1* (Edinburgh, 1862); *Census of Great Britain, 1851. Population tables I* (London, 1852); *Uitkomsten der derde tienjarige volkstelling in het Koningrijk der Nederlanden, 1849* (The Hague, 1852); J. Ehmer, *Familienstruktur und Arbeitsorganisation im frühindustriellen Wien* (Munich, 1980), 56; *Ergebnisse der Volkszählung . . . 1861. Preussische Statistik, 5* (Berlin, 1864); W. H. Hubbard, 'Städtische Haushaltsstruktur um die Mitte des 19. Jahrhunderts', in *Moderne Stadtgeschichte*, ed. W. H. Schröder (Stuttgart, 1979), 210 (Graz); *Statistisk tabelværk, N.R., 12* (Copenhagen, 1856); *Seventh Census of the United States: 1850* (Washington, 1853); S. E. Bloomberg *et al.*, 'A census probe into nineteenth-century family history: Southern Michigan, 1850–1880', *Journal of Social History* 5 (1971), 30; *Statistique de la France*, S. 2, Tome 2 (Paris, 1855).

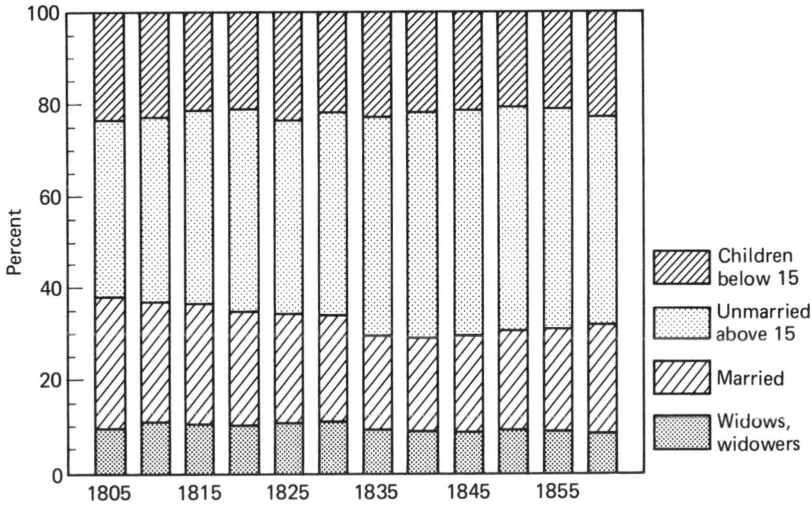

Figure 6.7 Distribution of Stockholm's population by marital status, 1805–1860. *Source: Statistisk årsbok för Stockholms stad* 38 (1905), 53.

Angeles, and 26 per cent in Graz.[26] This high proportion in Stockholm does not seem to be the result of instability or very high mortality within marriage; the proportion of widows was fairly normal compared with other Swedish towns, and wives are seldom reported as living apart from or having been deserted by their husbands.

In fact, the proportion of widows was falling during the first half of the nineteenth century as a delayed consequence of the declining nuptiality (see also chapter 8 below).[27] Figure 6.7 displays changes in the distribution of population by civil status 1805–60. Up to mid century, the proportion of unmarried above age 15 grows substantially at the expense of the other categories. Even the proportion of children tends to decline. After the 1840s, the situation changes in a favourable direction. Once more, family formation, not dissolution, is the critical variable.

When compared with other European towns, the pattern described

26 C. N. Conzen, *Immigrant Milwaukee 1836–1860* (Cambridge, Mass., 1976), 51; L. Davidoff and C. Hall, *Family Fortunes; Men and Women of the English Middle Class, 1780–1850* (Chicago, 1987); 406; Anderson, *Family Structure in Nineteenth-Century Lancashire*, 46; D. Ward, 'Environs and neighbours in the 'two nations': residential differentiation in mid-nineteenth-century Leeds', *Journal of Historical Geography* 6 (1980), 145; Armstrong, *Stability and Change*, 182; B. Laslett, 'Social change and the family: Los Angeles, California, 1850–1870', *American Sociological Review* 42 (1977), 276; Hubbard, 'Städtische Haushaltsstruktur', 201.

27 The increase in the proportion of widows/widowers in 1810 is no doubt connected with the 1808–9 war.

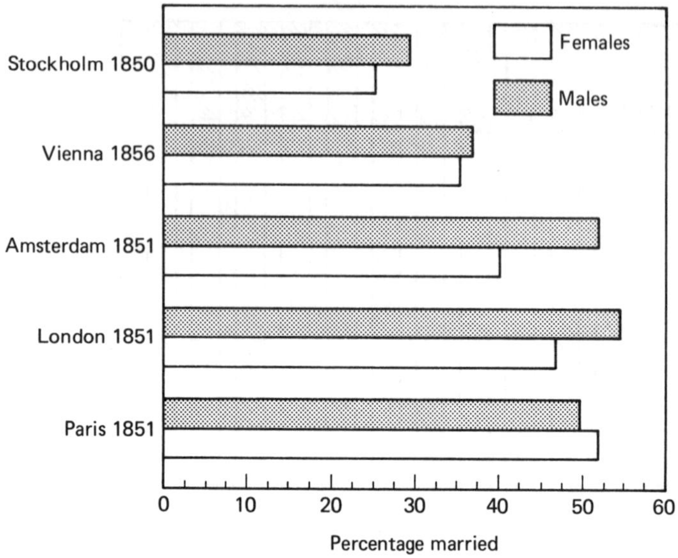

Figure 6.8 Distribution by marital status of population over 15 years of age in Stockholm, Vienna, Amsterdam, London, and Paris, around 1850. *Sources*: *Statistisk årsbok för Stockholms stad* 38 (1905), 53 (Stockholm); W. Wretlind, *Undersökningar rörande Stockholms mortalitet* (Stockholm, 1866), 36.

above is unusual. The peculiarity of the Swedish capital emerges clearly from figure 6.8, describing the distribution by marital status of the population above 15 years of age. The proportion married in Stockholm was far lower than in mid nineteenth-century Paris, London, or Amsterdam. Vienna, though closer to Stockholm, still gives the impression of less serious barriers to marriage.[28]

A comparative view of the occupational structure cannot be undertaken here; the difficulties would be great due to varying classificational systems. Only one aspect shall be briefly discussed. The occupational structure of Stockholm was very diversified, the capital lacking any dominating industry. By far the most common occupation was that of female servant, indicative of the still large pre-industrial nature of the economy. The proportion of households containing servants is probably not a bad indicator of the degree of industrialization and proletarianization of an urban area, the proportion expected to be lower in more advanced towns.

In Stockholm, 16 per cent of the households employed servants. On

[28] Copenhagen, Berlin, Brussels, and Madrid are other cities exhibiting significantly higher proportions of married than Stockholm at the time. See Wretlind, *Undersökningar rörande Stockholms mortalitel*.

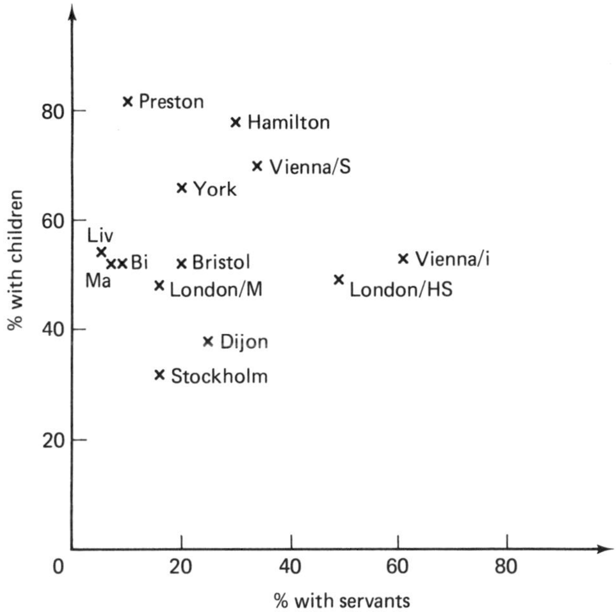

Figure 6.9 Percentage of households containing servants and children in selected cities.

Notes: Liv = Liverpool; Ma = Manchester; Bi = Birmingham; Vienna/S = Vienna, Schottenfeld; Vienna/i = Vienna, innere Stadt; London/M = London, Marylebone; London/HS = London, Hanover Square. *Sources*: Figures for Birmingham, Bristol, Liverpool, Manchester, Marylebone, and Hanover Square refer to registration sub-districts according to *Census of Great Britain, 1851. Population tables I* (London, 1852), table 13. *Other sources*: M. B. Katz, *The People of Hamilton, Canada West* (Cambridge, Mass., 1975), 221 (Preston, York, Hamilton); M. Mitterauer, 'Auswirkungen von Urbanisierung und Frühindustrialisierung auf die Familienverfassung an Beispielen des österreichischen Raums', in *Sozialgeschichte der Familie in Neuzeit Europas*, ed. W. Conze (Stuttgart, 1976), 146 (Vienna); J.-P. Viennot, 'La population de Dijon après le récensement de 1851', *Annales de démographie historique* 1969, 250 ff.

the one hand, this is more than in relatively industrialized British towns such as Preston and in the sub-districts of Birmingham, Leeds, Manchester, and Liverpool as reported in the 1851 census. On the other hand, the Stockholm figure is lower than in the little industrialized but possibly wealthier York, Graz, Dijon, and Berlin. The Stockholm proportion is far lower than the proportion found in the wealthiest districts included, Hanover Square registration sub-district in London and in the central part of Vienna.

Figure 6.9 illustrates the unusual position of Stockholm with regard to the percentage of households containing servants and children. While Stockholm resembles Dijon more than any other of the towns selected, it is clearly different from the cluster of British industrial towns (Birmingham, Liverpool, Manchester) as well as from the less industrialized cities and towns with a high frequency of servants.[29]

Determinants of individual poverty

In the sample, each individual above age 17 was classified as poor or non-poor according to the judgement of the tax authorities. Poverty status of children below 17 was regarded as being the same as that of the head of the household. The main results with regard to the characteristics of the poor segment of the population are reported in table 6.4, in which the risk of being poor is described for several categories of the sample.

In most cases these categories characterize the individual, but in some cases (which are specified in the table) categories pertain to the *head of the household* in which individuals were living. Thus, the proportion poor by sex is given not only for individual's sex (34 per cent of the females being poor) but also by sex of the head of the household (54 per cent being poor out of the members of households headed by females). Size of households and number of children below 17 years of age refer to individuals living in the respective categories; for instance, among the members of three-person households, 60 per cent out of a total of 129 in the category are classified as poor, and these 129 individuals represent 15 per cent out of the total sample of 836.

The poverty ratio for the sample is 38 per cent or somewhat higher than for the total population of Stockholm (table 6.3 above) where, however, children were not included whereas institutions were. Children are taken to belong to the same occupational category as their parents.

At first sight, a surprising result in table 6.4 is that the proportion of poor among males in the sample exceeds that of females (42 against 34 per cent), which is in sharp contrast to conditions in rural areas studied by the same method. In rich as well as poor rural districts, the incidence of poverty among females has generally been observed to be

[29] For urban centres not included in figure 4.2 see data on the share of households with servants in I. Thienel, *Städtewachstum im Industrialisierungsprozess des 19. Jahrhunderts* (Berlin, 1973), 413 (24 per cent in Berlin in 1861); Conzen, *Immigrant Milwaukee*, 56 (19 per cent in 1850), W. H. Hubbard, 'Forschungen zur städtischen Haushaltsstruktur am Ende des 19. Jh.: das GRAZHAUS-Projekt', in *Sozialgeschichte der Familie in der Neuzeit Europas*, ed. W. Conze (Stuttgart, 1976), 290 (32 per cent in 1857); van Dijk, *Rotterdam 1810–1880*, 451 (13 per cent in 1849).

Table 6.4 *Percentage share of poor among various categories of the total sample (N = 836), and category as percentage of the total.*

Category	% poor	N	Category as % of total sample
Sex (own)			
Male	42	357	43
Female	34	479	57
Sex (head's)			
Male	31	595	71
Female	54	241	29
Age (own)			
Below 20	33	272	33
20–59	39	529	63
Above 60	49	35	4
Marital status (head's)			
Unmarried or widower	50	246	29
Married	29	466	56
Widow	47	124	15
Household position			
Head of household	52	337	40
Other	28	499	60
Occupation			
Upper, professional	0	33	4
Small entrepreneur	5	66	8
Clerical, lower middle	12	130	16
Craftsmen (masters)	32	38	5
Domestic	5	81	10
Skilled labour	17	36	4
Unskilled/semi-skilled labour	57	264	31
Retired	67	44	5
Unspecified	64	144	17
Size of household			
1	66	164	20
2	46	108	13
3	60	129	15
4 or more	18	435	52
Number of children below 17			
0	41	347	42
1	54	153	18
2–3	34	246	29
4 or more	6	90	11

higher than among males, although the difference between sexes tended to be smaller for poor regions.

The better performance of Stockholm females is primarily to be explained in terms of the different labour markets facing each sex, a much higher proportion of women being employed as domestics and thus acquiring a fairly secure position at least in the short run. As is seen from the information on poverty by occupation in the table, the proportion of poor was extremely low among domestics, only 5 per cent.

Being female *and* head of a household, however, was quite another thing. Belonging to a female-headed household meant a far greater risk of being poor (54 per cent as compared with 31 per cent where the head was a male). In this perspective, there must have been strong incentives for a female to try and find domestic employment rather than to establish a household of her own.

With regard to the marital status of the head, it is not surprising that the unmarried and widower category (the component groups which cannot be separated), as well as that of widows, were characterized by higher proportions of poor than households headed by married couples. There were certainly economic barriers to marriage while at the same time this type of arrangement, once established, probably helped in the management of the household economy.

The relationship between marital status and poverty is, however, different for males and females. Among males the proportion of poor was *lower* where the head of household was married than where he was not (36 and 44 per cent, respectively). Among females on the other hand the proportion below the poverty line was *higher* among the married than among the unmarried or widows (38 and 33 per cent, respectively).[30] In terms of poverty, males gained from marriage whereas females did not.

It does not seem to have been exceptional that married women participated in the labour force. They could do so in a considerable range of activities: as saleswomen, working with textiles or baking, or as keepers of shops and inns, just to mention those observed in the sample. No quantitative assessment as to the extent of such female work supporting the family economy is possible, however, information being unavailable for the large majority of wives.

Large households and a large number of children were clearly positively related to the economic level of the household. The propor-

30 As table 6.4 shows poverty among widows was even higher. For the sake of comparison with the males, however, the categories unmarried and widows must be collapsed.

tion of poor was very low in households consisting of four persons or more, and it was even lower in households with four children or more (18 and 6 per cent, respectively). Having several children at home does not seem to have been possible except in well-to-do households. Children belonging to households in the lower strata probably had to leave home at young ages. Households with one child exhibit an unusually high proportion of poor (54 per cent), implying a life-cycle pattern of poverty involving special stress in the early stage of family formation. The high percentage of poor among three- as compared with two-person households points in the same direction.

Yet a significant difference as compared with rural Sweden concerns the relationship of poverty to age. The risk of being poor in Stockholm increased with age but not at all to the same extent as in rural Sweden. Poverty ratios are 33 per cent below 20, 39 per cent for ages 20 to 59, and 49 per cent above age 60. Investigated rural parishes exhibit lower proportions of poor among the young and middle-aged but higher ones above, say, ages 55 or 60. The relationship between poverty and the inability to work is likely to have been weaker in Stockholm than in rural areas, which implies serious problems of unemployment or irregular employment in the capital.

Finally, table 6.4 describes the risk of being poor by occupational category. The proportion of poor is much below average in the small entrepreneur (mostly shopkeepers) and clerical categories (referring to lower, in most cases public and municipal employees such as book-keepers or policemen). Skilled labourers, a rather small group including primarily compositors and some occupations within engineering and metal manufacturing, also managed rather well (27 per cent in poverty). Craftsmen (masters only) exhibit a surprisingly high proportion of poor, 32 per cent, just below the overall average. A contributing factor may have been that ages were relatively high among households in this category.[31]

The situation was far worse among unskilled or semi-skilled labour, more than half (57 per cent) being poor. We thus face very substantial differences between skilled labour on the one hand and the unskilled/semi-skilled on the other, which no doubt reflect a real and pronounced stratification within the working class. The mid nineteenth-century pay differentials between skilled and unskilled labour were wider than either previously or later (on pay ratio trends see the next chapter).

The highest proportions of poor are found in the retired category

[31] There is no comprehensive study of the social and economic conditions in Stockholm handicrafts during the first half of the nineteenth century that is comparable with the in-depth major works of Ernst Söderlund on the eighteenth century.

Table 6.5 *Results of discriminant analysis with poverty status as the dependent variable.*

Independent variable	F-value	Significance
Size of household	172.31	0.0001
Number of children	59.07	0.0001
Occupation = unskilled/semi-skilled	54.91	0.0001
Retired	33.05	0.0001
Female head of household	34.16	0.0001
Widow as head of household	5.36	0.0209

(including only cases where the occupational title clearly specifies retirement; no age criterion is involved) and among those with unspecified occupations (including many of the widows).

In order to determine the relative importance of variables discussed above affecting individual poverty, a discriminant analysis was carried out with poverty status as the dependent variable. The independent variables are those listed in table 6.5.

The overall fit of the model in table 6.5 is fair, correctly classifying 84 per cent of the poor and 76 per cent of the non-poor. The size of household and the number of children are, as already mentioned, clearly positively related to the economic status of the household. These variables prove to be the ones that best differentiate between poor and non-poor. Belonging to occupational category unskilled/semi-skilled or being retired substantially reduced the chance of finding oneself above the poverty line, as did, though to a lesser degree, belonging to a household headed by a female or widow.

Inclusion of the variables individual's age and gender (as distinct from that of the head of the household) does not significantly improve the results as reported above (the F-values are clearly insignificant). This underlines the fact that the structure of poverty in Stockholm was dissimilar from that of rural areas where poverty was to a large extent determined by age and gender. Though not yet an industrialized town, Stockholm poverty possessed less of a purely demographic dimension and more of a class dimension.

Concluding comments

The spatial distribution of wealth and poverty towards the end of the eighteenth century and in 1850 has been examined in this chapter.

The rich and poor areas of the capital were about the same in 1790 as in 1850. The central districts were the most well-to-do. The poorest districts, however, were of two different types: one proletarian comprising comparatively large numbers of wage labourers, and another more characterized by the segment of marginalized people often with some relationship to the military or civil parts of the public sector. Katarina is the most prominent example of the former type, while Johannes typifies the latter.

The cross-sectional character of the results presented here do not easily lend themselves to establishing trends over time. From a study of tax materials by Höjer, however, it appears that the degree of inequality in the spatial distribution of wealth (measured by the total amount of taxes paid per capita) was narrowing in the very long term between 1760 and 1855.[32] Nikolai in particular, although the richest district at all points in time during the period, was clearly less outstanding by the mid nineteenth century than it had been in 1760. Still, between 1835 and 1855 there is some indication of widening disparities, the richest districts of Nikolai, Klara, and Jakob advancing relative to the Stockholm average.

The poor districts of Katarina, Johannes, and Adolf Fredrik in the long term moved closer to the Stockholm average, though they were always below it. The district most dominated by military employment, Ladugårdslandet, on the other hand appears as relatively poorer by the mid nineteenth century than around the middle of the eighteenth. This may point to special problems connected with the military sector which we are not able to pursue here. The dominating pattern nevertheless seems to have been narrowing spatial differentials during the long period of stagnation, at least up to 1835.

The demographic structure of Stockholm was unusual in several respects. The mean size of households was extremely small, and a very high proportion of households (40 per cent in 1850) were headed by females. The small households and the prominent role of females is obviously to some extent related to the exceptionally high mortality level; as we shall see in chapter 8 below, one of the main characteristics of Stockholm mortality was the high rates among males in active ages. Still, the proportion of widows is not particularly high, implying that remarriage was frequent where the economic resources existed. Marriage rates were declining in the long term, suggesting growing economic or social barriers to marriage. As a counterpart to this process, illegitimacy was rising, reaching very high levels by the mid nineteenth century (see chapters 4 and 8). In fact, the term 'Stockholm marriage' was used as a label of cohabitation among unmarrieds. The

32 T. Höjer, *Sockenstämmor och kommunalförvaltning i Stockholm fram till 1864*, chapter 1.

interplay between economic and demographic series will be examined more closely in chapter 8.

A detailed analysis of the composition of the poor segment of the population (approximately the poorest third) was carried out for 1850. The results point to important differences between the structure of Stockholm poverty and that of rural poverty at the same time. Stockholm poverty was less tied to old age (and, as a consequence, inability to work) than was the case in rural regions. In the capital, poverty also affected males harder than females, in sharp contrast to the rural pattern. The most reasonable interpretation relies on differences in labour markets. In the urban context, males appear to have been more disadvantaged than females.

In one respect this chapter has failed to produce conclusive results. It cannot be decided to what extent the incidence of poverty by 1850, or the composition of the poor, differed from that of the latter part of the eighteenth century. The method of analysing poverty applied to the mid nineteenth century is not well suited to determine time trends. The reason is that the technique is based on certain features of the tax system, a system which was far from unchanging. The important question of trends in living standards must be approached by other methods, such as those employed in the analysis of real wages in the previous chapter.

Some other problems raised here will also be taken up later on. The next chapter will examine the question of trends in inequality. Did the tendency towards narrowing spatial differentials have a counterpart in the distribution of wealth at the individual level? Was stagnation accompanied by widening inequality or by levelling?

7

Trends in inequality, 1715–1850

Introduction

The relation between growth and distribution is a classic problem in economic history as well as in economic theory. It was paramount for the classical economists. Yet there are few studies of pre-industrial economies which actually explore these phenomena and the connections between them. While several previous chapters have focussed on the growth problems of Stockholm during the century following 1750, the distribution of economic resources will now be examined more closely.

A rather pessimistic picture of real wage trends in the eighteenth century emerged in chapter 5 above. This would be reinforced insofar as it could be shown that this was part of a broader process of widening social disparities. On the other hand, the overall perspective would be somewhat different if the stagnation of the capital was linked to a process of levelling, where the upper strata were losing ground as well.

The latter hypothesis, predicting growth to be associated with a surge in inequality, and depression or stagnation with a narrowing of differentials (or at least a stable distribution), would appear to be the more likely one. This is for instance the argument of the Slicher van Bath model referred to previously (chapter 5).[1] In his model, periods of expansion (in agriculture, to be precise) produce polarization between rich and poor. This happens largely because the price structure changes in a way that is disadvantageous to the lower strata as the prices

[1] B. H. Slicher van Bath, 'Les problèmes fondamentaux de la société pré-industrielle en Europe occidentale', *A. A. G. Bijdragen* 12 (1965).

of land and foodstuffs escalate. A phase of stagnation or depression, on the other hand, normally gives rise to a contraction of the social scale. Socioeconomic differentials tend to narrow during these periods of comparatively slow population growth.

Still, there is a scarcity of systematic empirical studies in a reasonably long-term time perspective. This chapter attempts to trace some secular trends in inequality from the earlier part of the eighteenth century up to the mid nineteenth. The following questions are asked. Can any clear long-term inequality pattern be discerned? How do trends in the capital compare with rural Sweden, where agrarian society is generally believed to have been characterized by growing inequality? Is the Kuznets curve relevant as a description of the historical pattern?[2]

We will deal partly with aspects of wealth inequality, partly with income inequality. The subsequent section concentrates on the distribution of real estate, where trends in Stockholm from 1715 to 1845 are compared with the corresponding trends for rural Sweden. The latter part of the chapter charts some changes with regard to the distribution of earnings, primarily in Stockholm.[3] The discussion of real estate ownership will be best suited to a description of change in the upper tail of the distribution, while the data presented on wages and salaries place greater weight at the lower tail.

The analysis of wealth and income thus can augment each other. In general, the more we focus on pre-industrial and agrarian conditions, the less relevant will an income approach be. While information on various aspects of wealth is fairly rich from the latter part of the sixteenth century onwards, direct measurement of even late nineteenth-century farm incomes is seldom feasible because of the scarcity of data.[4]

[2] It should be stated from the outset that the data and results in this chapter are of a more tentative character than those presented elsewhere in this volume. The reason is that inequality data are not as conveniently accessible as, e.g., demographic or price data, and that basic reference works focussing on historical inequality are lacking.

For a discussion of subsequent trends up to 1914 see J. Söderberg, 'Trends in inequality in Sweden, 1700–1914', *Historisch-Socialwissenschaftliche Forschungen* 21 (1987), 58ff.

[3] Neither wealth nor incomes can be captured fully. For example, we will not deal with human capital or ownership of other assets than real estate. To study rents or profits directly would be an extremely difficult task which cannot be undertaken here. Still, it is reasonable to expect that real estate was the most strategic single component of wealth and earnings the most important aspect of income in Stockholm during the period we are dealing with.

[4] J. G. Williamson, *Did British Capitalism Breed Inequality?* (Boston, 1985) argues that independently changing wealth distributions (due to emancipation, land reform, or revolution rather than to income changes) are historically rather rare. Such 'independence' would however be more frequent in the pre-industrial era, say prior to 1815,

Studies of historical inequality have a place in several research agenda. One of them, the macroeconomic analysis of capitalist developments, deals with inequality as part of a general equilibrium process. Within a growth and distribution model, inequality may be treated as a set of price signals flashing factor scarcities and triggering supply responses. Eventually, such a model may explain the joint behaviour of factor rewards, output, and inequality. Plausible macroeconomic modelling is however dependent upon the availability of fundamental data on inequality, factor markets, and output. More has been done on the British and American economies than on others. For Sweden and many other countries we first need to establish more of a systematic empirical basis.

As readers cannot generally be expected to know Swedish economic history well, it may be worthwhile to briefly present some basic features. Pre-industrial agrarian society was dominated by relatively independent peasants in large parts of the country. Most researchers maintain that Sweden was never feudalized.[5] Large estates were mainly found in the plainlands of the lake Mälaren region in eastern Sweden and in the south. The strategic industrial activity in the pre-industrial era was iron production.

Agrarian economic growth in the period 1750–1850 is now generally regarded as an important prerequisite to later industrialization. The expansion of the peasant economy was a major force in the transformation of agriculture and the beginning of modern economic growth.[6] The large landed estates do not seem to have possessed any

particularly with reference to the effects of war, demographic crises, and political instability. It is interesting to note that Eli F. Heckscher faced the problem squarely in his discussion of the distribution of wealth in seventeenth-century Sweden. Noting that 'one of the great controversies in political economy concerns the question whether wealth increases are rooted in especially valuable economic contributions – according to market valuation – or depend on the distribution of power in society, two viewpoints which, to be sure, do not altogether exclude each other', he thought that the conclusion based on Swedish seventeenth-century historical evidence would be that 'the great fortunes were created primarily by the political conditions; contributions to ordinary economic activity in seventeenth-century Sweden were not the main factors in the formation of large fortunes, although business transactions played their substantial part'. E. F. Heckscher, *Sveriges ekonomiska historia från Gustav Vasa*, I:2 (Stockholm, 1936), 318.

5 A classic statement on the absence of feudalism is E. F. Heckscher, *An Economic History of Sweden* (Cambridge, Mass., 1954), chapter 2. For diverging Marxist viewpoints see P. Anderson, *Lineages of the Absolutist State* (London,, 1974); J. Lindegren, 'Den svenska militärstaten 1560–1720', in *Magtstaten i Norden i 1600–tallet og de sociala konsekvenser*, ed. E. Ladewig Pedersen (Odense, 1984), 99–130.

6 On peasant expansion generally see S. Martinius, *Jordbrukets omvandling på 1700- och 1800–talen* (Lund, 1982); M. Fridholm *et al.*, *Industrialismens rötter* (Stockholm, 1976).

obvious productivity differences as compared with peasant farming based on family labour.[7]

The country was overwhelmingly agrarian well into the second half of the nineteenth century. As late as 1850 not more than one tenth of the population lived in towns. Industrialization was late but rapid; during the last decades of the nineteenth century exports of forestry products and iron ore grew dramatically. The industrialization process was extremely successful in terms of economic growth and raising standards of living. From about the turn of the century the domestic market increased in importance and industrial production was gradually reorientated from raw materials to processed products such as pulp and mechanical engineering. Industrialization and urbanization were to a considerable extent separate phenomena, as nineteenth-century exports relied on exploitation of natural resources in rural regions.

Wealth inequality

Rural Sweden

The only hypothesis concerning long-term inequality trends in the pre-industrial agrarian society so far advanced in Swedish research is Maths Isacson's (for references see table 7.3 below). His investigation of a parish in the county of Kopparberg (for the division into counties see figure 7.1) led him to separate two phases in the development of inequality among peasants. During the first phase, stretching from the end of the seventeenth century throughout the eighteenth, inequality was reduced. Larger farmsteads tended to be divided into two or more units, resulting in homogenization.

The second phase, according to this hypothesis, is connected with the agrarian revolution from the beginning of the nineteenth century. A stratum of 'large peasants' became more prominent. While still relying primarily on family labour, they possessed larger farms and employed more farm-hands than the other peasants. In Isacson's area of investigation, most peasants were involved in iron production as well. Agrarian production was growing at a faster rate than previously and substantial amounts of land were reclaimed. Isacson believes there were some advantages of scale for the relatively large farmers. By 1850, a marked stratification among the peasants is seen, and the

[7] See, e.g., U. Jonsson, A.-M. Köll and R. Pettersson, 'Eine Agrargesellschaft im Wandel', *Zeitschrift für Agrargeschichte und Agrarsoziologie* 28 (1980); U. Jonsson, *Jordmagnater, landbönder och torpare i sydöstra Södermanland 1800–1880* (Stockholm, 1980), chapter 5.

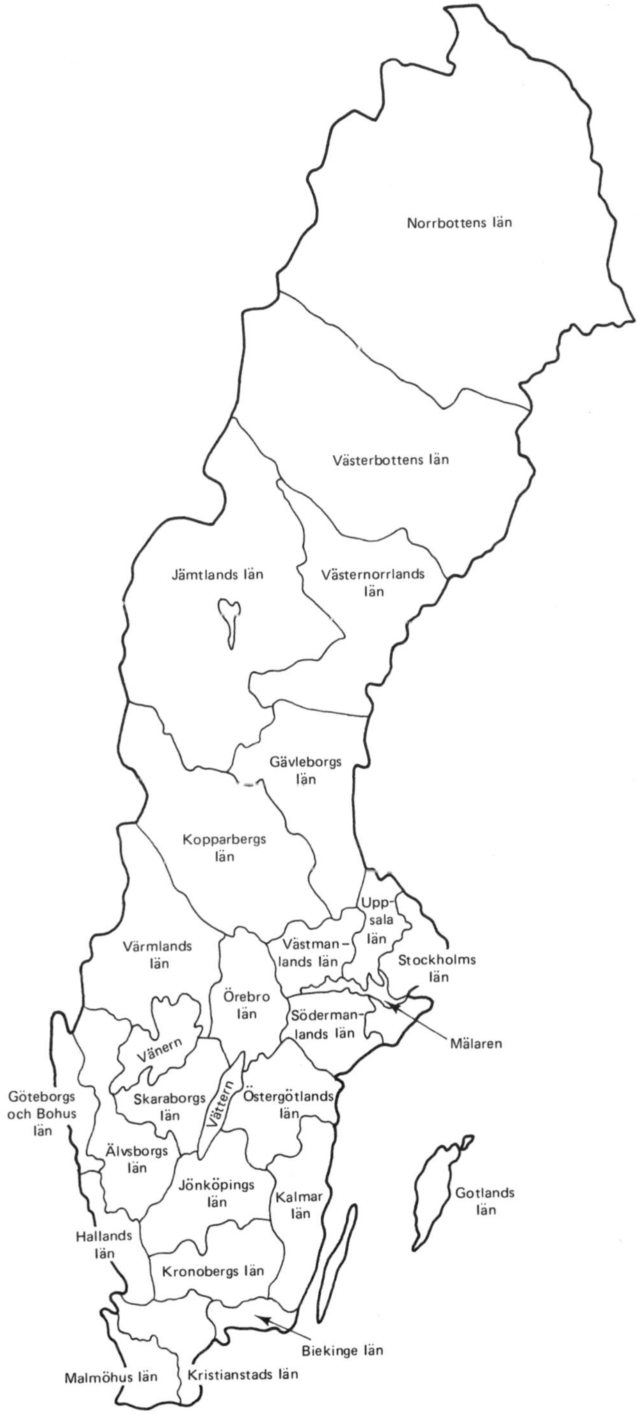

Figure 7.1 The division of Sweden into counties.

distribution of wealth was more unequal than it had been in 1715. The small group of large peasants by the mid nineteenth century was differentiated from the rest of the peasantry not only with regard to wealth and productive capacity but also socially, e.g., by the ownership of wagons, gold, and silver.

There is wide agreement among researchers that inequality among peasants was rising for the first half of the nineteenth century. Several regionally based studies in addition to Isacson's display such a pattern of differentiation (see table 7.3 below). Christer Winberg, dealing with a few parishes in the plains of Skaraborg county, reports a quite marked increase in inequality with regard to the distribution of land. He contends that the peasants in his area were so differentiated by 1850 as to make it meaningless to characterize this category as a social stratum.

Although several researchers have dealt with social stratification in rural Sweden particularly with respect to the nineteenth century, the degree in inequality is seldom described with any standard measure. This makes interregional and intertemporal comparison more difficult.[8] One of the few actual inequality measurements refer to two peasant-dominated parishes in southern Sweden, where inequality among landowners and farmers was on the rise between 1821 and 1862. The Gini coefficient (G) increased from 0.42 to 0.51 in the plainland parish of Fleninge and from 0.18 to 0.35 in the woodland parish of Loshult. Still, inequality among property owners in agrarian society is in general likely to have been lower than in the towns. The Gini coefficients are far lower than those that will be reported below for owners of real estate in Stockholm.[9]

So far we have dealt primarily with peasant farmers or owners. One of the most striking elements in the total process of differentiation was, however, the growth of the rural stratum below peasants in the century after 1750. Especially during the period ca. 1800–70, the lower stratum comprising crofters or landless increased dramatically. About 1750, groups below the peasants (primarily crofters, cottars, and landless labourers) were only a quarter as numerous as the peasants; a century later the lower stratum comprised as many people as the

[8] Inequality is here measured solely by conventional indicators such as the Gini index. In quantitative history there has sometimes been an overstress on the unusual or fanciful at the expense of standardization and comparability. The comparative dimension will be extremely important in future historical inequality research. Such work will be aided by the use of standard methods and measures as far as possible.

[9] L. Soltow, 'The Swedish census of wealth at the beginning of the 19th century', *Scandinavian Economic History Review* 33 (1985), indicates a higher level of inequality in Swedish and Finnish towns than in rural areas according to the wealth census of 1800. Unfortunately, Stockholm is missing in this material.

peasants. Regardless of trends within the peasantry, this expansion of the lower agrarian stratum must have contributed towards a widening of inequality in a broader perspective. In this sense there can be little doubt that the century after 1750 must be regarded as a period of growing overall inequality.[10]

Large landowners were declining in the long run. This was a temporally and regionally differentiated process, involving shifts between various groups of large landowners as well. The decline in the position of noble landowners began and grew strongest in areas outside the central plainlands. The central plains, where the largest estates were situated, were less affected. Especially in the decades around 1850, a not inconsiderable net transfer of land took place from nobles and non-nobles including bourgeois as well as peasants. By 1862, the 2.6 per cent of largest owners held 29 per cent of the value of landed property.[11]

Stockholm

In order to trace some broad trends in inequality in Stockholm, the distribution of real estate (land and buildings) will be studied by means of three cross-sections referring to the years 1715, 1799, and 1845. As only a minority of the population were owners of real estate, this sort of investigation is best suited to gauging inequality trends among (at the mid nineteenth century) approximately the upper 10 per cent of households.[12]

10 Several detailed social mobility studies demonstrate that downward mobility from the peasant to the lower stratum increased dramatically during the first half of the nineteenth century. Facing rapidly rising land prices, sons or daughters of peasants frequently failed to attain the position of their parents. Social mobility trends thus conform to what is reasonable to expect from inequality trends. Major studies include those of Winberg, Martinius, and Söderberg listed in table 7.3. See also J. O. Björkman, *Bonde och tjänstehjon; om social stratifiering i äldre svensk agrarbygd* (Uppsala, 1974), and I. Eriksson and J. Rogers, *Rural Labor and Population Change* (Uppsala, 1978). Köll, *Tradition och reform i västra Södermanlands jordbruk*, includes an interesting analysis of marriage patterns as an indicator of social distance. See also S. Carlsson, *Fröknar, mamseller, jungfrur och pigor* (Uppsala, 1977), and for an overview of social structure R. Miller and T. Gerger, *Social Change in 19th-Century Swedish Agrarian Society* (Stockholm, 1985).

11 On the position of noble and other large landowners see S. Carlsson, *Ståndssamhälle och ståndspersoner 1700–1865* (Lund, 1973). By the mid eighteenth century, less than half a per cent of Sweden's population held approximately a third of the land. Although this may seem a high figure, it is far from extreme in a European perspective. The distribution was more uneven in, e.g., England and Wales, Prussia, Lombardy, and Spain, but perhaps somewhat more even in France on the eve of the Revolution. The 1862 distribution: S. Martinius, *Jordbruk och ekonomisk tillväxt i Sverige 1830–1870* (Gothenburg 1970), chapter 2.

12 In 1845, the 3,394 owners of real estate in Stockholm constituted 3.8 per cent out of the total population of 88,242 (out of which 18,901 or 21.4 per cent were children

The study is based on the following sources. Between 1713 and 1716, a yearly wealth tax was levied on real and personal property in Sweden. For Stockholm only the 1716 returns, pertaining to valuations carried out during late 1715, are preserved. The registers report estimated values of sites, buildings, and personal property. Values of sites and buildings are here added for the purpose of obtaining comparability with the other cross-sections. Personal property is left aside.[13]

Apart from the wealth tax of the 1710s, no eighteenth-century valuation of real or personal property exists at the national level. Taxation of real property remained a municipal matter until 1810. For Stockholm, the source situation is better than for most of Sweden, since real property was re-evaluated on three occasions during the eighteenth century (1737, 1787, and 1799). Here, only the 1799 records are used.[14]

Starting in 1810, yearly real property valuations were carried out throughout the century. All of this valuable material is preserved. In rural areas valuations were generally fixed in money terms between about 1815 and 1862. For instance, a farmstead assessed at 1,000 rdr (*riksdaler banco*) in 1815 would still exhibit the same value in the 1861 volumes, although ownership changes would be recorded correctly. Of course this means that the sources do not reflect market values well during most of this period. In Stockholm, however, valuations were

below 15 years). The number of *properties* was of course higher, 3,813, since one owner could possess several properties. See T. Höjer, *Sockenstämmor och kommunalförvaltning i Stockholm fram till 1864*, 205, 469, *Statistisk årsbok för Stockholms stad* 38 (1905), table 11, and Taxeringslängder 1846, Stockholm City Archive. With a mean household size of 2.5 (see chapter 6 above) this would imply that close to 10 per cent of the households owned real property.

The number of properties changed only slowly; in 1813 it was 3,633. The number of owners that year is not known. Assuming the same number of properties per owner as in 1845, the number of owners in 1813 would have amounted to 3,234 or 4.7 per cent of total population. It is very likely that the proportion of property owners was gradually declining as the values of properties rose, raising the cost of entry. See F. Berg, 'Statistiska minnesblad öfver Stockholm', *Statistisk tidskrift* 3 (1869) for data on the number of properties.

For 1715 we lack the basic demographic data required to estimate the proportion of property owners.

13 For a general account of the wealth tax of 1713–16 see J. E. Almquist, 'Om kontributionsränteriet', *Karolinska förbundets årsbok* (1917).

14 The 1737 municipal real property tax records are partly damaged.

Table 7.1 *Percentage of real estate in Stockholm held by specified shares of property owners in 1715, 1799, and 1845.*

	Share			Cumulative shares		
Percentile	1715	1799	1845	1715	1799	1845
0–1	12	9	11	12	9	11
1–5	30	24	23	42	33	34
5–10	21	20	19	63	53	53
10–20	20	21	19	83	74	72
20–30	9	10	10	92	84	82
30–40	4	7	6	96	91	88
40–50	2	4	5	98	95	93
50–60	1	3	3	99	98	96
60–70	0	1	2	99	99	98
70–80	1	0	1	100	99	99
80–90	0	1	1	100	100	100
90–100	0	0	0	100	100	100
Gini coefficient				0.78	0.70	0.68
N				390	364	366

Sources: 1715: Karl XII:s kontributionsarkiv, skattningslängd 1716. 1799 and 1845: Brandvaktskasseadministrationens arkiv, taxeringslängder 1799 and 1846. All in Stockholm City Archive.

far more flexible in the short run.[15] For practical reasons, a municipal register based on the 1845 tax register has been used.[16]

A stratified random sample was drawn from each register. All registers contain the same information: the title and name of the proprietor and the estimated value of the property, but no other

15 See Berg, 'Statistiska minnesblad öfver Stockholm', for annual data on the aggregate valuations of the real estate in Stockholm 1813–65 according to the tax records. The mean valuation per property doubled from 1813 to 1845 and doubled once more from 1845 to 1862. This rate of growth, although it cannot automatically be taken to reflect the growth in market values, certainly by a wide margin outstripped the rise in the general price level of the period. The Swedish cost of living index rose modestly from 72 in 1810/14 to 80 in 1840/4 and 100 in 1860/4 (L. Jörberg, *A History of Prices in Sweden II*, 350).

Though the trend in real wages and salaries was upward during the first half of the nineteenth century, the rise in property values must have been steeper, in Stockholm as well as in Sweden generally. This process was of course driving inequality upwards, raising the cost of entry into the real estate market. It should be noted, however, that the major changes in the distribution of real estate reported below clearly fall on the upper tail of owners, while changes attributable to the lower are negligible.

16 On nineteenth-century real property tax registers see R. Adamson, *Järnavsättning och bruksfinansiering 1800–1860* (Gothenburg, 1966), chapter 9, and S. Martinius, *Peasant Destinies* (Stockholm, 1977), chapter 2.

Table 7.2 *Distribution of real estate in Stockholm by social category.*

	Percentage of wealth			Percentage of sample		
Category	1715	1799	1845	1715	1799	1845
Persons of standing	74	41	35	23	20	18
Merchants, industrialists	12	33	37	8	20	21
Artisans	13	23	23	47	37	43
Lower stratum	1	3	3	22	23	18
Total	100	100	100	100	100	100
Female owners	35	14	11	21	20	14

personal characteristics such as age, and few descriptions of houses or sites.[17]

Table 7.1 reports the share of real estate held by specified percentiles of proprietors, ranked from largest to smallest, and sample sizes.

The key result is that inequality among property owners declined. Most of the change occurred between 1715 and 1799, when G fell from 0.78 to 0.70.[18] What shifts between social strata account for the narrowing differentials? Who were the winners? Who were the losers?

Table 7.2 divides the samples into four strata. The first comprises persons of standing or rank (*ståndspersoner*) except merchants, dealers, and industrialists, who make up the second group.[19] The third consists of artisans and some other people of similar social standing, while the fourth comprises individuals with a social position below that of the craftsmen: journeymen, labourers, soldiers and civil servants in low positions, and unspecified widows. The table also reports the share held by females (summed over all social strata).

[17] The 30 largest proprietors were located in each register. The rest were drawn by simple random sampling. As is well known with regard to highly skewed distributions such as these, simple random sampling throughout will underestimate inequality. See, e.g., F. Nygård and A. Sandström, *Measuring Income Inequality* (Stockholm, 1981), chapter 10.

[18] A narrowing in inequality in Stockholm during the first half of the nineteenth century is also suggested by Soltow's study of the distribution of wealth among deceased. G declines from 0.84 in 1790 and 1800 to 0.78 in 1850. The source is the municipal death lists (*dödlistor*). This material is however highly incomplete, including only a minority of the deceased. The consequences of the gaps are not discussed. See Soltow, 'The Swedish census of wealth', 23.

[19] The ståndsperson concept (from German *Standesperson*) refers to persons of high extraction and particularly those standing above the burgher and peasant estates. Nobles and priests were included, but from the latter part of the eighteenth century the concept also was taken to comprise growing numbers of non-noble iron masters, officers, doctors, etc. See Carlsson, *Ståndssamhälle och ståndspersoner*, chapter 2.

Persons of standing suffered a rather dramatic decline in their share of real estate during the eighteenth century, from 74 to 41 per cent of the total. Their shares were overtaken primarily by merchants and industrialists, and the artisans also advanced noticeably. Between 1799 and 1846 the distribution was more stable; the small changes taking place were continuations of eighteenth-century trends. The lower stratum, while comprising about a fifth of the number of proprietors, always held a fairly negligible portion of total real estate.

When discussing the causes of the redistribution we have to keep in mind that the 1715 taxation took place during the later stage of the Great Nordic War, ending in 1721 when Sweden lost her Baltic provinces and her great power position. By 1715 the war had been raging for a decade and a half and Sweden had suffered heavy losses in Russia. Of course the war involved great strains for the country. Still, modern research has tended to play down the adverse effects, which clearly were not as disastrous to the economy as an older tradition maintained. Stockholm was never attacked, but at the time discussed here the capital had received quite a number of refugees from Åland which had recently been conquered by the Russians. These people are often described as destitute in the 1715 register.

The eighteenth-century levelling tendency particularly affected the nobles. They very much dominated the upper tail of the 1715 distribution. Among the top ten proprietors only one was a non-noble (the merchant, Paul Johan Heublein). The largest owner was a noble woman, Elisabet Funck (1642–1719). The daughter of a rich mayor of Stockholm, she married Johan Funck, a dynamic iron master and entrepreneur regarded as one of the richest persons of burgher extraction in his time. He was ennobled in 1672 and died in 1679 at the height of his career.[20] Among the rest of the top proprietors a small number of well-known noble families were well represented (e.g., Sparre, Tessin, De la Gardie, Piper, Fleming, Stenbock, and Horn).

By the 1799, the situation had changed significantly. Only three nobles remained among the top ten (representing the families De Geer, Cronhjelm, and Rosenadler). The largest proprietor was a textile manufacturer, Carl Gustaf Apiarie, possessing the largest mill in Stockholm. The rest of the top ten was quite diversified, including a merchant, an ironworks entrepreneur, another textile manufacturer, a high government official, an officer, and a wealthy widow.

In 1845, the largest owner was the doctor, M. C. Retzius. The rest of the top ten included a stronger element of merchants, occupying positions two to five. Furthermore, there were three nobles (families

[20] On the Funck family see *Svenskt biografiskt lexikon* 16 (1964), 650.

De Geer, Nordenfalk, and Staël von Holstein), a textile manufacturer, and a brewer.

In a classic interpretation of Swedish economic history, Heckscher emphasized two major changes in the eighteenth-century economy. The first was the emergence of a new, largely non-noble upper class based on the leading merchants, particularly in Stockholm (the *Skeppsbroadel*), and the iron masters. The second was the growing importance of the peasantry, similarly based on economic expansion. Heckscher thought that the eighteenth century in some respects could be regarded as the century of the merchants, who were still being favoured by mercantilist policies aimed at stimulating the feeble towns. The merchants not only controlled the important exports but also were more closely involved in industrial production, especially iron, than they were to be during the next century.

Heckscher on the other hand very much played down the role of urban handicrafts and manufacturing in economic growth. They did not form a point of departure for the industrialization gaining momentum during the nineteenth century. The roots of modern industrialization rather were to be found in rural cottage production, particularly in textiles.[21]

Heckscher's conception of the cottage industry is supported and reinforced by recent Swedish research stressing the importance of the domestic market for consumption goods. In a major study of the rise of mechanized textile factories, Lennart Schön observes a close connection between agricultural growth, raising domestic demand for textiles, and the expansion of the rural cottage industry.[22] Heckscher located strategic elements in the proto-industrialization debate which pointed to the existence of such a positive link between cottage industry and subsequent industrialization.

The limited investigation of Stockholm presented here can of course only partially form a basis for an appraisal of Heckscher's interpretation of the Swedish eighteenth-century economy. Nevertheless, we will try to relate the results to a larger framework.

With regard to the expansion of iron merchants and iron masters emphasized by Heckscher, this cannot be expected to have made much of an impact on the Stockholm real estate market. Investments in current assets and ironworks were more strategic to the exporters than was investment in real estate within the capital.[23] For this reason

21 E. F. Heckscher, *Svenskt arbete och liv* (Stockholm, 1968), 148, 212, 219.

22 L. Schön, *Från hantverk till fabriksindustri* (Lund, 1979), chapter 5; L. Schön, *Industrialismens förutsättningar* (Lund, 1982).

23 K. Samuelsson, *De stora köpmanshusen i Stockholm 1730–1815* (Stockholm, 1951), chapter 3.

the economic strength of the leading merchants (or iron masters) will not show up in the holding of large amounts of real property in Stockholm. Other sources and methods will have to be used in order to determine the economic expansion of these groups.

The advance of the merchant and industrialist group in table 7.2 mainly involved individuals other than those associated with the major merchant export firms. Traders in grain, spices, or general groceries were prominent.

Particularly in 1799, there was a considerable number of industrialists among the larger proprietors. Even though the manufacturers of the capital on the whole had been declining since the 1760s, this should not lead us to believe that possibilities of capital accumulation were absent. A few textile and tobacco manufacturers were able to compete at the highest level of the urban real estate market.

During the eighteenth century not only merchants and industrialists but also the artisan category in table 7.2 clearly improved their position in relationship to persons of standing. While artisans formed a diminishing share of the proprietors, those remaining increased their share of total real estate. Artisan proprietors in other words became fewer and richer. Brewers, representing a relatively capital intensive industry, are among the most prominent in 1799. At the other end of the scale were the few and small owners from large trades with small costs of entry such as shoemaking and tailoring.

This pattern may be compared with Ernst Söderlund's study of the Stockholm artisans, based on tax registers. On one hand, he stressed the secular stagnation of handicrafts in the capital during most of the eighteenth century. Small-scale rural cottage production and other towns offered stiffening competition. On the other hand stagnation did not affect all handicrafts equally and did not preclude polarization tendencies. Some small groups among the masters succeeded in establishing capitalistic forms of enterprises, employing dozens of journeymen and labourers in the building trades. Brewers, butchers, bakers, and goldsmiths formed an upper stratum at a considerable economic distance from the majority of masters.[24] Results in table 7.2 seem to agree with a view of widening inequality within the artisan group when this is taken to include the unpropertied masters. Economic stagnation among artisans should not be overemphasized since the category was expanding at the expense of persons of standing.

The decline of persons of standing is the dominating feature of table

24 E. Söderlund, *Stockholms hantverkarklass 1720–1772* (Stockholm, 1943), chapter 8; Söderlund, *Hantverkarna II* (Stockholm, 1949), 85–99.

7.2. There is a lack of economic studies dealing with the nobility, among whom the decline was striking. One possibility is that some withdrew from the capital in order to specialize as landowners. The counties surrounding Stockholm were a stronghold of noble landowners well into the second half of the nineteenth century. One of the very few investigations into landed estate during the eighteenth century suggests fairly high levels of profitability. There is no reason to expect any economic crisis among noble landowners in this region.[25]

Far from all nobles possessed land, however. A cohort study of the nobility by Ingvar Elmroth reveals a secularly declining proportion holding landed estate. This share was high among those born or ennobled in 1650–9 (56 per cent) but far lower for the late seventeenth-century cohorts onwards. After 1720, the proportion holding landed estate never exceeded one third. Demographic reproduction was significantly lower among the unpropertied, indicating less favourable economic circumstances.[26] A growing share of the noblemen became civil servants or military men. This was partly an inevitable effect of the *reduktion* of the late seventeenth century, withdrawing to the crown a considerable amount of landed estate previously granted to the nobility. The amount of land belonging to the nobility is thought to have been reduced by about one third.[27]

The weakened position of the Stockholm nobility during the eighteenth century may be seen as an expression of growing inequality within the estate, being particularly felt in the capital where the number of nobles in civil service was very high. The subsequent section will describe how the money-salaried functionaries in the capital suffered from a massive decline in their real earnings from service during most of the period 1720–1809. It is only logical that the stable position of the landed nobility in the lake Mälaren valley should contrast the retrogression in the capital.

There are reasons to believe that the major features of Heckscher's interpretations are realistic. Summarizing the discussion above, some minor points may still be made. First, reference to social categories should be supplemented by the observation that differentiation within the peasantry as well as within the nobility and within the Stockholm

25 L. Magnusson, *Ty som ingenting angelägnare är än mina bönders conservation* (Uppsala, 1980), chapter 5.

26 I. Elmroth, *För kung och fosterland* (Lund, 1981), chapters 4, 6. The figures mentioned refer to the national level; no regional breakdown is available.

27 The classic account of the impact of the *reduktion* is E. F. Heckscher, *Sveriges ekonomiska historia från Gustav Vasa* I:2, 336–59. For more recent assessments see K. Ågren, 'The reduktion', in *Sweden's Age of Greatness*, ed. M. Roberts (London, 1973), and L. Magnusson, *Reduktionen under 1600-talet: debatt och forskning* (Malmö, 1985).

artisans in all likelihood was widening. Second, Heckscher may have had a too negative view of the role of urban burghers and manufacturers. While it is true that handicrafts and manufacturing very often did not transform into modern factory industries, possibilities of capital accumulation within the handicraft and manufacturing sectors were far from totally lacking.[28]

Third, regarding the Stockholm merchants, the advance of some iron exporters may have been overstressed at the expense of other merchants and dealers who often seem to have been fairly successful. Fourth, the diversity of regional patterns makes generalization at the national level a less straightforward matter than Heckscher was aware of. The establishment of national trends more often than not requires large amounts of regional investigations of which only a few have as yet been carried out.

The results regarding female proprietors in table 7.2 remain to be commented upon. A surprisingly high share of real estate in 1715 (35 per cent) was held by women. This share was not more than 14 per cent in 1799 and 11 per cent in 1845. In 1715 as well as in 1799 females comprised about 20 per cent of the sample. The 1715 female proprietors thus were remarkable wealthy but not unusually numerous. Wartime male mortality alone is not a sufficient explanation. Possibly the Great Nordic War led to a disproportionate rise in mortality among noblemen as many officers were killed. Anyhow this period seems to be associated with an economically strong position of propertied women. It is not then wholly surprising to find a woman as the largest owner in 1715, in contrast large to the situation in 1799 and 1845.

The long-term levelling tendency in Stockholm does not parallel either of the competing hypotheses regarding Swedish rural society referred to above. Table 7.3 summarizes most of the available results on secular trends.

Kuznets' well-known inverted U hypothesis supposes inequality to widen during early periods of industrialization, later to narrow. Kuznets assumed that inequality among the urban population would be far wider than for an agricultural population organized in relatively small enterprises. This would be the case particularly when the urban population was being swelled by immigrants, either from the country's agricultural areas or from abroad. Once the turbulent phases

[28] This somewhat more positive interpretation resembles Stadin's concerning the small-town burghers in the decades around 1700. K. Stadin, *Småstäder, småborgare och stora samhällsförändringar* (Uppsala, 1979).

Table 7.3 *Schematic presentation of results on secular inequality trends in Sweden, c. 1720–1850.*

Area, county	Social category	Inequality trend 1720–1800	1810–50
By, Kopparberg	Peasants	Falling	Rising
Most of Skaraborg	Peasants	Rising	
Dala, Skaraborg	Peasants		Rising
Skåning, Skaraborg	Peasants		Rising
Julita and Österåker, Södermanland	Peasants		Rising
Fleninge, Malmöhus	All owners		Rising
Loshult, Kristianstad	All owners		Rising
Västerlövsta, Västmanland	All owners		Rising
Luleå, Norrbotten	All owners	Rising	
Stockholm city	All owners	Falling	Falling

Sources: By: M. Isacson, *Ekonomisk tillväxt och social differentiering 1680–1860* (Uppsala, 1979). Skaraborg: L. Herlitz, *Jordegendom och ränta* (Gothenburg, 1974); Dala: C. Winberg, *Folkökning och proletarisering* (Gothenburg, 1975), 184–5; Skåning: S. Martinius, *Peasant Destinies; the History of 552 Swedes Born 1810–12* (Stockholm, 1977). Julita and Österåker: A.-M. Köll, *Tradition och reform i västra Södermanlands jordbruk 1810–1890* (Stockholm, 1983), 46–7. Fleninge and Loshult: J. Söderberg, *Agrar fattigdom i Sydsverige under 1800–talet* (Stockholm, 1978), 60–1. Västerlövsta: M. Morell, 'On the stratification of the Swedish peasant class', *Scandinavian Economic History Review* 28 (1980), 29. Luleå: Calculation based on G. Enequist, *Nedre Luledalens byar* (Uppsala, 1937), 139, 221.

of industrialization and urbanization had passed, the relative position of the lower urban strata would improve, reducing overall inequality.[29]

The inverted U hypothesis in this original formulation is based on the assumption of the emergence of a dynamic growth process in which industrialization and urbanization are closely tied. This does not provide a good description of the Swedish experience in the century after 1750 where industrialization and urbanization were

[29] S. Kuznets, *Economic Growth and Structure* (London, 1966), 273–5.

largely separate phenomena. Agrarian growth is likely to have surpassed urban economic growth. Under these conditions most of Sweden experienced a widening and subsequent narrowing in inequality during the eighteenth and nineteenth centuries, exhibiting an inverted U curve albeit within another growth context than that envisaged by Kuznets.

The larger framework within which Stockholm producers operated differed radically from the agrarian arena. Contrary to advancing on a widening market, as agricultural producers did, those in Stockholm were facing long-term economic stagnation and strong tendencies towards de-industrialization in the century after 1750. Trying to adapt to market contraction, Stockholm firms were often on the Schumpeterian negative side of development. Indications of low profitability should of course not be taken to imply that no individual enterprise was gaining large profits; examples of success among manufacturers and craftsmen have already been presented. Secular economic stagnation still should have put serious barriers to capital accumulation, inhibiting a cumulative process of differentiation.[30]

Notes on the distribution of earnings

Focussing on the distribution of real estate as an important aspect of wealth, the discussion above had little to say about incomes. Since only a limited segment of the population possessed real estate, the analysis did not inform us about distributional trends with regard to larger portions of the population.

Recent historical inequality research has stressed the pattern of pay ratios as a key phenomenon in the evolution of overall inequality. In particular, a growing empirical data base referring to Britain and the United States suggests that the pay differentials between skilled and unskilled labour tend to closely parallel inequality trends at large. Other sources of inequality trends, such as compositional shifts in the labour force or movements in intraoccupational inequality, appear to have been less important.

The trends in earnings or income inequality in Sweden are largely unknown before 1850. Being a predominantly agrarian country, the sources are better suited to describing the distribution of wealth (in particular that of real estate) than income. The pattern of pay differentials can, however, be studied for Stockholm (and certainly a number of other towns as well), but as yet there is no basis for regional comparisons.

30 On Stockholm's economic stagnation see chapter 2 above.

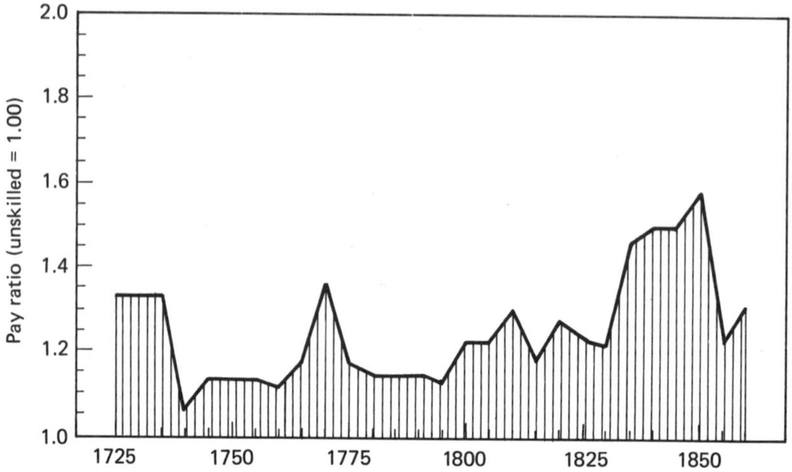

Figure 7.2 The pay ratio of carpenters to unskilled labour in Stockholm, 1725–1860.

One of the relationships often discussed in the literature on historical inequality is that of the wage rate of skilled labour (w_s) to that of unskilled labour (w_u). The main question posed is whether or not the skilled to unskilled pay ratio w_s/w_u tended to rise during the early phase of industrialization, in accordance with observations from British and American data that skilled occupations typically enjoyed greater gains than the unskilled from the early phases of economic growth.[31]

The City Archive of Stockholm contains a wealth of wage information relating to various jobs performed for the municipality (mostly construction, maintenance, and repairs). Starting during the sixteenth century and with no large gaps after 1573, the wage series are probably the longest in Sweden. The accounts report the day wages actually paid to day labourers and others employed by the city. This source is the same as was exploited in the previous analysis of real wage trends (chapter 5).

The pay advantage of carpenters over common labour is displayed in figure 7.2. The pay ratio was at a generally lower level during the eighteenth century than during the nineteenth. It rises noticeably during the deflationary period of the late 1760s. It then declines until the turn of the century. During the first half of the nineteenth century the level is higher than during the last quarter of the eighteenth

[31] For a discussion emphasizing post-1870 trends see J. Söderberg, 'Wage differentials in Sweden, 1725–1950', in *Income Distribution in Historical Perspective*, ed. Y. S. Brenner *et al.* (Cambridge University Press, forthcoming).

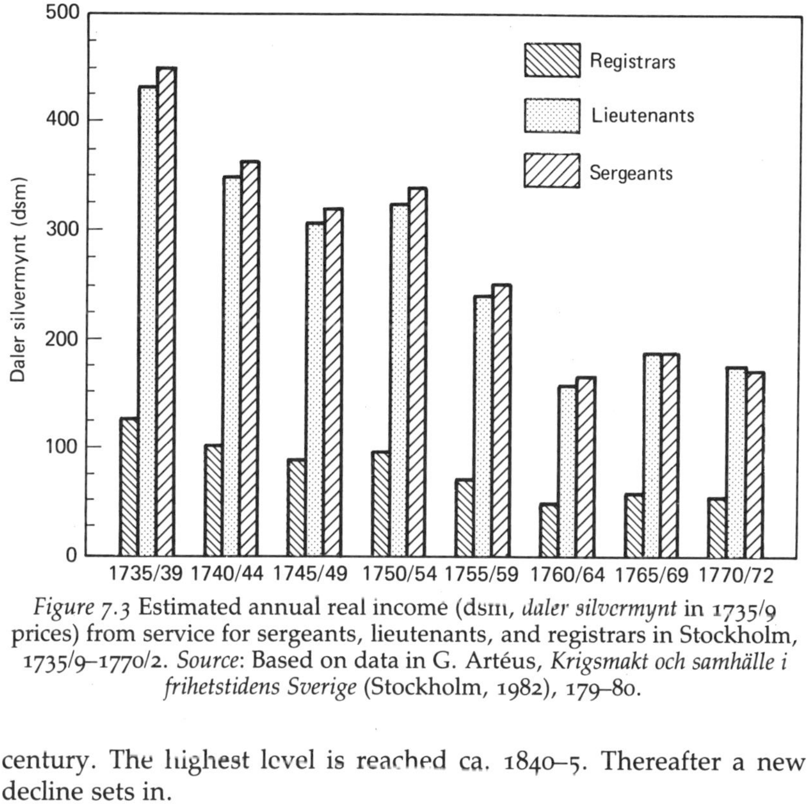

Figure 7.3 Estimated annual real income (dsm, *daler silvermynt* in 1735/9 prices) from service for sergeants, lieutenants, and registrars in Stockholm, 1735/9–1770/2. *Source*: Based on data in G. Artéus, *Krigsmakt och samhälle i frihetstidens Sverige* (Stockholm, 1982), 179–80.

century. The highest level is reached ca. 1840–5. Thereafter a new decline sets in.

There are not many other available series to which these results for Stockholm can be related. Few published investigations provide any information on pay ratios before 1860. Larsson, however, reports time series of pay for various categories of labour at Bredsjö ironworks in central Sweden (Örebro county).[32] Pay ratios based on daily wage rates for furnace masters and blast-furnace workers exhibit an upward trend around mid century peaking in 1860. This is followed by a general levelling tendency during the rest of the period covered.

Although the peak occurs later in Bredsjö than in Stockholm, the mid nineteenth-century rise and later decline in pay ratios is similar to the results obtained for Stockholm above. The general trends are also similar to the curve traced by British pay ratios which surge around mid century, later to level.

Another side of the earnings distribution refers to the pay of functionaries. For the eighteenth century, the work of Artéus on real

[32] M. Larsson, *Arbete och lön vid Bredsjö bruk; en studie av löneprinciper och lönenivåer för olika yrkeskategorier vid Bredsjö bruk 1828–1905* (Uppsala, 1986), table 11.

incomes of the military was referred to previously (see page 82). Figure 7.3 below, based on his data, charts the estimated real income from 1735/9 to 1770/2 for two military and one civilian in Stockholm: sergeants, lieutenants, and registrars.[33]

The most striking feature is the extent of the real income decline for all these groups who were money-salaried (in contrast to those county functionaries who had part of their income in kind and did not experience the same deterioration).[34] The 1770/2 level is not more than 41 and 40 per cent of the 1735/9 level for sergeants and lieutenants, respectively; the corresponding figure for the registrars is 38 per cent. Differentials between these occupations thus were practically unchanged. These data rather suggest a considerable stability in the pay structure around the mid eighteenth century, in spite of very marked shifts with regard to levels. Other studies indicate that the pay gaps between the civil servants of the central administration in Stockholm were stable during the whole period 1720–1809.[35]

It should also be noted that the trend in the salaries of all these functionaries in the capital was clearly far more adverse than the trend in the daily wage rates of unskilled manual labour reported in chapter 5. While the annual earnings of the labourers cannot be computed due to the lack of employment data, only a dramatic deterioration in employment (which there is little reason to expect) could have gener-

33 There are several methodological and technical problems in the measurement of the salaries of the various categories of personnel discussed subsequently in this section. The reader is referred to the studies cited for details on sources and methods. It should be stressed that none of the investigations referred to includes earnings other than those from the service in question. Incomes from possible other services are thus disregarded as well as, e.g., rents. For critical remarks pointing to some of the difficulties see B. Odén, 'Socialhistoria i blickpunkten', *Historisk tidskrift* 83 (1963), and G. Rystad, 'Till frågan om tjänster och löner inom kansliet under frihetstiden', *Historisk tidskrift* 86 (1966).

34 During the Age of Liberty (1720–72) the majority of the employees of the central government administration were paid wholly in cash. The pay of the Stockholm clergy and of the employees of the court were more complicated, involving a part in kind. On the pay of the rural clergy during the first half of the nineteenth century see S. Alsne, *Från prästtionden till reglerad lön; pastoraliekonventionerna i Uppsala ärkestift 1810–1862* (Uppsala, 1966). Shortly after the mid nineteenth century there was a transition from a variety of local remuneration contracts to regular salary.

35 Elmroth's investigation into the salaries of servants and officials at the central government offices supplements that of Artéus well by concentrating on the civil functionaries. The dispersion is practically constant from 1720 to 1809, when his study ends. There appear to have been strong institutional forces serving to maintain the established differentials. See I. Elmroth, *Nyrekryteringen till de högre ämbetena 1720–1809* (Lund, 1962) chapter 3.

ated as unfavourable a trend for the unskilled as for the money-salaried personnel.[36]

These remarks on the structure of wages and salaries are of a partial nature. The research needed to trace the trends for a broader spectrum of occupations remains to be done. As they stand, however, the results presented here at least suggest two things. First, there was no substantial change in the pay of unskilled as compared with more skilled manual labour, nor among the categories of Stockholm civil and military functionaries mentioned. Pay relations within the administration were very stable. The sources of overall changes in the distribution of earnings rather must be sought between larger groups, perhaps primarily between the money-salaried personnel in a rigid pay structure and labourers with far more varying pay rates. This observation is in line with the corresponding argument put forward in the research referred to above on the sources of inequality in Britain and America.

Second, when these observations are taken together, the preliminary conclusion must be that no marked widening in earnings inequality in Stockholm appears to have taken place during most of the eighteenth or the beginning of the nineteenth century. Since the money-salaried functionaries were the most adversely affected, there should rather have been a tendency towards levelling as skilled and unskilled labourers approached them from below. This levelling tendency was at work during most of the period 1730–1809, although it was suspended for a rather short period at the end of the 1770s when the functionaries finally succeeded in raising their pay.

In Sweden as a whole, the tendencies towards growing differentials probably was the dominating one. Figure 7.4 summarizes data on nominal earning of officials, indicating the widening disparities between county officers who had part of their pay in kind, and the

36 Elmroth concludes that 'a large proportion of the lower bureaucracy thus must have been living in very depressed circumstances particularly towards the end of the Era of Liberty' (that is, towards 1772). The strong downward pressure on the money-salaried officials appears to have continued at least up to 1809. Even though salaries were raised substantially in 1778, the improvement was not more than temporary since inflation was even stronger at the close of the century. Prices thus rose rapidly during the 1790s and the first decade of the nineteenth century, while salaries improved little. See Elmroth, *Nyrekryteringen till de högre ämbetena*. The civil servants experienced a marked fall in real earnings during the first decade of the nineteenth century, while the downward trend in the daily wage rates, in real terms, of labourers did not continue beyond 1800.

The municipally employed personnel of Stockholm received a major salary increase earlier than the government personnel, as in 1761, but afterwards salaries were unchanged for several decades. See B. Boëthius, *Magistraten och borgerskapet i Stockholm 1719–1815* (Stockholm, 1943).

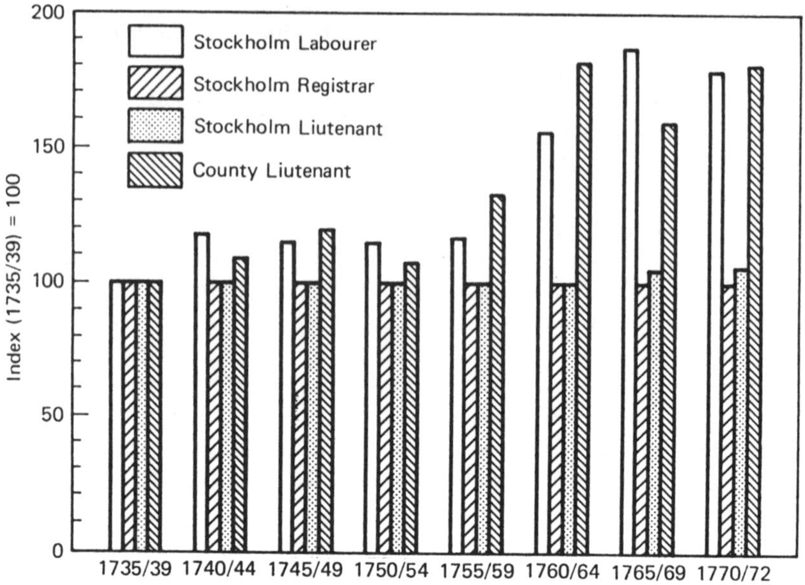

Figure 7.4 Change in nominal earnings of various county and Stockholm occupations, 1735/9–1770/2 (index 1735/9 = 100). Data for Stockholm labourers refer to daily wage rates.

money-salaried in Stockholm. The Stockholm unskilled labourers' daily wage rates are included as well. The exposed situation of the functionaries of the capital emerges clearly, while the far more advantageous development of wages of labourers is closer to the increase in the earnings of the county officers. Even though labourers suffered from the long-term inflation of the eighteenth century, they were not the main losers. The most afflicted are to be found higher in the social hierarchy.

Figure 7.4 also illustrates how inequality could widen at the national level, taking into account the growing differentials between town and country, while at the same time inequality may well have narrowed in Stockholm. The widening inequality among functionaries during several decades of the mid eighteenth century parallels the trend that seems to have been dominant among peasants and in agrarian society as a whole, where those producing for a market could benefit from the rising foodstuff prices and agricultural labourers experienced a real wage decline. The relative price shifts favouring the agrarian sector serve equally well to explain the inequality tendencies among peasants and among functionaries.

The overall pattern of the first half of the nineteenth century is quite

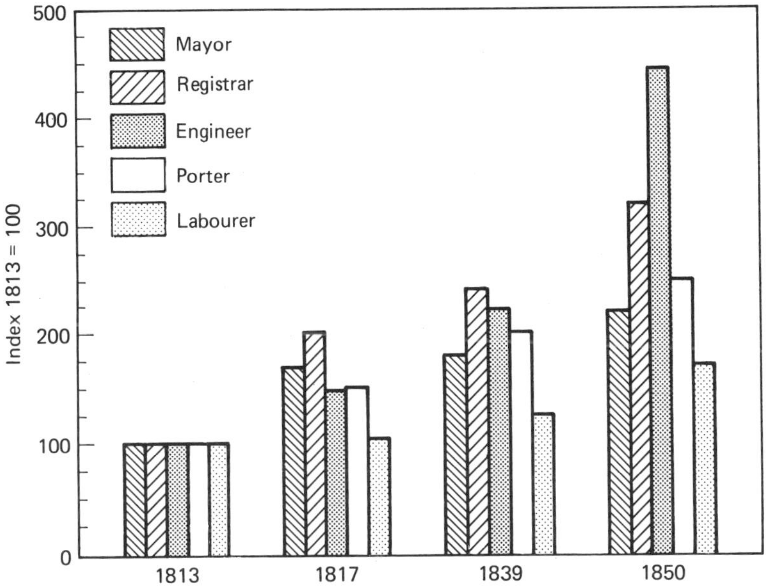

Figure 7.5 Change in nominal earnings of certain functionaries employed by Stockholm City and in the day wages of unskilled labour, 1813–50. *Source:* Based on data in T. Höjer, *Stockholms stads drätselkommission 1814–1864* (Stockholm, 1953), 70–1.

another one. Data on the salaries of the personnel employed by Stockholm City indicate strong increases between the 1810s and mid century, outstripping the improvement in day wages of common labour. Contrary to the eighteenth century, then, the functionaries were more successful than the unskilled in advancing their pay. In real terms, the trend was clearly upward.

At the same time, also unlike the preceding century, the structure of pay among the salaried changed. The middle range now advanced more than the others. In other words, a certain levelling among the functionaries took place. Figure 7.5 shows how the day wages of labourers lagged behind the increases in the salaries of the municipal functionaries, who are ordered from left to right with respect to the 1813 level of their annual salary.[37] It is evident that the rise in the salary of the mayors (and some other highly paid officials) was less promi-

37 Höjer's study of the municipal salaries has the merit of taking into account that certain categories were allowed to draw part of their earnings from a commission in municipal incomes from charges on trade and seafaring (*provision*). This affects, for instance, some personnel in the administration of the harbour.

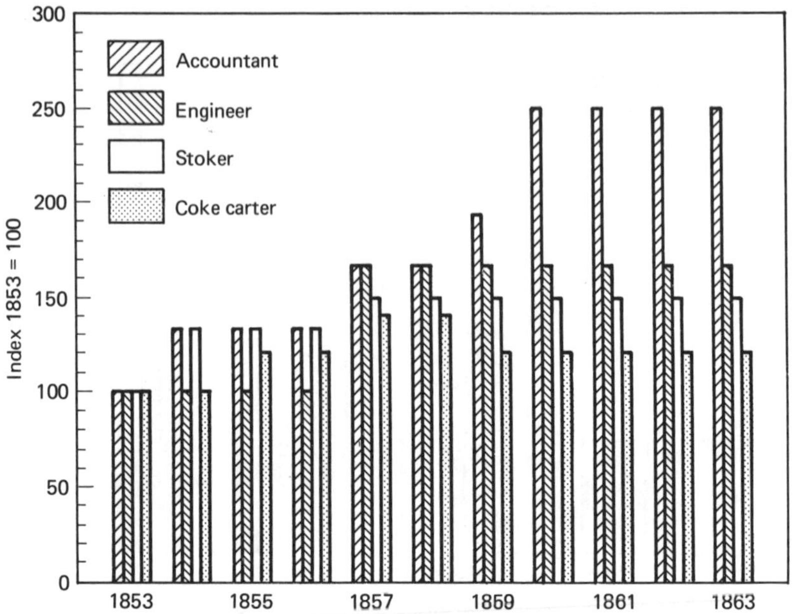

Figure 7.6 Change in nominal earnings of accountants, engineers, stokers, and coke carters of *Gaslysningsbolaget*, 1853–63. *Source*: Based on data in T. Höjer, *Sockenstämmor och kommunalförvaltning i Stockholm fram till 1864* (Stockholm, 1967), 422–3.

nent than that of middle groups in the administration such as the city engineer and the registrars.[38]

It is quite possible, then, that the period from about 1810 to 1850 is characterized by a widening in earnings inequality. After having experienced a long-term deterioration not only in real terms but also compared with the labourers, the functionaries are progressing

[38] Regarding government employees see the data on salaries in the National Archives reported by S. Bergh, Svenska Riksarkivet 1618–1837. *Meddelanden från svenska Riksarkivet, N.F., II:5* (Stockholm, 1916), 127. The changes in the pay structure during the decades after 1810 resemble those of the municipal administration. In real terms, salaries increased substantially, while there was some narrowing in pay differentials. The officials in lower and middle positions gained relative to the highest paid. Both trends, being partly a result of a Parliamentary decision in 1815 to raise salaries by a certain percentage, ranging from 75 per cent for the lowest paid to not more than 10 per cent for the highest, should have affected other government offices as well. For other examples of rapid improvement after 1810 see J. A. Almquist, Kommerskollegium och riksens ständers manufakturkontor samt Konsulsstaten. *Meddelanden från svenska Riksarkivet, N.F., 4* (Stockholm, 1912–15), 145ff.

strongly after 1810. The levelling of the eighteenth century is reversed.[39]

The tendency towards widening differentials may well have been particularly strong around the 1850s, as figure 7.6 suggests. These data refer to the annual salaries (of the accountant and engineer) and day wages (of the coke carters and stokers) of the company responsible for the gas lighting of Stockholm (*Gaslysningsbolaget*). The changes in pay follow a perfectly regular pattern of widening differentials. The best paid in 1853 received the most substantial pay rises up to 1863, while the carters and stokers clearly were lagging behind. Skill rewards were on the rise.

Concluding comments

The previous analysis may be summarized by the following points.

1. During the period 1720–1809, there appear to have been considerable egalitarian forces at work in Stockholm. At the same time inequality was probably on the rise outside the towns. In some respects differentials were widening between the capital and rural Sweden. The distribution of real estate among property owners became levelled in the capital, while the tendency in the agrarian sector seems to have been the opposite. The real earnings of many functionaries in the capital deteriorated, while their country colleagues managed better. The earnings gaps between the functionaries and large groups of manual labourers are likely to have narrowed, as the labourers approached the money-salaried officials from below. Pay gaps among functionaries were very stable, and neither did the pay of skilled labourers change appreciably as compared with unskilled labour.

The nobility, having had a dominating position in 1715, was retrogressing in the long term while other strata apparently were unable to advance to similar prominence. The real estate distribution indicates the degree of inequality among the top stratum of the population, while the data presented on earnings are probably more

39 After the Napoleonic Wars, there was a depression in agricultural prices in Sweden as elsewhere in Europe, which particularly affected grains. According to Jörberg's national price index, the increase in grain prices was only 1 per cent from 1815/19 to 1850/4. In contrast to the eighteenth century, being money-salaried probably ceased to be a disadvantage. Though we know of no study comparing earnings of the money-salaried with those linked to the *indelningsverket*, the former gains of the county officials as compared with their urban colleagues cannot be expected to have been at work during the decades after 1810.

consequential when it comes to interpreting overall inequality trends. Trends in the distribution of real estate and of earnings were thus moving in the same direction in Stockholm during this period. The erosion of the pay of the functionaries of the capital should be seen largely as an unintended consequence of the system of pay, linking the salaries of county officials (but not those of the capital) to rents and thereby to agrarian price trends.

2. The trends during the first half of the nineteenth century (in particular between 1810 and 1860) in several ways appear as the reverse of those of the previous period. Unlike the eighteenth century, the real earnings of administrators as well as the wages of labourers turn upward. From about 1819 the salaries of functionaries seem to rise more than the wages of labour, making for widening differentials between sectors. During the same period, pay differentials between skilled and unskilled labourers also widen. The overall tendency in earnings inequality thus was on the rise. The surge in inequality may well have been particularly strong in the 1850s, when there are indications that skill rewards rapidly became more pronounced.

With respect to real estate, there was little change in the distribution among owners. There are however indications that the real estate market step by step grew more exclusive. Costs of entry were rising, and it is reasonable to expect that a decreasing proportion of the population succeeded in establishing themselves as owners of real estate.

The observation of a mid nineteenth-century widening is supported by pay ratios series from an ironworks in central Sweden exhibiting a surge ca. 1840–60 after which date a secular levelling took place.

How do these trends regarding Stockholm and Sweden compare with international inequality trends? Interpreting American inequality data, Williamson and Lindert argue that long-term stability appears to be the best description regarding the eighteenth century. The main period of increasing inequality was between 1820 and 1860, while the latter part of the century exhibits no evidence of rising inequality.[40]

The British pattern is somewhat different, indicating a rise in income inequality from the end of the seventeenth century to the mid Victorian era. While the timing of the changes is still not well known, a

[40] J. G. Williamson and P. H. Lindert, *American Inequality* (New York, 1980), chapters 1–4. Our comparison focusses on trends in rather than levels of inequality. On levels, see the comparison between Sweden, Finland, and the United States in Soltow, 'The Swedish census of wealth at the beginning of the 19th century'. According to him, Swedish wealth inequality was higher than in Finland because of the stronger position of the nobility in the former country. Swedish inequality also surpassed that of the United States.

phase of wage stretching seems to have taken place from the 1820s to mid century. After the 1860s there is a decline in inequality.[41]

Sweden then joins the United States and Britain in exhibiting a period of growing inequality during the first half of the nineteenth century, in particular around 1850. This would seem to apply to Swedish agrarian society as well as to Stockholm. The surge in inequality in Sweden should be seen partly as a result of rising land prices, partly as an effect of increased demand for skills. The simultaneous strong population growth in Sweden has in all likelihood been a contributing factor through producing increasing supplies of unskilled labour while at the same time driving land prices upwards.

The eighteenth-century patterns are more complex and varying. The century is characterized by widening inequality in Britain as well as in London, and this is probably the dominating trend in Sweden as well (when we take into account the trend towards redistribution of growth and incomes between town and country). Stockholm, however, exhibits egalitarian trends to which we see no counterpart in the other countries mentioned. Particular institutional arrangements in Sweden (*indelningsverket*) have played their part in generating distinctly diverging trends in the earnings of county and town officials, depending upon the relative price shifts of agricultural products. On a more basic level, the levelling tendencies in Stockholm may to a certain extent be interpreted as a consequence of the urban economy being unable to keep pace with the rural one.

[41] Williamson, *Did British Capitalism Breed Inequality?*; see, however, the critical comments by R. V. Jackson, 'The structure of pay in nineteenth-century Britain', *Economic History Review* 40 (1987), 561–570. Re-analysing Williamson's series, Jackson notes that the pay ratio estimates are sensitive to small changes in the underlying data. Still, the wage stretching of the mid nineteenth century persists in Jackson's revised estimates. On the other hand very little of the British mid-century rise in inequality remains if Feinstein's criticism, discarding several of Williamson's series as being unreliable, is accepted. C. H. Feinstein, 'The rise and fall of the Williamson curve', *Journal of Economic History* 48 (1988), 703ff. The best way to resolve the issue would of course be to extend the database to include a larger number of wage series.

8

The economic-demographic system

Introduction

In his classic discussion on eighteenth-century Sweden, Eli F. Heckscher assumed a close short-run link between economic and demographic fluctuations. The variation in the crude death rate was according to Heckscher strongly influenced by the harvests, usually with a lag of one year. His interpretation was that living standards were close to the minimum level and that the Malthusian positive check regularly was activated.[1]

Heckscher also thought that mortality was more responsive to short-run economic fluctuations than was nuptiality and fertility. His view of the Swedish economic-demographic system was similar to the model of the high-pressure French system with low standards of living, a high death and birth rate, and a population vulnerable to short-term shocks through mortality fluctuations.[2]

Recent Swedish research has tended to further emphasize some basic features of Heckscher's interpretation. Basing their analysis on better economic time-series data than were available to Heckscher, Tommy Bengtsson and Rolf Ohlsson conclude that fluctuations in vital rates were to a substantial degree determined by fluctuations in the standard of living (as measured by the real wage), and they adhere to the opinion that the Swedish economy had a clearly Malthusian character during the latter half of the eighteenth century. The first half of the nineteenth century should be seen as a transitional phase in which the importance of Malthusian mechanisms was reduced, although they are still observable.

1 E. F. Heckscher, *Svenskt arbete och liv* (Stockholm, 1968), 150–7.

2 E. A. Wrigley and R. S. Schofield, *The Population History of England, 1541–1871* (London, 1981), 478–9.

However, Bengtsson and Ohlsson also stress that the relationship between real wages and mortality was weak in short fluctuations below five years. Short-run mortality changes seem to have been primarily determined by non-economic factors (epidemics, climate, etc.). The relationships between real wages and mortality was of a cyclical character, medium-length real wage cycles with a period of 5–10 years leading mortality and fertility cycles.[3] Real wage changes thus affected vital rates in a less direct way than Heckscher assumed.

The view of the mortality-sensitive demographic system which Bengtsson and Ohlsson share with Heckscher may be contrasted with the low-pressure system discussed by Wrigley and Schofield. The low-pressure model, appropriate for England and probably also for Holland in the eighteenth century, involves a lower level of mortality and a weak mortality response to economic fluctuations. English real wage fluctuations were more closely related to nuptiality and fertility change than to mortality. In Malthusian terms, we are dealing with the preventive rather than the positive check.

Because of the source situation, most historical demographers have restricted themselves to rural areas. Urban economic-demographic relationships have been far less studied. This chapter attempts to characterize the links between economic and demographic change in Stockholm, where both kinds of information are more readily available than is usual for the rest of Europe in the century after 1750.

Long-term demographic trends

Most of the century after 1750 is characterized by economic stagnation in Stockholm. Especially during the latter half of the eighteenth century the capital was declining industrially as well as commercially. Stockholm represented a decreasing share of Sweden's total foreign trade. Economic growth was very weak until the 1830s or 1840s. Population only grew from 73,000 in 1763 to 80,000 in 1830.[4]

Economic stagnation is likely to have been accompanied by a downward pressure on standards of living, at least among labourers and functionaries (see chapters 5 and 6 above). Real wages of unskilled labourers employed by the municipality were declining during most of the eighteenth century. There was a sharp rise after the Napoleonic wars and no clear trend during the second quarter of the nineteenth

[3] R. Ohlsson and T. Bengtsson, 'Population and economic fluctuations in Sweden 1749–1914', in *Pre-Industrial Population Change*, ed. T. Bengtsson *et al.* (Stockholm, 1984).

[4] On Stockholm's economic development see chapter 2 above.

century. The eighteenth-century deterioration, related to the rise in foodstuff prices and the changing terms of trade between agrarian and non-agrarian sectors in favour of the former, is discussed more fully in chapter 5 above. Largely similar real wage reductions are seen in many European towns as well as rural areas.

Three economic series will be referred to below. One is the real wage curve of unskilled labourers employed by the municipality, as described in chapter 5 above.

The other is the annual percentage change in the number of bankruptcies (more precisely, the number of applications presented to the legal authorities). Several years of the 1750s and 1760s were characterized by a rising number of bankruptcies, especially in connection with the deflation crisis of the late 1760s and the serious harvest failures of 1772–3. Other troublesome business years were the generally difficult years around 1800 as well as 1806–7, when the silk industry collapsed. Around 1810 the number of bankruptcies declined but then rose up to the late 1830s (the highest figure reached in 1838), the 1840s and 1850s exhibiting no clear trend.[5] The series is to be regarded primarily as a general handicrafts and petty bourgeois business index. The majority of bankruptcies stemmed from handicraft masters, small dealers, and other individuals who were not engaged in medium-sized or large manufacturing. The number of bankruptices (not detrended) are shown in figure 8.1.

A third economic series describes employment year by year in manufacturing. The statistical sources of Swedish manufacturing were described in chapter 3 above, to which we refer. It was stressed that the falling number of workers did not mean a corresponding decline in production volumes. In fact, there were signs of a considerable rise in productivity during the latter part of the eighteenth century.[6]

The long-term development of the aggregate number of factory workers in Stockholm and the rest of Sweden was shown in figure 4.2 above. The beginning of the period is characterized by expansion, starting in the 1720s and continuing until the beginning of the 1760s. The national financial crisis of the 1760s resulted in a halving of the number of workers in Stockholm, and the national figures were reduced by more than one third in a few years. Though recoveries took

5 The year 1838 is reported to have been a year of unemployment, with an increasing number of vagrants coming to the capital, and the number of thefts doubling. In summer serious riots took place, partly with an antisemitic bias. See T. Nerman, *Crusenstolpes kravaller* (Stockholm, 1938).

6 E. F. Heckscher's archive, deposited in Riksarkivet by the Department of Economic History, Stockholm University. See also O. Krantz, 'Production and labour in the Swedish manufactories during the 18th century', *Economy and History* 19 (1976).

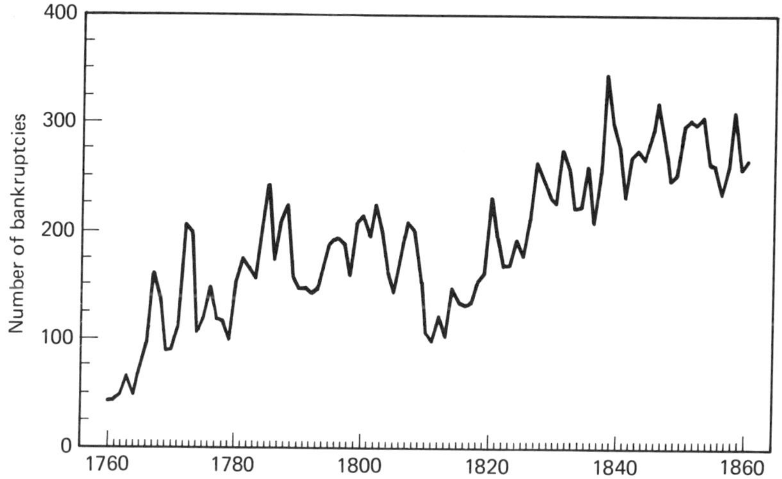

Figure 8.1 Annual number of bankruptcy applications in Stockholm, 1760–1860. *Sources*: K. Samuelsson, *De stora köpmanshusen i Stockholm 1730–1815* (Stockholm, 1951), 228; P.-E. Brolin, *Hattar och mössor i borgarståndet 1760–1766* (Uppsala, 1953), 127; Magistraten och rådhusrätten. Ingående konkursdiarier (1773–1850). Stockholm City Archive; T. Hedlund-Nyström, *Svenska kriser och internationella konjunkturer* (Lund, 1970), 133.

place in the 1770s, 1790s, and 1800s, the number of employed in 1760 was never reached again during the period in the capital, and not until the 1840s in Sweden.

The correlation between employment figures for Stockholm and the rest of the nation is fairly strong ($r_{xy} = 0.66$ for the period 1751–1830). Stockholm's share of the national figure amounted to about 50 per cent during these years, with a secular downward tendency from approximately 60 per cent in the 1750s to 45 per cent in the 1820s. In the period 1831–50 the number of workers in Stockholm were diminishing slightly while the national figures rose sharply. Stockholm's share of the national manufacturing labour force declined to about 30 per cent in the 1830s and to 20 per cent in the next decade.

During this latter period Stockholm consequently lost its dominant position within Swedish manufacturing. The leading role was instead taken by Norrköping, a traditional industrial town with a population of about 10,000 in 1830. By 1846, Norrköping had 20 per cent of Sweden's manufacturing workers as compared with only 12 per cent for Stockholm. The traditional explanation for this shift has been that Norrköping had access to the water-power that became

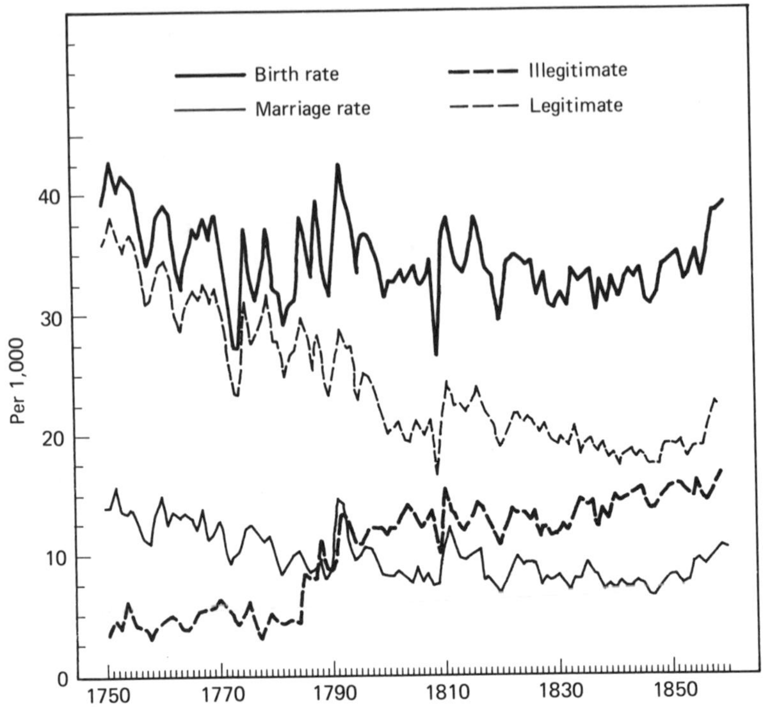

Figure 8.2 Crude birth rate, legitimate and illegitimate birth rates, and nuptiality in Stockholm, 1750–1860. Per 1,000. *Sources: Statistisk årsbok för Stockholms stad* 38 (1905) (crude birth rate and nuptiality); *Statistisk tidskrift* 1 (1860), 45–7 (legitimate and illegitimate births).

necessary as mechanization was successively introduced during this period.[7]

A crude division by sector reveals that the dominating position of textiles within manufacturing, at about 90 per cent in the mid eighteenth century, diminished to about 45 per cent by the 1840s. The non-textile sectors consisted of, besides the sugar and tobacco enterprises, primarily small workshops with few, if any, employees engaged in a great number of different activities.

The most specific trait of the long-term demographic development of Stockholm was the persistently high level of mortality. Contrary to a large number of European towns, Stockholm continued to exhibit excess mortality during the first half of the nineteenth century. Not only the level but also the age- and sex-specific pattern of mortality

[7] Nyström, *Stadsindustriens arbetare före 1800-talet*, 160ff.

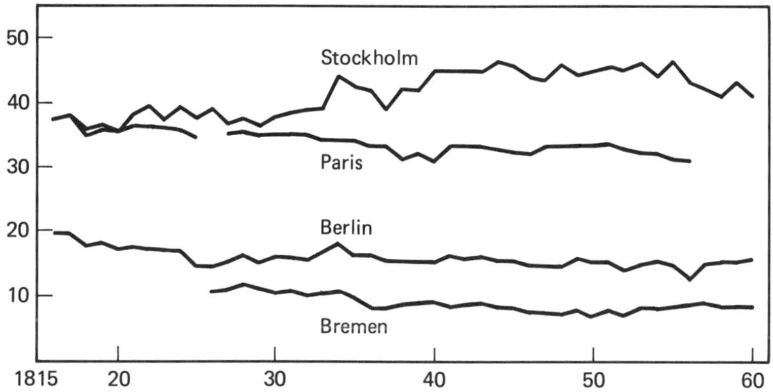

Figure 8.3 Illegitimate births as per cent of total births in Stockholm and Berlin 1816–60, Bremen 1821–60, Paris 1817–25 and 1827–55. *Sources:* Stockholm: *Statistisk årsbok för Stockholms stad* 38 (1905). Berlin and Bremen: *Quellen zur Bevölkerungs-, Sozial- und Wirtschaftsstatistik Deutschlands 1815–75, 1* (Boppard am Rhein, 1980). Paris: *Recherches statistiques sur la ville de Paris* I–II, V–VI.

was extreme. Adult male mortality often was more than twice that of contemporary British and continental cities.

Stockholm cannot generally be considered either as a low or as a high fertility town. Birth rates did not reach the impressive levels of cities like nineteenth-century Vienna or eighteenth-century Lyon. Compared with continental centres such as Berlin or Hamburg there was no dramatic difference at least in the first part of the nineteenth century.[8] In spite of a slight increase in crude birth rates in the 1850s there was a moderate decline over the period 1750–1860.

However, behind this rather stable crude birth rate was a dramatic decline in legitimate and subsequent rise in illegitimate births. The strong rise in illegitimate births was associated with a significant drop in nuptiality (figure 8.2).

It is a well-established fact that there was a general rise in bastardy all over Europe in the century after 1750. Some authors speak of a 'sexual revolution' in the second half of the eighteenth century.[9] The level of extramarital fertility in Stockholm was, if not uniquely high, on the high side. Vienna in the 1840s and 1850s, where 49 per cent of the children were born out of wedlock, slightly exceeds the Swedish

[8] Fertility data for some German cities are presented in *Quellen zur Bevölkerungs-, Sozial- und Wirtschaftsstatistik Deutschlands*, 1 (Boppard am Rhein, 1980).

[9] E. Shorter, *The Making of the Modern Family* (New York, 1975), 103.

capital.[10] On the other hand Stockholm figures for the first part of the nineteenth century were more than twice as high as for Berlin and almost four times as high as for Bremen, a town of Stockholm's size. After 1830 the rate of bastardy for Stockholm also exceeded that for Paris (figure 8.3).

When children born out of wedlock are almost as numerous as those born within marriage, extramarital fertility cannot be a product of brief encounters alone. Family formation in Stockholm during the latter half of the nineteenth century has been studied extensively by the historian, Margareta Matović.[11] This is a period when bastardy rates are only slightly lower than in the first part of the century. Her investigation reveals a hidden structure of extralegal family formation. A large part of the illegitimate children were born in marriage-like settings.

The interpretation of Matović is very interesting. Contrary to the established view of bastardy, convincingly formulated by Edward Shorter, she does not regard extralegal family formation as a failure of women to achieve marriage.[12] According to Matović it cannot be taken for granted that women always wanted legal marriage. Marriage was not automatically advantageous for lower-class women earning an income. When married, the husband had a legal right to her earnings. Lower-class men with insecure income prospects had little to offer their mates; on the contrary the women could have strong reasons to fear exploitation within marriage. Trying to avoid legalization was then, from a female point of view, a perfectly rational response. The official norm system of course strongly disapproved of this form of family formation, but was unable to influence unpropertied classes. A harsh reality dictated its own norm system.

It is difficult to judge the extent to which the hypothesis of Matović is plausible for the whole century after 1750. Some important indicators do tend to support her thesis. The constant male mortality disadvantage in the active years of life, which was far from the general rule in Europe, suggests that the male sex was economically disfavoured.

At the same time we know that among popular classes it did not need to be a social catastrophe to give birth to an illegitimate child even

10 S. Ehmer, 'Produktion und Reproduktion in der Wiener Manufakturperiode' in R. Banik-Schweitzer *et al.*, *Wien im Vormärz* (Vienna, 1980), 127.

11 M. Matović, *Stockholmsäktenskap; familjebildning och partnerval i Stockholm 1850–1890* (Stockholm, 1984).

12 E. Shorter, 'Female emancipation. Birth control and fertility in European history', *American Historical Review* 78 (1973).

in rural areas, much less so in the relative anonymity of the capital.[13] Thus we cannot exclude the possibility that the initiative to form extralegal families was to some extent taken by women.

The cross-sectional study of poverty in 1850 (see chapter 6 above) also gives some interesting clues. Contrary to the situation in rural areas, the incidence of poverty among Stockholm males in economically active ages exceeded that of females. The male labour market seems to have been characterized by many casual jobs and by frequent unemployment. For instance, an official report from the 1820s describes the huge seasonal variations in employment. Most outdoor jobs employing day labourers were carried out only during seven or eight months of the year. During winter, the report continues, there was little chance of getting such jobs. From spring to autumn, on the other hand, there was a scarcity of labourers.[14]

The female labour market, dominated by servant jobs, was quite different; these women were usually employed on a yearly basis.

Being a female servant certainly involved a lot of heavy work. Some foreign visitors were surprised at the amount of hard, manual work carried out by these women. Travelling in a rural area in southern Sweden, Mary Wollstonecraft Godwin reported in 1796 having seen the girls washing clothes during winter, their hands chapped by the cold or scratched by the ice and bleeding.[15] This kind of labour was hardly different in the capital. 'In Stockholm, where everything else is expensive, the keeping of servants is cheap', remarked the German professor, D. H. Hegewisch, in 1794. The reason, he explained, was that servants were paid only a minimal cash wage and received low quality food.[16] Nevertheless, female servants probably enjoyed substantially more stable living conditions than did large segments of the male labour force.

From the close of the eighteenth century, when the rising cost of living probably led to a substantial downward pressure on living standards, there are several accounts of the widespread custom among the upper classes of keeping a mistress. The Polish canon, J. B. Albertrandi, asserted in 1790 that 'almost every woman of the lower classes of society is the mistress to some high gentleman'.[17] In 1799,

13 For a discussion of social consequences of bastardy see S. Carlsson, *Fröknar, mamseller, jungfrur och pigor; ogifta kvinnor i det svenska ståndssamhället* (Uppsala, 1977), 93.

14 *Överståthållarämbetets underdåniga femårsberättelse 1822–1826* (Stockholm, 1829), 26.

15 Quoted from A. Strindberg, *Arbetare och radikaler i 1700–talets Sverige* (Stockholm, 1935), 267.

16 A. Julius, *Sverige sett med främlingsögon* (Stockholm, 1930), 115.

17 D. Anckarsvärd, 'Stockholm 1789–90 skildrat av en polsk kanik', *Sankt Eriks årsbok* (1933), 105.

the Italian diplomat, Giuseppe Acerbi, wrote that girls such as these were generally rather badly paid by their lovers and therefore must distribute their services among seven or eight gentlemen simultaneously.[18]

While this might indicate some change in customs and attitudes since mid century, a change contributing to the rise in bastardy, it is more likely that the major part of this rise was due to an increase in the proportion of more stable extramarital unions within the lower and middle strata. As is clear from an inspection of figure 8.2, the year-to-year fluctuations in illegitimate fertility are very close to those of the marital fertility rate. This implies that both were affected largely by the same mechanisms. In the short term, extramarital and marital fertility were very much the same, increasing during good years and decreasing during bad years.

Part of the system of relatively stable extramarital cohabitation was described by the author K. A. af Kullberg, living in Stockholm in the mid 1840s. He reported that the standard form of prostitution was concubinage. Holding a 'housekeeper' or '*mamsell*' recruited from the class of female servants was regarded as an accepted middle road between being married and unmarried. Kullberg found it very often among the civil servants, who defended this kind of cohabitation with reference to the low costs compared with marriage. Under these conditions he did not wonder that hardly any other European town exhibited as high a proportion of illegitimate births as did the Swedish capital.[19]

Equally unsurprised by the extent of illegitimacy was a German traveller, Theodor Mügge, who described the same system stating that a man and his *mamsell* would outwardly appear as unmarried and without mutual obligations. 'The *mamsell* will not bother us, her demands and pretentions are modest, she is dependent on us and will so remain, and we can make us free from her whenever we wish to', the men had told him. The males emphasized the economic barriers making marriage impossible, but also the advantages offered to them by the concubinage system.[20]

A study of the frequency of divorce among the female street-vendors and inn-keepers in Stockholm during the first half of the nineteenth

[18] V. Hellberg, 'Turist i Stockholm 1799', *Sankt Eriks årsbok* 1946, 106. Acerbi's account was published as *Travels Through Sweden, Finland, and Lapland, to the North Cape* (London, 1802). For another late eighteenth-century account see G. Näsström, 'Med gubben Gjörwell i det gustavianska Stockholm', *Sankt Eriks årsbok* (1972/73), 24.

[19] F. Rouel [K. A. af Kullberg], *Minnen från en vistelse i Stockholm åren 1844–45* (Norrköping, 1845), 39.

[20] T. Mügge, *Sverige 1843–1844* (Stockholm, 1845), 257, 262.

century reveals some interesting patterns in this connection. Divorce was more frequent among the economically successful women than among the population at large. Christine Lindquist points out that these females had succeeded in making themselves economically independent and they did not have to stand the drunkenness or beatings of their husbands.[21]

It seems likely that there was a harsh economic dimension to the pattern of low nuptiality. To the economically stronger men it offered opportunities of forming convenient relationships with females involving very few obligations on the part of the males. At the same time some relatively successful women, no doubt fewer in numbers, would have the chance to benefit from not marrying (or divorcing). It would not be realistic to suppose that the decline in nuptiality is primarily explained by large numbers of females having preferred to stay unmarried. At least a not insignificant portion of the males have found extramarital cohabitation preferable, regardless of the preferences of the women. The interpretation of Matović may be more relevant to the somewhat better-off females than to those who had little choice but to accept extramarital unions without the mutual and formal obligations that marriage involved.

With the decline in manufacturing and the stagnation of handicrafts, there are reasons to expect growth in what we may call the informal sector of the Stockholm economy. This is a process which is extremely difficult to describe with any precision. Next to nothing, for instance, is known about what happened to those who lost their jobs when factories were closed down. Several hundred Stockholm workers were reported to have emigrated after the crisis of 1763, about half of them to Russia. Some remaining unemployed labourers applied to Kommerskollegium, a government office in charge of the trades, for permission to start making their living by brewing and baking in their homes. This proposal met with strong protests from the established guilds, however, and the government decided to leave it to the labourers to 'find out on their own how they may legally earn a scanty living for themselves and their families'.[22]

Part of this informal sector consisted of female laundry-work etc; little is known about the dimensions of such employment. The same applies to another component of the informal sector, the illegal handicrafts production which was persecuted by the guilds. During

[21] C. Lindquist, 'Kvinnor i tvåförsörjarfamiljen. Gifta krögerskor och månglerskor under första delen av 1800-talet', *Manliga strukturer och kvinnliga strategier. En bok till Gunhild Kyle*, eds. B. Sawyer and A. Göransson (Gothenburg, 1987).

[22] J. F. Nyström, *Bidrag till svenska handelns och näringarnas historia*, 1 (Stockholm, 1884), 25.

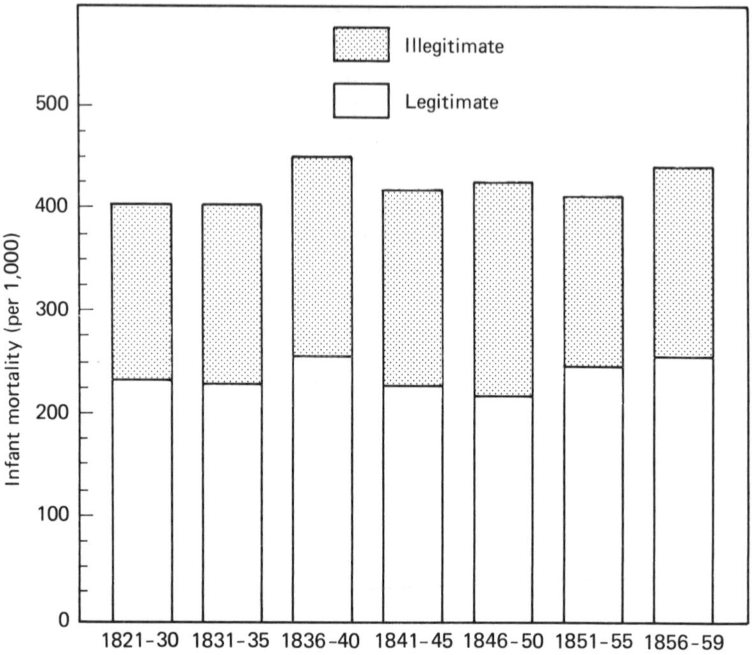

Figure 8.4 Infant mortality among legitimate and illegitimate children in Stockholm, 1821–59. Per 1,000. *Sources*: *Statistisk årsbok för Stockholms stad* 38 (1905), 82, 87 (1821–30); W. Wretlind, *Undersökningar rörande Stockholms mortalitet* (Stockholm, 1866), 37.

the eighteenth century production outside the guilds seems to have been most frequent in activities requiring small amounts of capital, e.g., weaving, tailoring, and shoemaking. This work was performed by a variety of people of lower strata, for example soldiers, labourers, and civil servants.[23]

Illegitimate births began to rise in the mid 1780s, when the female-dominated textile industry declined. The chances of lower-class women finding employment in the formal manufacturing sector must have deteriorated step by step. On the other hand informal self-employment may well have been rising, as was argued in chapter 4.

It is impossible to determine in a more precise way to what extent the rise in illegitimate births was a result of rational choices by lower-class women or of a failure of the same women to establish marital unions. What we safely can say is that a rising number of

[23] E. Söderlund, *Stockholms hantverkarklass 1720–1772* (Stockholm, 1943), 300.

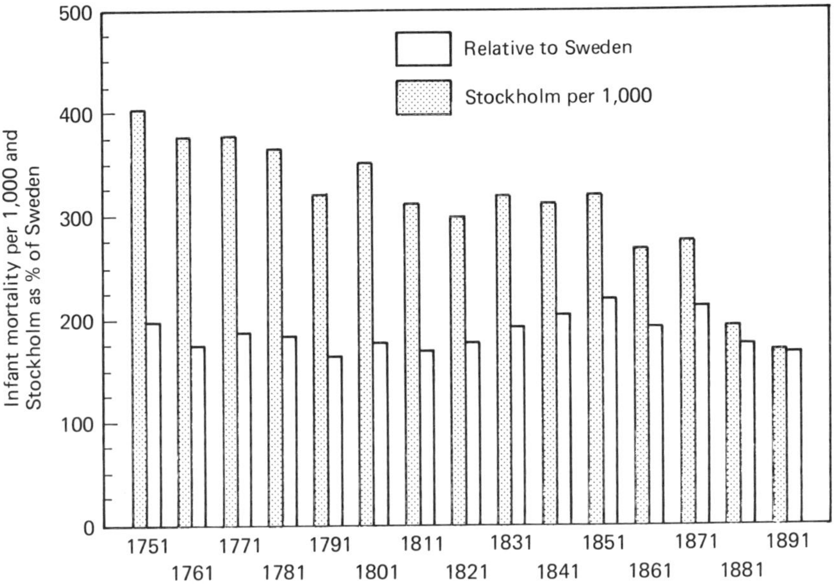

Figure 8.5 Infant mortality per 1,000 in Stockholm, 1751–60 – 1901/10, and Stockholm infant mortality rates as percentage of the national average. Decennial figures. *Sources*: E. F. Heckscher, 'Städernas plats i Sveriges samhällshistoria', *Ekonomisk tidskrift* 40 (1938), 112 (1751–1800); *Statistisk årsbok för Stockholms stad* 84 (1953), 50; G. Sundbärg, *Bevölkerungsstatistik Schwedens 1750–1900* (Stockholm, 1970), 131 (national data).

couples, for whatever reason, chose to develop different kinds of extralegal family forms rather than the officially sanctioned marriage.

Infant mortality was clearly higher among the illegitimate children. For the period 1821–59 aggregate statistics on infant mortality by marital status of the mother are available. The mortality differential between legitimate and illegitimate children culminated during the later 1840s, as figure 8.4 shows, when mortality was nearly twice as high among the illegitimate. Throughout the period more than 40 per cent of the illegitimate children died before they were one year old.

From these data it appears unlikely that hygienic conditions or other aspects of child care improved during the first half of the nineteenth century. Some decline had, however, taken place already during the second half of the eighteenth century.[24] The modern reduction in

24 Determining the causes of the later eighteenth-century drop in infant mortality would require a detailed investigation that cannot be undertaken here. It need not imply an improvement in sanitation or hygienic measures. Lacking any direct evidence in this direction on Stockholm before the mid nineteenth century, it is more

infant mortality starts in the 1860s, about the same time as most other demographic series point to substantial improvements. The long-term changes from the mid eighteenth century to the end of the nineteenth, though they cannot be disaggregated by marital status of the mother, emerge from figure 8.5. It appears that the downward trend during the period 1750–1810 was halted and possibly even reversed during the next half century. Infant mortality in the capital was usually about twice as high as in Sweden as a whole, but Stockholm's position relative to the national average deteriorated during the period 1810–50.[25]

The extralegal family is primarily a phenomenon of the pre-industrial Stockholm economy. With industrialization and the subsequent rise in real wages and in the regularity of employment, bastardy declined although for a long time rather moderately. By the 1890s, children born out of wedlock had decreased to less than 30 per cent of the total number of births.[26] A growing share of the working class could afford to adhere to the official norm system. However, we shall not overestimate the change. It was not until the 1930s that illegitimate fertility in the capital returned to the low level of the 1750s.

Short-term fluctuations

In the analysis of the short-term relationships between economic and demographic variables in this section, the trend in all economic and demographic series was removed by transformation into yearly relative deviations of the form X_t/X_{t-1}. Such a transformation was not necessary regarding the climate variable described below, since this exhibits no trend.

Table 8.1 presents a comparison between English, French, Finnish,

plausible that the virulence of certain diseases affecting the infants was reduced. Recent international research has often argued that improvements in hygiene or medical practice hardly played a prominent role in the mortality decline until the latter part of the nineteenth century. See A. Perrenoud, 'Mortality decline in its secular setting', and G. Fridlizius, 'The mortality decline in the first phase of the demographic transition: Swedish experiences', both in *Pre-Industrial Population Change*, ed. T. Bengtsson *et al* (Stockholm, 1984). Part of the negative trend in infant as well as in maternal mortality during the second quarter of the nineteenth century is due to the fact that the main maternity hospital in Stockholm (*Allmänna BB*) increasingly was used in the training of the midwives. As hygienic measures were neglected, infections were more easily passed on to the mothers and to the infants.

25 The observation of some secular decline in infant mortality 1750–1850 of course strengthens the argument of the latter part of this chapter, where adult mortality in active ages is seen as the most interesting component when accounting for the overall high level of mortality in Stockholm up to 1860.

26 *Statistisk årsbok för Stockholms stad* 38 (Stockholm, 1905), 82.

Table 8.1 *Comparison between English, French, Finnish, Swedish, and Stockholm vital rates responses to price and mortality fluctuations, c. 1750–1850.*

Explanatory variable	Lag	England 1750–1850	France 1750–1850	Finland 1755–1850	Sweden 1750–1850	Stockholm 1750–1850
Fertility						
Price (or real wage)	0	−0.146**	−0.024	0.156**	−0.118**	−0.103**
	1	−0.036	−0.079+	0.015	−0.036	−0.222
	2	0.136**	0.333	−0.023**	0.063+	−0.045
	3	−0.016	−0.088+	0.010	0.009	0.050
	4	0.052	0.060	0.014	−0.055+	0.041
Mortality	0	−0.016	−0.049	−0.178**	−0.178	−0.071 +
	1	−0.043	−0.024	0.063*	0.016	−0.091*
	2	0.102+	0.061	0.051	0.090+	0.054
	3	0.043	−0.040	0.018	−0.005	−0.031
	4	−0.034	−0.030	0.016	0.028	0.050
R^2		0.42	0.32	0.56	0.54	0.40
Nuptiality						
Price (or real wage)	0	−0.326**	−0.282*	0.162*	−0.200**	−0.148**
	1	−0.020	−0.091	−0.143+	0.065	−0.018
	2	0.315**	0.099	−0.011	0.021	0.000
	3	−0.075	0.086	−0.089	0.034	0.038
	4	−0.004	0.062	−0.035	−0.004	0.026
Mortality	0	−0.126	−0.048	−0.137*	−0.056	−0.091
	1	0.155	0.188	0.313**	0.153*	0.092
	2	0.135	0.067	0.168**	0.142*	0.081
	3	−0.050	−0.205	0.038	0.108+	0.048
	4	−0.046	0.123	−0.079	0.009	−0.200
R^2		0.38	0.38	0.57	0.42	0.18
Mortality						
Price (or real wage)	0	0.051	0.079	−0.271+	0.141+	0.093
	1	−0.078	0.082	−0.031	0.037	−0.014
	2	0.113	0.192	0.305*	−0.132+	−0.006
	3	−0.157+	−0.345**	−0.170	−0.097	−0.067
	4	−0.080	0.053	−0.095	−0.079	−0.025
R^2		0.09	0.27	0.12	0.18	0.05

Note: A double asterisk indicates a regression coefficient significantly different from zero at the 1 per cent level based on a two-tailed test. A single asterisk denotes the 5 per cent level; a + represents the 10 per cent level of significance.

Table 8.1 (*cont.*)
For Finland, a real wage measure (the nominal daily wage rate for unskilled agricultural labourers deflated by the price of rye) was used instead of the rye price. The reason is that the calculation of a long-term price series is complicated by several changes in the monetary system. Assuming that wages and rye prices were always expressed in the same currency, the real wage series should be more reliable. Of course this means that the signs of the real wage regression coefficients are in general the opposite to the case when price is an explanatory variable.

Sources: E. A. Wrigley and R. S. Schofield, *The Population History of England 1541–1871* (London, 1981), 533–5 (vital rates); E. H. Phelps Brown and S. V. Hopkins, 'Seven centuries of the prices of consumables', *Economica* 23 (1956). France: Y. Blayo, 'Mouvement natural de la population française de 1740 à 1829', *Population* 30 (1975); B. R. Mitchell, *European Historical Statistics 1750–1970* (London, 1975), 106–9 (vital rates); E. Labrousse, *Le prix de froment en France au temps de la monnaie stable* (Paris, 1970), 9–11. Finland: Mitchell, *European Historical Statistics*; (vital rates); V. F. Johanson, 'Markegångspris i Finland åren 1731–1870', *Statistiska översikter* 3 (1926), No. 8 (rye price and daily wage rates of agricultural labourers). Sweden: G. Sundbärg, *Bevölkerungsstatistik Schwedens 1750–1900* (Stockholm, 1907, reprinted 1970), tables 3, 25; L. Jörberg, *A History of Prices in Sweden I* (Lund, 1972), 632–5, 710–3 (rye price). Stockholm: see *figures 5.1 und 8.2*.

Swedish, and Stockholm vital rates responses to prices (or, in the case of Finland, to real wages) and mortality.

Finland, followed by Sweden and England, represent the most clear-cut cases of low-pressure demographic response. Especially in the case of Finland, fertility and nuptiality are heavily influenced by prices (or real wages) and mortality. In all these countries, short-term mortality variations are only weakly linked to economic fluctuations.

France is more of a high-pressure system than the others. Here, mortality is more sensitive to price fluctuations. However, it is also obvious that France constitutes a high-pressure system only in a relative sense. Not much more than a quarter of the variance in mortality is eliminated by prices. Fertility and nuptiality are at least as affected by economic fluctuations as is mortality.

Stockholm presents a different picture. In very general terms, the system is a low-pressure rather than a high-pressure one; mortality is less responsive to prices than anywhere else. Only 5 per cent of the variance in Stockholm mortality is accounted for by prices, a percentage which does not increase if prices are replaced by real wages as the explanatory variable. There is, in other words, practically no connection between short-term price fluctuations and mortality.

The main difference as compared with Sweden as a whole as well as with the other countries is in nuptiality. The effects of prices and

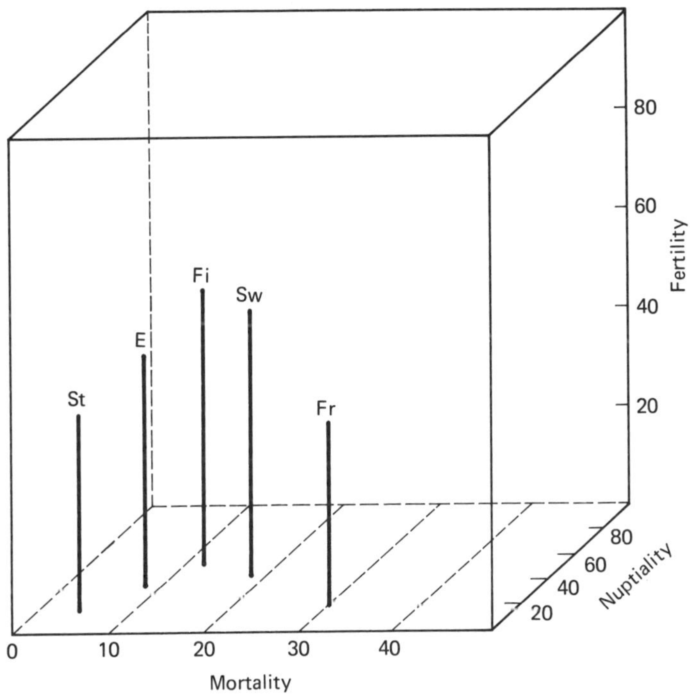

Figure 8.6 Percentage of variance in vital rates eliminated by the explanatory variables in Table 8.1. Stockholm (St), England (E), Finland (Fi), Sweden (Sw), and France (Fr)

mortality on nuptiality are quite weak in Stockholm where only 18 per cent of the variance in the latter variable is eliminated. This is a far smaller portion than in Sweden (42 per cent) and in the other countries.

Not only nuptiality but also Stockholm fertility is less affected by prices and mortality than is the case in Sweden as a whole. The overall Stockholm pattern is one of a comparatively high degree of independence *between* the economic and the demographic systems as well as of weak linkages *within* the demographic system.

A clearer overall picture of the differences between the areas studied emerges from figure 8.6. It depicts the percentage of the variance eliminated (that is, the coefficient of determination multiplied by 100) in the three vital rates, respectively, by the explanatory variables in table 8.1.

Stockholm is not far from the front left of the cube, indicating a situation of generally weak demographic responses. The further we move to the right in the figure, the more of a high-pressure, mortality-sensitive system we face. The further we are from the front of the cube, the more of a low-pressure system we have, especially with increasing heights of the columns. France stands out from the others in being more of a high-pressure system.

The relative independence of Stockholm mortality to the other variables could no doubt partly be attributed to the fact that the capital constituted a far more open economy than the country as a whole. The heavy migratory movements to and from the city contributed towards a large exposure to disease. As a port, Stockholm was open to epidemics such as the 1834 cholera epidemic which produced the enormous crude death rate of 86 per thousand, the highest figure recorded after 1750.

The influences on mortality do not help much, however, in explaining the major difference between Swedish and Stockholm demographic response, that is in nuptiality. The unresponsiveness of nuptiality to other vital rates and to economic changes rather suggests differences in life styles. Stockholm evidently was less restricted by considerations regarding a certain material basis for marriage. Correlations between nuptiality and mortality on the one hand and real wages on the other have the expected signs but are remarkably weak (0.33 and −0.17, respectively).

With regard to vital rates responses as a whole, Sweden occupies a position between responsive England and unresponsive Stockholm. If the short-term demographic response to economic fluctuations is regarded as the essential ingredient of the Malthusian model (as Heckscher did), then this model is obviously less powerful for Sweden than for Finland, and dramatically less impressive for Stockholm.

The more subtle interpretation of the Malthusian model referred to earlier by Bengtsson and Ohlsson, in which medium- rather than short-term relationships are stressed, is not affected by the argument above. What is the Stockholm counterpart of the periodicities discussed by them for the national Swedish level?

In discussing possible periodicities, we use the periodogram since this facilitates hypothesis testing. Before drawing conclusions concerning the existence of cycles of a certain period, we feel that the null hypothesis should be tested that the periodogram ordinate corresponding to this period does not deviate from the average of the series. As a time series gets longer, the likelihood of recording a high value in the periodogram will increase due to chance alone. If the null hypothesis cannot be rejected at a reasonable level of significance, there is little point in constructing a theory accounting for the suspected cycle.

Table 8.2 *Ratio of largest periodogram ordinate to the average: vital rates and real wages in Stockholm and Sweden, 1749–1850.*

Series	Stockholm	Sweden
Mortality	3.81	4.03
Nuptiality	3.70	5.34
Fertility	4.46	6.74
Real wages	5.94	3.93

Although not used regularly in spectral analysis, the need for hypothesis testing is no less than in regression analysis.[27]

As it turns out (table 8.2), only the Swedish birth rate, with a dominating five-year fluctuation, displays a value at the periodogram ordinate which is significant at the 5 per cent level (that is, reaching the ratio 6.57).

The climate series also lacks a single, dominant periodicity (ratio = 4.29). This series, reporting the break-up of ice on Lake Mälaren at Västerås about one hundred km west of Stockholm, is plotted on figure 8.7. It has previously been discussed by Utterström who regards it as providing valuable information since the date at which the ice breaks up may be considered to mark the beginning of the growing season.[28] There is some indication that winters become more prolonged during the eighteenth century (from the start of the series in 1721) up to about 1810, after which date climate seems to have been slightly milder in the sense described here.

At the present level of our knowledge, then, it does not appear to be a good research strategy to invest much in searching for univariate cyclical explanations as long as the existence of such periodicities usually is in doubt.

The more important questions, however, concern the relationships between economic and demographic series rather than the properties of the variables taken one at a time. Results of such an analysis by cross-spectral methods are reported in table 8.3. The coherency square, varying between 0 and 1, measures the degree of covariation between two series at specified frequencies and may be thought of as analogous to a correlation coefficient.

The amplitude represents the sum of squares accounted for, while

[27] The test used here is described in W. A. Fuller, *Introduction to Statistical Time Series* (New York, 1976), 282ff.

[28] G. Utterström, 'Some population problems in pre-industrial Sweden', *Scandinavian Economic History Review* 2 (1954).

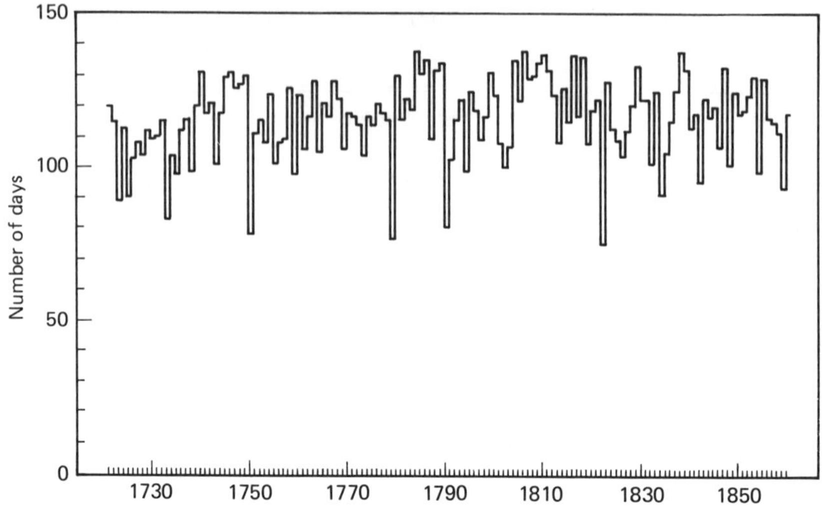

Figure 8.7 Date of the break-up of ice on Lake Mälaren, 1721–1860, expressed as number of days since New Year. *Source*: H. H. Hildebrandsson, Sur le prétendu changement du climat européen en temps historiques. *Nova Acta Regiae Societatis Scientiarium Upsaliensis*, 4th Series, vol. 4:5 (Uppsala, 1915), 26f.

the lag has been calculated from the phase spectrum, measuring the extent to which two series are in step. If there is a causal relation between variables, we should also be able to find a plausible lag.

With regard to the relationships mortality-real wages and mortality-climate, results are plausible except for the longest cycles. In Stockholm as well as in Sweden, one short-term and one medium-term cycle (2–4 years and 6–9 years, respectively) can be discerned in the relationships deaths-real wages and deaths-climate. The periodicity is practically the same in Stockholm as in the country, and deaths are everywhere lagging.

Stockholm coherencies between mortality and climate exceed those between mortality and real wages, while the opposite is true for Sweden. Possibly, the effect of climate on mortality was greater in Stockholm than in the country, but the reservation must be made that the same climate series is used in both cases, which may not give a good overall picture of Swedish climate.

The marriages-real wages relationships are different as far as lags are concerned. Real wages usually lag behind marriages which does not seem plausible. The lags are so short, however, that it can be doubted if we should assume any lags at all. We may recall that table

8.1 above indicated a very quick nuptiality response to prices (lags below zero were of negligible importance). As the periods of the cycles are about the same in Stockholm and Sweden, it seems that we are dealing with one short- and one medium-term fluctuation (with periods of 2 and 6–7 years, respectively) in the relationship between marriages and real wages.

Much the same as was said about marriages applies to births, too. Lags are small in the short- and medium-term fluctuations and should probably not be interpreted as differing from zero. Table 8.1 above also showed rapid responses in births to prices.

All coherencies in the short- and medium-term fluctuations of the marriages-real wages and births-real wages relations are higher in Sweden than in Stockholm, suggesting that these links were weaker in the capital. This is in line with the results from table 8.1 discussed previously, where a higher share of fertility and nuptiality could be accounted for at the national level than in Stockholm.

Altogether, we are observing short-term as well as medium-term cycles in the mortality-real wages, mortality-climate, and marriages-real wages relationships, in Stockholm and in Sweden.

What are the implications of the results above for the Malthusian interpretation of the Swedish economy? Even if the existence of a relationship between variables in certain periodicities is accepted, this does not amount to demonstrating that mechanisms of the Malthusian type were decisive when it comes to accounting for demographic fluctuations.

In terms of coherencies and amplitudes, the short-term cycles of 2–4 years in table 8.3 are about as important, and maybe even somewhat more prominent, than the medium-term cycles of 6–9 years. If the short-term links were important in explaining the behaviour of the vital rates over time, this would have shown up in the lags in table 8.1. The contribution of lags of one year or more are, however, usually negligible.

Although the medium-length, cyclical real wages-mortality hypothesis seems unlikely to account for a very substantial share of mortality variance, the discussion is difficult within the format of spectral analysis. It would be useful to try and reformulate the thesis of a close, cyclical link between living standards and mortality in a time series model that lent itself more easily to hypothesis testing. While there can be little doubt about the existence of economic-demographic cycles, it is much more questionable that economic fluctuations were a major (or even main) determinant of mortality. A reformulation would make it possible to draw more definite conclusions regarding the

Table 8.3 *Dominating fluctuations, coherency squares, amplitudes, and lags between vital rates and real wages in Stockholm and Sweden, 1749–1850.*

Variables	Dominating fluctuation	Coherency square	Amplitude	Lag
Stockholm				
Deaths-real wages	3.6	0.70	107	Deaths lag 1.3 years
	9	0.71	80	Deaths lag 4 years
	14	0.50	26	Real wages lag 2 years
Deaths-climate	2.0	0.77	54	Deaths lag 11 months
	7	0.79	22	Deaths lag 3 years
	10	0.47	37	Climate lags 2.4 years
Marriages-real wages	2.2	0.55	40	Real wages lag 5 months
	7	0.49	53	Marriages lag 5 months
	14	0.76	31	Real wages lag 4 months
Births-real wages	2.2	0.78	42	Real wages lag 4 months
	6	0.67	38	Births lag 4 months
	94	0.65	32	Real wages lag 2 months
	14	0.58	11	Births lag 1.6 years
Sweden				
Deaths-real wages	3.4	0.84	39	Deaths lag 1.2 years
	9	0.64	37	Deaths lag 4 years
Deaths-climate	2.6	0.48	20	Deaths lag 3 months
	6	0.67	16	Deaths lag 1.6 years
	13	0.55	14	Climate lags 6 months
Marriages-real wages	2.0	0.93	15	No lag
	6	0.83	40	Real wages lag 5 months
	14	0.62	11	Real wages lag 3 years
Births-real wages	4.6	0.82	36	No lag
	10	0.82	10	Real wages lag 5 months

magnitude of such effects. Regression methods are also better suited to discussing multivariate relationships, e.g., the joint effects of real wages, mortality, and climate on fertility and nuptiality, and to estimating simultaneous models, e.g., allowing for demographic effects on real wages.

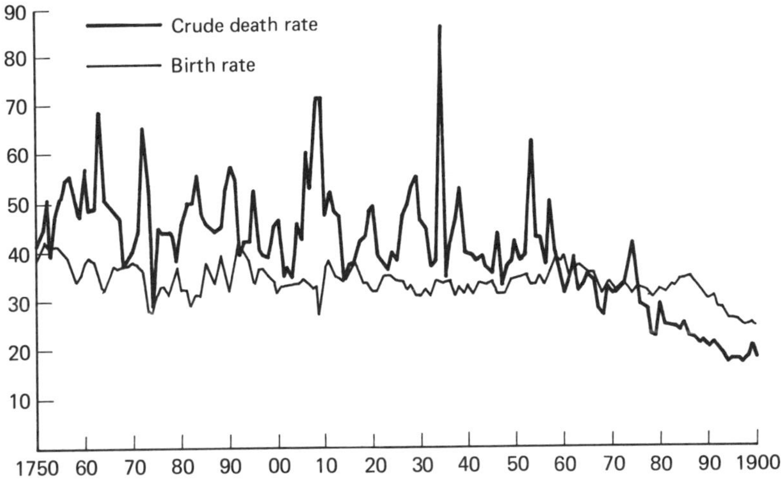

Figure 8.8 Crude death and birth rates in Stockholm, 1750–1900. Per 1,000
Source: *Statistisk årsbok för Stockholms stad* (1905).

Long-term development of mortality in Stockholm

Stockholm in the eighteenth and early nineteenth century was a city of extremely high rates of mortality. The long-term pattern of mortality and fertility is presented in figure 8.8. Excess mortality was the rule even in years with comparatively low death rates. Between 1750 and 1850 we can only count four single years when the crude birth rate was higher than the crude death rate (1753, 1768, 1792 and 1816). Moreover the natural increase these years was very modest, ranging between 3.5 per thousand in 1792 and 0.03 in 1816. In a European perspective this was a remarkable pattern. Although natural deficits were usual in the eighteenth century there was a change in the nineteenth century, when many European cities began to show natural increases in all but years characterized by heavy epidemics.

Among western and central European cities it is only Vienna that displays a higher level of mortality (figure 8.9). However, due to extremely high birth rates Vienna counted 16 years with natural increases between 1800 and 1850.[29]

Berlin, a city of a considerably greater size than Stockholm, did not have more than six years of natural deficits between 1816 and 1850 although crude birth rates were not especially high. Hamburg, twice the size, counted nine deficit years between 1821 and 1850. Bremen, a city of about the same size as Stockholm, had only two years of excess

[29] *Statistische Tableaus über die Bewegung der Bevölkerung* (Vienna, 1869).

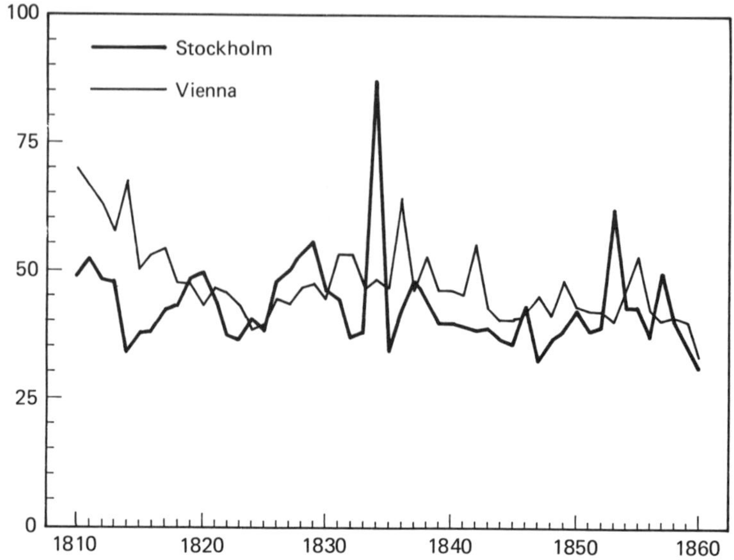

Figure 8.9 Crude death rates in Stockholm and Vienna, 1800–1860. Per 1,000
Sources: Vienna: *Statistische Tableaus über die Bewegung der Bevölkerung* (Vienna, 1869). Stockholm: see *figure 8.8*.

mortality in the period 1823 to 1850. Birth rates in Hamburg and Bremen were not generally higher than in Stockholm.[30] When comparing the long-term development in Stockholm with continental cities, at first glance it seems as if we have a clear case of retarded development. The changes in mortality patterns observed in the more advanced European cities became manifest in Stockholm about half a century later. Arthur Imhof's portrait of mortality in Berlin may serve as an illustration of this phenomena (see figure 8.10).

The curves of crude death rates in eighteenth- and nineteenth-century Berlin and Stockholm show many resemblances. Natural deficits are the rule. Open crises are fairly common. Both cities seem to have a mortality pattern which historical demographers have characterized as the mortality of 'l'ancien régime'. After 1810 the Berlin pattern is changing in a distinct way. Fluctuations in crude death rates do not reach more than a third of their former level and natural increases become the rule. Demographic crises in the period from 1810 to the early 1870s have a more hidden character.[31] In Stockholm it is not

[30] *Quellen zur Bevölkerungs-, Sozial- und Wirtschaftsstatistik Deutschlands 1815–1875*, (Boppard am Rhein, 1980), 190ff., 250ff., 262ff.,

[31] A. Imhof, 'Mortalität im Berlin vom 18. bis 20. Jahrhundert', *Berliner Statistik*, Nr. 8 (1977).

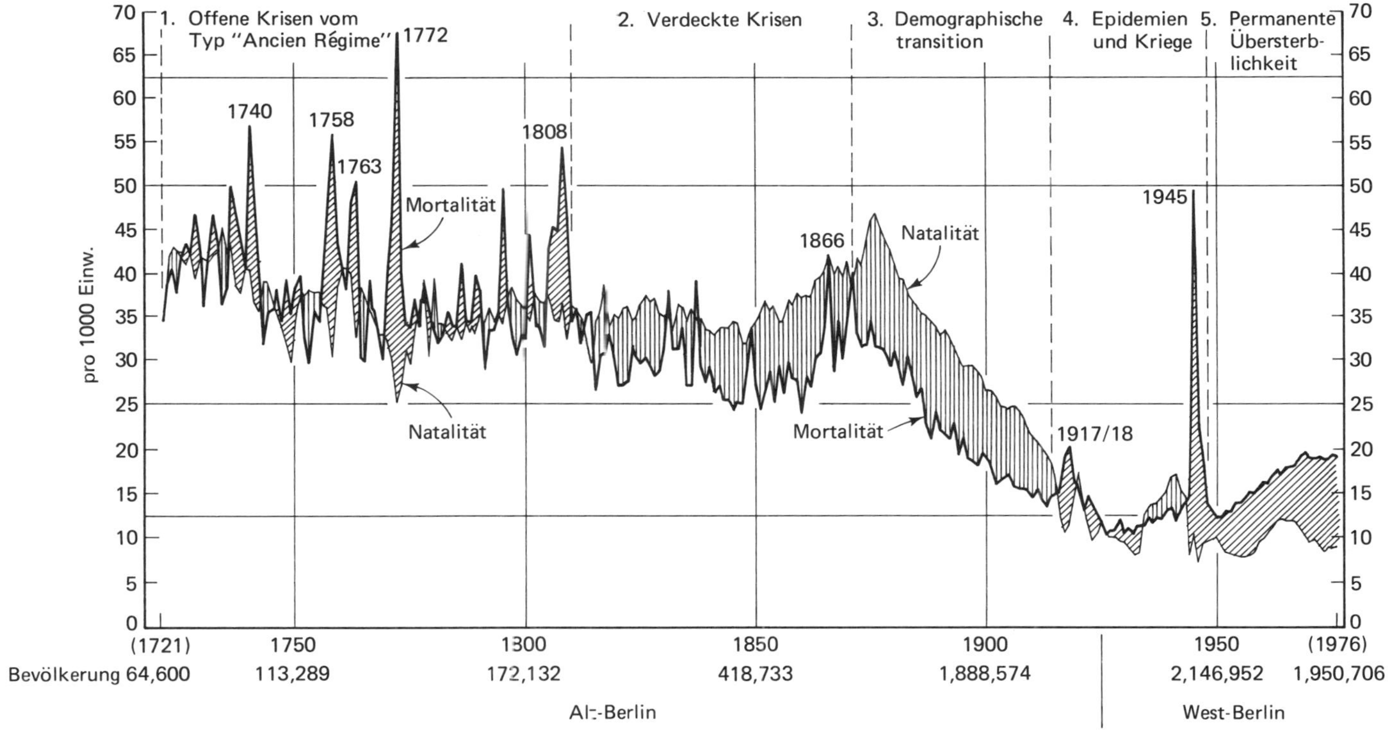

1. Offene Krisen vom Typ "Ancien Régime"
2. Verdeckte Krisen
3. Demographische transition
4. Epidemien und Kriege
5. Permanente Übersterblichkeit
1740
1758
1763
1772
1808
1866
1917/18
1945
Mortalität
Natalität
Natalität
Mortalität
pro 1000 Einw.
pro 1000 Einw.
70
65
60
55
50
45
40
35
30
25
20
15
10
5
0
(1721)
1750
1300
1850
1900
1950
(1976)
Bevölkerung 64,600
113,289
172,132
418,733
1,888,574
2,146,952
1,950,706
Al:-Berlin
West-Berlin

possible to identify a clear break with the eighteenth-century pattern until at least 1860.

Nevertheless, it would be inadequate to consider Stockholm in the first part of the nineteenth century as stuck in an old pattern where the effects of subsistence crises governed fluctuations in mortality, while an important part of urban Europe delivered itself from the constraints of that demographic regime. As demonstrated in a previous part of this chapter there are no significant correlations between real wages, changes in real wages and mortality rates during the whole period 1750–1860. Although the level of mortality was very high there was no direct response to changes in real wages.

The correlation between fertility and nuptiality and real wages was, however, significant. Certain demographic variables thus behaved as in a low pressure system described by Wrigley and Schofield, where changes in real wages influenced fertility and nuptiality rather than mortality.[32] It is of course highly inappropriate to define eighteenth- and nineteenth-century Stockholm in these terms. Still, possible connections between mortality and economic conditions are of a more subtle kind than a direct response to changes in real wages. In that respect Stockholm differs significantly from the results obtained by Tommy Bengtsson and Rolf Ohlsson for the country as a whole. These authors have demonstrated that there was a strict response in mortality for ages over 20 to changing real wages, stronger in the eighteenth century but still significant in the first part of the nineteenth century.[33]

Are the reasons behind Stockholm's relative backwardness to be searched for in the domain of public health and sanitary conditions? The bad sanitary state was a source of constant complaints from concerned citizens in nineteenth-century Stockholm. Water supply and sewage disposal were regarded as especially deficient.[34]

On the other hand sanitary conditions were intolerable in urban Europe as a whole. The heroic age of sanitary reform is very much a product of the second half of the nineteenth century. We meet the same kind of charges in almost every city monograph concerning the first part of the nineteenth century.[35] It is beyond any doubt that the

32 E. A. Wrigley and R. S. Schofield, *The Population History of England 1541–1871*, 466–80.

33 T. Bengtsson and R. Ohlsson, 'Population and economic fluctuations in Sweden 1749–1914', in *Pre-Industrial Population Change*, ed. T. Bengtsson *et al.*

34 See for example Wretlind, *Undersökningar rörande Stockholms mortalitet*.

35 For London of the pre-sanitary reform era see, e.g., A. S. Wohl, *The Eternal Slum* (London, 1977). Sanitary conditions in a number of cities in Victorian Britain are discussed in *The History of Working Class Housing*, ed. S. Chapham (London, 1971); see also Wohl's contribution, 'Unfit for Human Habitation', and G. Rosen, 'Debility and Disease', in *Victorian cities*, eds. H. J. Dyos and M. Wolf (London, 1973). The classic on nineteenth-century Paris is of course L. Chevalier, *Laboring Classes and Dangerous*

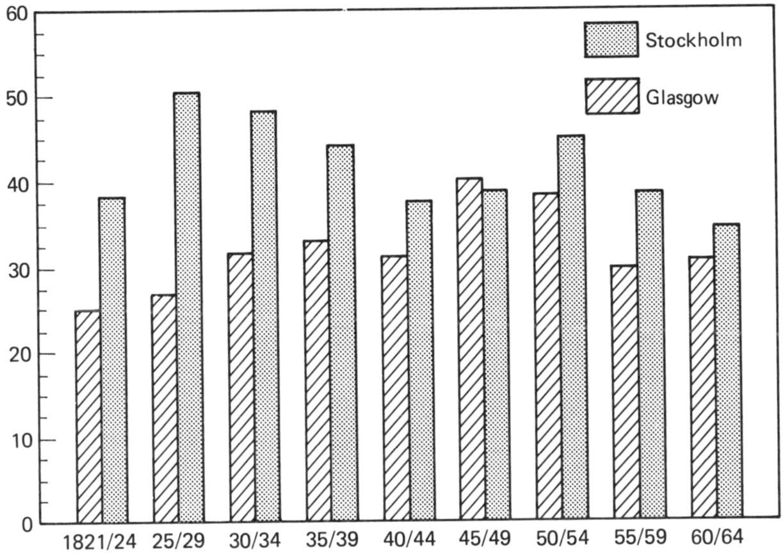

Figure 8.11 Crude death rates in Stockholm and Glasgow, 1821–1864.
Sources: Glasgow: *Scottish Population History*, ed. M. Flinn, 377. Stockholm: see *figure 8.8*.

failure of contemporary authorities to provide their citizens with a decent sanitary standard was an important reason behind the urban/rural mortality gap in Europe as a whole. Samuel Preston and Etienne van de Walle have convincingly demonstrated that the different timing of sanitary improvements is the most plausible explanation of the divergent trends of mortality in Paris, Lyon, and Marseille in the second half of the nineteenth century.[36]

For the first part of the nineteenth century it is extremely difficult to argue a priori that sanitary conditions could have been so much worse in a relatively small and stagnant town like Stockholm than in the expanding cities of the industrial revolution in Britain. British cities like Manchester, Liverpool, and Glasgow, under the pressure of an uncontrolled urbanization, had far lower death rates than Stockholm. In figure 8.11 crude death rates in Glasgow, after Liverpool the fastest

Classes in Paris during the First Half of the Nineteenth Century (Princeton, N.J., 1973). For a more recent contribution see E. Confora-Argadona and T. H. Guerrand, *La répartition de la population et les conditions de logement des classes ouvrières à Paris au 19ᵉ siècle* (Paris, 1976), chapter 2.

36 S. Preston and E. van de Walle, 'Urban French mortality in the nineteenth century', *Population Studies* 32 (1978).

growing city in Britain in the period, are compared with Stockholm 1821–64.

Although mortality in Glasgow rose from the 1830s to the second half of the 1850s, the Scottish metropolis only occasionally reached the level of Stockholm. For most of the period crude death rates in Stockholm were more than 10 per thousand higher. Nineteenth-century Glasgow was known as the unhealthiest and dirtiest city in Britain. It is highly difficult to imagine that the environments of Glasgow in the 1840s so vividly described by the Scottish physician Neil Arnott could have been so much better than Stockholm in the same period.[37] Differences in the state of public health are most unlikely to account for more than a fraction of the mortality gap between the two cities.

In the remaining part of the chapter we will concentrate the discussion on age- and sex-specific rates of mortality in order to get a picture as complete as possible of the specificities of Stockholm.

Age- and sex-specific mortality in Stockholm in the first part of the nineteenth century

Compared with a number of European cities, the most striking trait of age- and sex-specific mortality in nineteenth-century Stockholm is the large difference between male and female mortality in general, in particular in the age group 25–50. The male crude death rate was for most of the period 1760–1860 more than 10 per thousand higher than the female. In England and Wales, in the overview provided by the Registrar General in his 1848 report, not a single town displayed the same large male/female difference. The gap between the sexes was normally under 5 per thousand.

The extent to which male mortality in the active period of life differed from a number of European cities is illustrated in tables 8.4 to 8.6. The first of these tables compares age- and sex-specific mortality in 1821/5, a period of comparatively low mortality in both cities.

Although child mortality was significantly higher in Stockholm the biggest difference in relative terms is found in the group 40–49 years. This pattern of age- and sex-specific mortality was fairly constant during the first half of the nineteenth century. The male disadvantage was greater in periods of severe epidemics as in the cholera year 1834 and during the typhus/typhoid epidemic in the second half of the 1820s (figure 8.12).

The extent to which the higher crude death rate in Stockholm,

37 *Report on the Sanitary Conditions of the Labouring Population of Great Britain*, ed. M. Flinn (Edinburgh, 1965), 95.

Table 8.4 *Age- and sex-specific mortality in Stockholm and Glasgow, 1821–1825 (Per 1,000).*

	Males		Females	
Age	Stockholm	Glasgow	Stockholm	Glasgow
0–4	129.1	80.8	124.8	76.6
5–9	11.3	13.1	9.8	12.6
10–19	8.5	7.4	6.2	7.1
20–29	21.8	12.3	10.8	8.8
30–39	37.0	13.5	15.8	12.4
40–49	58.7	18.2	22.6	16.6
50–59	71.1	24.8	32.6	26.8
60+	114.3	88.1	72.3	73.2

Sources: Mortalitets- and folkmängdstabeller 1821–25, SCB; *Scottish Population History*, ed. M. Flinn, 378.

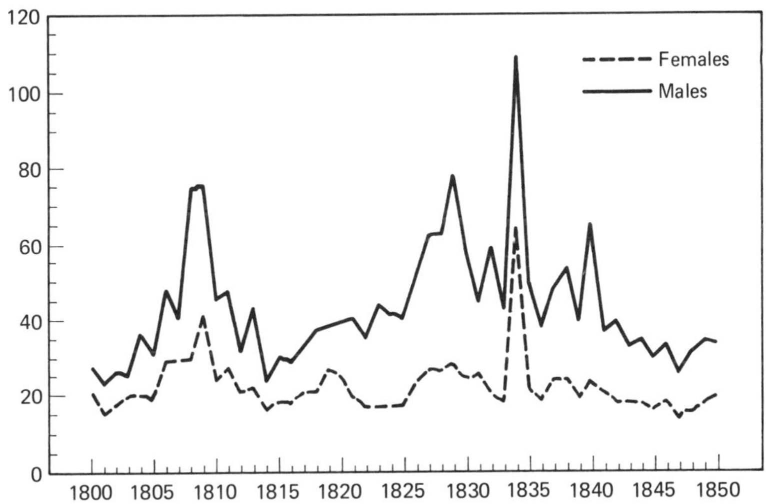

Figure 8.12 Male and female mortality in Stockholm 1800–1850 for the age group 25–49. Per 1,000. *Source*: Mortalitets- and folkmängdstabeller, SCB.

Table 8.5 *Age- and sex-specific mortality in Stockholm, 1835 and Paris, 1836 (Per 1,000).*

	Males		Females	
Age	Stockholm	Paris	Stockholm	Paris
0–4	136.7	125.7	116.7	110.4
5–9	14.7	15.9	8.7	17.8
10–14	4.0	6.3	5.2	9.8
15–19	8.4	10.0	3.3	9.7
20–24	14.0	16.0	10.7	13.2
25–29	19.0	13.5	11.7	13.7
30–39	33.7	11.9	14.9	13.7
40–49	48.9	17.4	20.6	17.3
50–59	62.7	29.9	31.8	26.5
60 +	102.0	82.1	70.0	82.7

Sources: Mortalitets- and folkmängdstabeller 1835, SCB. *Recherches statistiques sur la ville de Paris* (1844).

compared with most other European cities, could be a function of adult mortality is exposed below in a somewhat extreme example. Age-specific mortality in Stockholm in the year 1835, when the crude death rate was exceptionally low (34.6) per thousand, is compared with Paris 1836, a year close to the average level of mortality (28.6) in the first part of the nineteenth century for the French capital. In this example the difference in the crude death rates observed was almost exclusively due to the wide gap in male mortality in the age span 30 to 50 years.

The extreme position of Stockholm concerning adult mortality is further revealed in table 8.6. Age-specific mortality in the three most disadvantaged English cities and in the worst sub-district of London exposed by the Registrar General in his survey of the period 1838/44 is contrasted against Stockholm 1836/45.

The pattern displayed in the previous tables is repeated in an almost monotonous way. It is in their prime years that the male inhabitants of Stockholm were exposed to greater dangers than in most other parts of urban Europe. The comparatively high level of mortality in nineteenth-century Stockholm was then to a large extent a consequence of an extreme adult male mortality. It is of course necessary to be cautious when trying to explain the divergence between Stockholm and contemporary European towns. Nevertheless the age- and sex-specific structure tends to support the thesis that sanitation cannot

Table 8.6 *Age-specific male mortality in Stockholm, 1836/45 and in Liverpool, Manchester, Bristol, and Whitechapel (London), 1838/44 (Per 1,000).*

Age	Stockholm	Liverpool	Manchester	Bristol	Whitechapel
0–4	180.4	142.3	136.6	107.0	114.4
5–9	16.3	17.4	14.4	16.4	13.9
10–14	6.4	6.3	5.7	7.8	4.3
15–24	12.8	9.8	9.3	10.5	8.5
25–34	27.4	12.7	12.9	15.7	12.7
35–44	50.8	21.6	19.8	21.1	21.2
45–54	66.4	33.7	30.4	28.8	32.6
55–65	76.5	53.1	52.5	49.9	57.4
65 –	115.2	124.2	117.2	122.8	132.8

Sources: Mortalitets- and folkmängdstabeller 1836–45, SCB; *Ninth Report of the Registrar General* (1848).

have been a central factor behind Stockholm's deplorable position. Even if males were more exposed, men and women to a large degree were victims of the same environmental hazards. The quality of drinking water must have had the same effect on both sexes.

When disqualifying sanitary conditions as a main component behind the peculiar pattern of age- and sex-specific mortality in nineteenth-century Stockholm, there are two broad fields where it is fruitful to search for possible explanations: (1) to what extent was the economic and social structure, especially the labour market, discriminating against either sex, (2) to what extent can the mortality gap be linked to the consequences of different ways of life, for example, differentials in alcohol and tobacco consumption. There are substantial difficulties in securing any precise measurements in either of these fields. Consequently, the discussion must have a tentative character. This section concentrates on the effects of the economic and social context on sex differentials. The second aspect will be treated as a brief analysis of causes of death.

Sex-specific mortality differentials is a complex subject. In order to insert the age- and sex-specific pattern in Stockholm and in the cities displayed in the previous tables in a broader framework, it is necessary to take a brief digression on the literature of sex-specific mortality in general.

In his classical summary of sex mortality differentials, Stolnitz demonstrated that higher male mortality was not as usual as commonly believed.[38] A recent contribution by Samuel Preston constitutes a fruitful extension of Stolnitz' approach. Preston's investigation includes 165 observations of national populations between 1861 to 1964. Most of his observations, however, stem from the twentieth century. In his sample, high mortality populations with life expectancies under 45 years have (in contrast to nineteenth-century Stockholm) higher female mortality for a number of age groups, not only in childbearing ages. With improving levels of mortality the female disadvantage disappears. As most of Preston's high mortality populations are located in agrarian societies he reaches the conclusion that there tends to be a systematic discrimination against women in agrarian societies. With economic modernization and subsequent urbanization this discrimination vanishes. A distinct pattern of more or less permanent male overmortality emerges.[39]

In German historical demography Arthur Imhof and Robert Lee have pointed out that the intensification of agriculture in the nineteenth century resulted in an increased female participation in direct agricultural work, with rising maternal and infant mortality as a consequence. Recent German investigations comparing urban and rural areas have established a general female mortality disadvantage in the reproductive ages from 1780–1899.[40]

In the German discussion, as already pointed out, this pattern is regarded as a consequence of growing female participation in different kinds of work outside ordinary household tasks. When analysing adult mortality differentials it is of course highly relevant to look upon the total burden of work pressing on each of the sexes. Mortality divergences can tell us or draw our attention to the fact that we are facing a change in the workload to the disadvantage of either men or women. There are of course a number of other relevant factors, such as sex-specific incidences of unemployment, etc.

A brief inspection of Scandinavian and English data also gives a somewhat more complicated picture than the German one. As in the German context, a tendency towards higher female mortality is found in both England and Scandinavia. For the period 1838/44 we have

[38] G. A. Stolnitz, 'A century of mortality trends II', *Population Studies* 10 (1956).

[39] S. H. Preston, *Mortality Patterns in National Populations. With a Special Reference to Recorded Causes of Death* (New York, 1976).

[40] A. Imhof, 'The amazing simultaneousness of the big differences and the boom in the 19th century – some facts and hypotheses about infant and maternal mortality in Germany, 18th to 20th century'; R. Lee, 'Mortality levels and agrarian reform in early 19th century Prussia: some regional evidence', both in *Pre-industrial Population Change*, ed. T. Bengtsson *et al.*

Table 8.7 *Frequency of higher female death rate by age in 19 rural districts in Sussex, Essex, and Suffolk, 1838/44.*

Age	Districts with higher female death rate	Districts with higher male death rate
15–24	18	1
25–34	19	0
35–45	17	2
45–55	13	6

Source: Ninth Annual Report of the Registrar General (1848).

examined 19 rural districts in Sussex, Essex, and Suffolk, characterized by highly intensive agriculture. In the age span 15 to 55 years there is only rarely a higher male mortality (table 8.7).

Modern British historical demography has another explanation for this divergent pattern. In the areas of intensive farming specializing in cereal production, the participation of women in agricultural production tended to decrease rather than increase. The position of women in the agricultural labour market grew increasingly precarious.[41]

From 1840, official Danish mortality statistics are divided into urban and rural districts. For rural Denmark as a whole there was generally a female mortality disadvantage in the ages 25 to 45 from 1840 to the end of the century.[42] Swedish evidence does not entirely contradict this picture of a female disadvantage in the reproductive years in rural areas. In a broad overview of the demographic transition in Sweden, Gunnar Fridlizius presents age-specific death rates from a sample containing regions with highly different agrarian structures. In the Swedish case it is not possible to discern a general female disadvantage in the ages 25–49. Nevertheless there are examples of areas with distinctly higher female mortality.[43]

When we turn to the urban scene a different picture emerges. In Denmark, male mortality was significantly higher than female from 30 years in Copenhagen and from 25 years in the provincial towns during the whole period from 1840 to the end of the century.[44] A higher male

[41] K. D. M. Snell, *Annals of the Labouring Poor. Social Change and Agrarian England 1660–1900* (Cambridge, 1985), 51–66.
[42] *Befolkningsforholdene i Danmark i det 19. aarhundrede* (Copenhagen, 1905), 128ff.
[43] G. Fridlizius, *The Demographic Transition of Sweden 1750–1930* (Lund, 1976), mimeo.
[44] See note 40 above.

Table 8.8 *Age- and sex-specific death rates in 40 English towns, 1838/44.*

Age group	Gender	Industrial	Non-industrial	Difference
25–34	Men	10.5	11.5	−1.0
	Women	11.2	9.5	1.7
	Difference	−0.7	2.0	
35–44	Men	13.6	15.5	−2.0
	Women	14.6	12.5	2.1
	Difference	−1.0	3.0	
45–54	Men	21.3	21.8	−0.5
	Women	18.6	14.8	3.8
	Difference	2.7	7.0	

Source: see *table 8.7.*

mortality in the reproductive years was the rule in urban Sweden although the differential between the sexes was not as large as in Stockholm.[45]

Urban England constitutes an interesting example. It is the only area of Europe in the first part of the nineteenth century with a sufficient number of towns with distinctly different characteristics. In England and Wales of the 1840s there existed, besides expanding industrial cities, a comparatively great number of towns not too small (above 20,000 inhabitants) and relatively untouched by the Industrial Revolution.

It is thus possible to get a rough idea whether there was any systematic difference of the age- and sex-specific structure of mortality between industrial and non-industrial urban environments. We have examined a sample of 40 English towns 1838/44 with 20,000 inhabitants or more. More than half the sample constituted non-industrialized towns.[46] Age- and sex-specific death rates for the groups 25/34, 35/44, and 45/54 are presented in table 8.8.

45 Mortalitets- och folkmängdstabeller, 1800–50. SCB.

46 The sample contains the following towns: Dover, Brighton, Reading, Northampton, Ipswich, Norwich, Yarmouth, Exeter, Plymouth, Bath, Bristol, Cheltenham, Worcester, Wolverhampton, Stoke, Birmingham, Coventry, Warwick, Leicester, Nottingham, Derby, Liverpool, Blackburn, Preston, Rochdale, Bolton, Manchester, Salford, Sheffield, Bradford, Leeds, York, Hull, Sunderland, Newcastle, Merthyr Tydfil, Kidderminster, Wigan, Ashton/Oldham. The classification follows the typology proposed by A. D. M. Phillips and J. R. Walton, 'The distribution of personal wealth in English towns in mid-nineteenth century', *Transactions. Institute of British Geographers* (1975).

Men in their best years were the most favoured group in the industrial towns. In the age when they were reaching their maximal earning capacity between 35–44, the mortality gap versus non-industrial towns was at its greatest. While non-industrial towns had a higher male mortality throughout the whole active period of life, industrial centres showed a female disadvantage until the age of 45. Even after 45 the male/female differential was much greater in non-industrial towns. These results tend to support the thesis that the economic and social structure, especially the labour market, discriminated against females in industrial cities while the opposite was true for non-industrial urban environments.

Women in industrial towns to a large extent shared work-sites with men. Consequently they were exposed to the same kind of risks. In general, women were lower paid and most certainly victims of greater fluctuations in employment. For married women, work outside the household meant an exhausting double-work. The position of men was strengthened by the greater regularity of employment and higher wages than in non-industrial towns, where different kinds of casual work dominated the local labour market. The higher crude death rate in industrial centres was, thus, to an important extent a consequence of higher infant mortality. It does fit into the contemporary view of the bad sanitary conditions prevailing in the rapidly growing industrial cities. From a restricted mortality point of view, adult men can be regarded as the winners in the process of industrialization with women and infants as the great losers.

The age- and sex-specific pattern of mortality in Stockholm emerges as an extreme variant of the non-industrial urban type. However, it still remains to discern possible explanations for Stockholm's extraordinary position. As demonstrated in chapters 4 and 6, we have reasonably good indicators from the mid nineteenth century that the economic stagnation seems to have hit men harder than women. Contrary to the general Swedish pattern, poverty was more prevalent among men in active ages than their female counterparts. Our measurement of poverty is a fairly good indicator of the employment situation. The poverty gap between men and women was most extended in the age group 20–29 (figure 4.2). Still men remained the disfavoured sex until the age of 50. Young men entering the labour market in their early twenties faced severe difficulties in finding regular employment. Women in this age group went to a large extent into the servant sector. Life as a servant was not exactly a sinecure, but it provided a reasonable degree of security. The labour market available for young men dominated as it was by casual trades meant that they had to cope with long periods of unemployment. Low and irregular incomes increased the risk of malnourishment. It also forced them to choose the cheapest possible housing. Even when far from actual starvation, malnourishment seriously affects the host's defence against infections. Living in overcrowded habitations meant a frequent exposure to infectious diseases. Young men in casual trades hence faced a double disadvantage.

This interpretation suffers from some disturbing weaknesses. The biggest difference in poverty ratios is found in the age group 20–9, while the mortality differential is greatest after the age of 30. Male mortality continued to rise steeply after a significant drop in the poverty ratios from 55 per cent for ages 20–9 to 44 per cent for the ages 30 to 49. Female mortality on the other hand remained low even after their economic position deteriorated. Furthermore women in their thirties increasingly left the relatively protected occupation as a servant.

From the poverty ratios we should have expected a mortality pattern close to what has been observed in Paris. As demonstrated in table 8.5 male mortality in Paris tended to rise between 20–4 and then to recover in the following age-groups until the age of 40. This pattern was even more marked during the Restoration. In figure 8.13 mortality in ages 15 to 59 are calculated from the first usable Parisian census 1817.

Pierre Guillaume has observed a similar pattern in nineteenth-century Bordeaux. Guillaume attributes this configuration to the greater obstacles men had to cope with when entering the labour market.

In Stockholm these difficulties were presumedly not relieved to the same extent as men grew older. As already noted men continued to be the disfavoured sex until the age of 50. After 50 considering the high male mortality prevailing in earlier age-groups we may assume that the population was heavily biased towards the richer stratum. Although women in their active years had to pay a heavy toll as demonstrated by the rising levels of still births and maternal mortality (see chapter 4 above), they obviously met the hazards of urban life more successfully than men.

Of course, it is not possible to assign the sex mortality differential to the situation in the labour market alone. Men tended to live a life more wasteful to their health than women. Alcoholism was predominantly a male phenomenon. Men were also more often involved in fatal accidents. In the following part of the chapter in connection with a brief discussion of causes of death we will try to estimate the possible influence of different ways of life on the sex mortality differential.

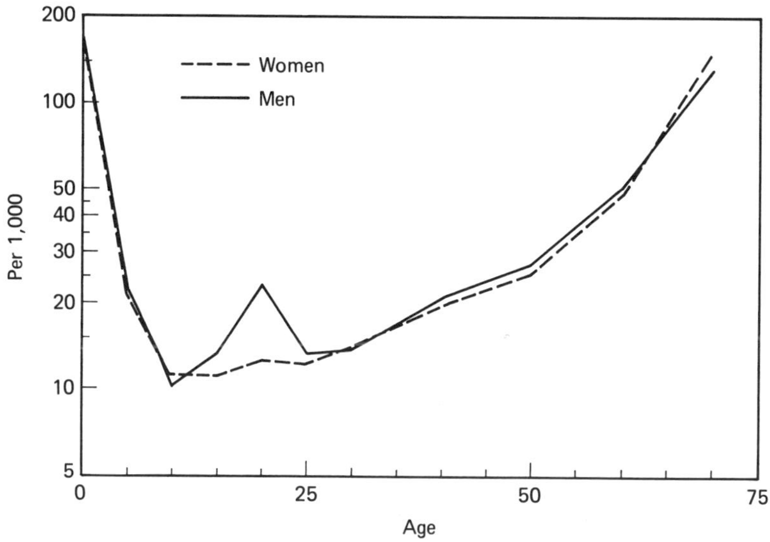

Figure 8.13 Adult mortality rates in Paris 1817. Per 1,000. *Source*: *Recherches statistiques sur la ville de Paris*, *I* (1821).

Causes of death

The Swedish official statistics contain information on causes of death from 1749 to 1830, then there is a gap until 1860. The system of classification changed several times over this period. In the subperiod 1805–30 examined here there was only one big modification. Between 1803 and 1820, 33 causes of death were registered. In cause-specific rates seven age groups were used (under 1, 1–2, 3–4, 5–9, 10–24, 25–49, and 50 years or older). The greatest change was a split of the rather 'broad' cause of death, fevers of all kinds, into inflammatory, nerve, and putrid and remittent fevers.

The difficulties and problems concerning classification of causes of death in former times are well known. For the eighteenth century, Swedish statistics on causes of death have been analysed by A. Imhof and B. Lindskog. Although the nomenclature is slightly different in this period their warnings against an interpretation in twentieth-century terms is highly relevant.[47]

However, for some causes of death as sensitive to the standard of living and way of life as consumption and dropsy, the ability of nineteenth-century men to make a reasonable judgement was fairly

[47] A. Imhof and B. Lindskog, 'Dödsorsakerna i Sydsverige 1749–1773', *Sydsvenska medicinhistoriska sällskapets årsskrift* (1973).

good.[48] The dominating causes of death in Stockholm during the first three decades of the nineteenth century were consumption, fevers, stroke, and dropsy. Over this period these causes accounted for between 55 and 70 per cent of the total. The very vague cause of death, stroke and sudden death dominated above all infant mortality. Among infants 50–70 per cent of all deaths were attributed to this cause. Consumption answered for 15 to 20 per cent of all deaths. The share of fevers was of about the same size. Dropsy was responsible for 5 to 10 per cent. For adults, especially in the age-group 25–49, respiratory tuberculosis was by far the most significant cause of death.[49]

Gustav Sundbärg, the pioneer of Swedish historical demography, analysed the extreme rate of consumption mortality in Stockholm in two articles in *Statistisk tidskrift* 1905. The figures for Stockholm in the first three decades of the nineteenth century were three times higher than the national average. Sundbärg also emphasized the great sex-specific differential. In the period 1821/30 men in the age group 25–49 had a death rate of 16.5 per thousand, while female mortality from tuberculosis stopped at 7.2. This sex-specific differential seems to have been fairly stable. In the period 1891/1900, when tuberculosis mortality had declined dramatically, the relation between the sexes was practically the same as 70 years earlier.

Sundbärg also noticed an increase in tuberculosis mortality between 1800 and 1830 both at the national level and in Stockholm.[50] However, this increase was rather modest even in the capital. If we look at the group 25–49 years (figure 8.14) we can detect a very interesting pattern. The curves for male and female consumption mortality diverged in a very distinct way. Although the female death rate rises as the male one in the second half of the 1820s, still it does not reach the same level as at the beginning of the period.

The male death rate for tuberculosis was positively correlated with time, 0.64, while the same correlation for females was weakly negative, −0.32. The connection between male and female mortality from consumption was much weaker than for other causes. The correlation was only 0.25 compared with 0.80 for fevers and 0.59 for dropsy.

Regarding the sharp divergence in the development of male and female tuberculosis mortality it is difficult to deny that different ways of life, especially concerning alcohol consumption, may have influ-

48 On the ability of contemporary authorities to identify tuberculosis see B.-I. Puranen, *Tuberkulos* (Umeå, 1984), 70ff.

49 Mortalitetstabeller, 1800–30. SCB.

50 G. Sundbärg, 'Dödligheten i lungtuberkulos i Sverige åren 1751/1830', *Statistisk Tidskrift* (1905).

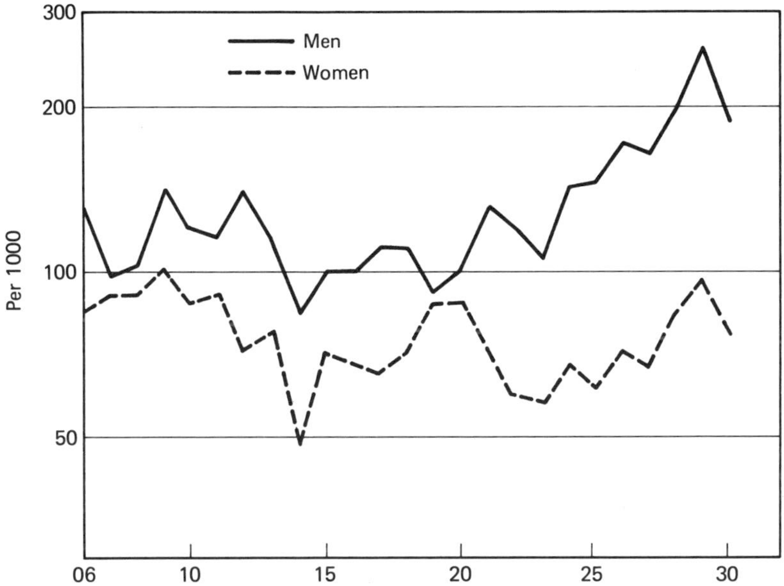

Figure 8.14 Mortality from respiratory tuberculosis in Stockholm 1806/30 for the age group 25–49. Per 10,000. *Source*: Mortalitets- and folkmängdstabeller 1805–1830, SCB.

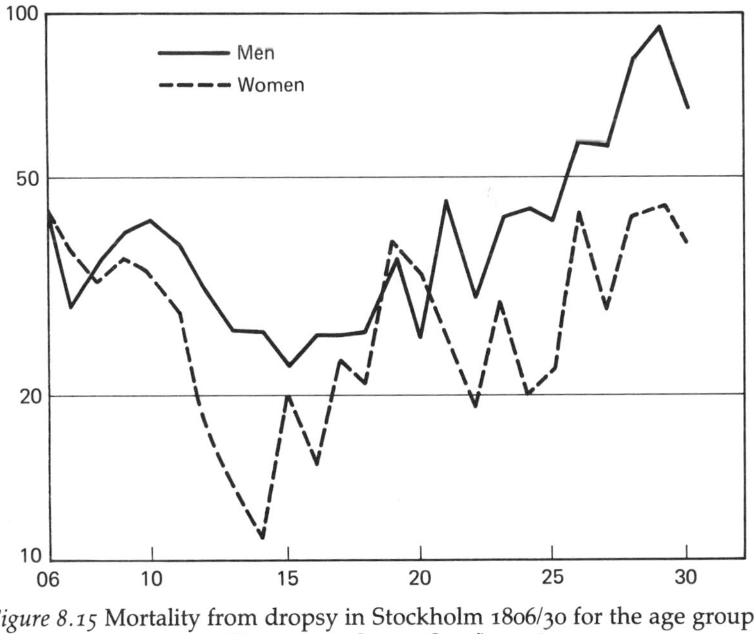

Figure 8.15 Mortality from dropsy in Stockholm 1806/30 for the age group 25–49. Per 10,000. *Source*: See *figure 8.14*.

enced the sex mortality differential. It is well known that excessive drink tends to weaken the resistance against tuberculosis infections. This suspicion is further strengthened by the fact that the rate for dropsy behaves in a similar way, with a rise in male mortality from dropsy in the 1820s (figure 8.15). Male dropsy mortality was, furthermore, very strongly correlated to the death rate for tuberculosis, 0.90. The corresponding female figure was somewhat lower, 0.70. Dropsy was a very complex cause of death. Symptoms that convinced contemporaries to classify a death as caused by dropsy could be the result of a number of different diseases, such as hunger, oedema, or heart and kidney infections. Heavy drinking could also produce manifestations that resulted in the dropsy diagnosis.

Many contemporaries believed that drinking was increasing during the 1820s. With the exception of winter 1826 and spring 1827, food prices were low. Real wages were rising. Thus low food prices created a margin for consumption of things other than the bare necessities of life. Certain observers presumed that men used an important part of this widening margin to consume alcoholic beverages.[51] To a certain extent this view was an expression of upper-class prejudices. However, it cannot be denied that alcoholism constituted a severe problem in early nineteenth-century Stockholm.

'This is an exceedingly thirsty city', remarked the poet, Carl Michael Bellman. He knew this well from first-hand participatory observation. The drinking of *brännvin*, the brandy distilled from potatoes or grain, certainly was more excessive than it would be during the later part of the nineteenth century. *Brännvin* was often served with the daily meals, not only in the evening but also with breakfast as well as with the midday meal.[52] While male overconsumption of alcohol may explain part of the male excess mortality, there are reasons to doubt that the whole difference between the sexes can be attributed to it.

Contemporaries remarked that drinking in Stockholm was by no means confined to the males. Females took part as well. 'The habit of brandy drinking', wrote the Polish canon quoted in the previous chapter, 'is so widespread that even women, girls, yes, even children

51 Överståthållarämbetets underdåniga femårsberättelse 1827–32 (Stockholm, 1834).

52 Alexandre Daumond, a Frenchman visiting Stockholm in 1830, stated that a burgher usually had coffee early in the morning and breakfast at ten or eleven o'clock, including sandwiches, ham, salted or smoked fish and *brännvin*. The midday meal was served at two, consisting of a piece of beef or veal which had been cooked on Sunday to be used during the whole week, supplemented by a fish dish and potatoes; once more *brännvin* was served, now with small beer. A. Daumont, *Resa i Sverige år 1830* (Stockholm, 1834), 212.

seldom let a day go by without several times taking a dram'.[53] Drinking, according to him, was one of the two major faults of the Stockholmers, the other being the 'limitless' sexual looseness of the females (the males escaping his reproach in this respect).

Drinking was far from an exclusive male privilege.[54] The diary of Märta Helena Reenstierna at Årsta manor just outside Stockholm dates from the late eighteenth and early nineteenth century. It has been published in three large volumes and is full of comments and reproaches on the servants for their heavy drinking. The most notorious alcoholic of the household ('well overloaded early in the morning', 'excellently drunk', 'mighty drunk', 'enormously drunk', 'drunk all day long', 'drunk as a jackdaw' or '3/4 drunk but completely useless') was the otherwise quite skilful and industrious maidservant, Catharina.[55]

Still, drinking no doubt constituted more of a problem among males. This was for instance the opinion of the author, G. H. Mellin, noting in 1857 that:

> the poorer class has regrettably acquired the habit of not being happy indoors. . . . Their savings are wasted at the tavern. Often the wife, to whom her husband does not grudge the earnings he receives or at least could get, maintains not only herself but also husband and children through efforts which no one who has not seen them will be able to appreciate.[56]

In this context it should be remembered that drinking at the tavern in the pre-industrial city was not merely a matter of getting drunk and enjoying oneself. Although matters may appear so in Bellman's songs, this would be too anti-Lutheran an interpretation. Work, drink, and leisure were more intertwined than they were to be in the industrializing city.

53 D. Anckarsvärd, 'Stockholm 1789–90 skildrat av en polsk kanik', *Sankt Eriks årsbok* 1933, 105. Albertrandi was surprised to find as many places serving brännvin in Stockholm 'as there are beer taverns in Warsaw'. He stayed in the central street Drottninggatan where 'there is a tavern in every third house but hardly a single café in the whole street'.

54 'The maidservant Sophia Lovisa Nordström, who has been employed by the undersigned since the beginning of last month, is from this date free from my service with regard to her during this time not only having overloaded herself with strong drink on several occasions, but also having been insolent and rude. She is, as far as I know, faithful and honest. Stockholm, July 12, 1830. C. G. Ramstén, Tobacco dealer.' The certificates of service required by the authorities in connection with emigration are usually not as blunt as this one from Katarina parish. Avflyttningslängd 1830, Katarina församlings kyrkoarkiv. Stockholm City Archive.

55 M. H. Reenstierna, *Årstadagboken 1–3. Journaler från åren 1793–1839 utgivna genom S. Erixon, A. Stålhane och S. Wallin* (Stockholm, 1985). Catharina had been fired twice on account of her drunkenness, but been allowed to return to the manor.

56 Quoted from M. Matović, *Stockholmsäktenskap* (Stockholm, 1984), 133.

A Stockholm example from the memoirs of the shoemaker Sven Anders Hägg illustrates, amongst other things, the next to non-existent border between work, drink, and leisure.[57] Hägg arrived at the capital in October 1841 as a journeyman. He was 23 years old and came from Linköping, having grown up in Småland in reduced circumstances. He was employed at the shop of the master Joseph Asklöf, where eight other journeymen worked. Hägg now received $2\frac{1}{2}$ riksdaler for a pair of boots, and from $1\frac{2}{3}$ to $1\frac{3}{4}$ riksdaler for shoes, a piece wage far higher than he had ever seen before. Avoiding luxuries, he kept to 'strong and nutritional' but inexpensive foodstuffs, which he could consume in larger quantities than before while still being able to save money. When he fell ill for several weeks in early 1842 this was, however, a serious intermission. In October 1843, after having been at another shop for half a year, he moved to Arosin's, the largest shop of the capital.

According to Hägg's experience, the middle-sized shops used to be fairly proper while the larger ones seemed to operate under the credo 'that a journeyman was capable if wearing a worn coat and on Mondays somewhat overcome and with blue eyes'. The older journeymen found their greatest pleasure in the 'free' or 'blue monday' spent away from the shop, gambling, and 'with low adventures'.

Still, the 'blue monday' did not preclude drinking at the shop. The distilling of brännvin was still unrestricted (this changed by the mid-1850s), and prices were low. The journeymen often met with friends, and the noticeable thing about these events is that they took place at the shop. At Arosin's, there were almost daily visits by soldiers or others, 'when brännvin should be offered'. An old journeyman would never take less than a 'blecka' or somewhat more than 8 cl at a time. As a result of this social intercourse, 'the lighter tools on my workbench were next to swimming in brännvin that had spilled over'.

For an industrious and proper journeyman like Hägg this was not an attractive workplace, and his stay lasted only for three weeks. He came to perceive the environment of the capital as increasingly disagreeable. In the late spring of 1844 he felt that 'the Stockholm life had produced such feelings of unpleasantness and cheerlessness, that I decided to travel to another country, no matter which one'.[58]

Hägg's description in several ways resembles the account of drinking in Eskilstuna as presented by Magnusson. Tavern life is not

[57] S. A. Hägg, *Mina levnadsminnen* (Stockholm, 1950).

[58] Hägg went to St Petersburg and later to Paris, where he experienced the 1848 Revolution and was impressed by the respected and valued position of the 'at least one million intelligent labourers' of the latter city. Unlike other places in the 'so-called civilized world', the Parisian labourer was not treated with contempt.

depicted by Hägg, most likely because he did not take much part in it, but it is obvious that the tavern was not the only place for social drinking. Though the number of officially permitted taverns was reduced in 1813, in an attempt by the authorities to reduce drinking, their number was still considerable. There were 715 taverns in 1810 (a figure practically unchanged for several decades), which should have been more than sufficient to serve a population of about 70,000.[59] In 1815 their number had been reduced to 417.[60] In addition to the legal taverns there were also illegal ones, whose existence may well have been stimulated by the restrictions.

One of the elements stressed in Lars Magnusson's thoughtful analysis of the significance of taverns and drink in Eskilstuna is its role in the pre-industrial social network.[61] Taking part in tavern life was a means of establishing contacts and gathering information that might be vital.[62] One might receive knowledge about jobs, buy or sell informal sector products, or succeed in persuading somebody to lend you some money.[63]

59 Some taverns were relatively large and aimed at specific categories such as The Lynx, a seamen's tavern. Most were small places such as the one called 'Sodom', described as 'dirty and narrow' with just a few tables and chairs. Most taverns were run by widows and persons who had some other occupation on the side. See P. B. Austin, *The Life and Songs of Carl Michael Bellman* (Malmö, 1967), 24.

60 From 1747 to 1813 the number of taverns was officially confined to 700. B. Boëthius, *Magistraten och borgerskapet i Stockholm 1719–1815* (Stockholm, 1943), 308, 441. The efforts to constrict drinking have been interpreted as a reaction against the rise in production following the Parliamentary decision of 1809 to abolish regulations on rural distilling and marketing of brännvin. Relying on police records Staf believes that consumption in Stockholm increased during the next few years, noting that the number of prosecutions for drunkenness grew from 255 in 1808 to 370 in 1810 and further to 445 in 1811. N. Staf, *Polisväsendet i Stockholm 1776–1850* (Uppsala, 1950), 345.

61 L. Magnusson, 'Drinking and the Verlag system 1820–1850: the significance of taverns and drink in Eskilstuna before industrialization', *Scandinavian Economic History Review* 34 (1986). Eskilstuna was a town of ironworking and smithery in eastern Sweden. See also B. Horgby, *Den disciplinerade arbetaren; brottslighet och social förändring i Norrköping 1850–1910* (Stockholm, 1986). Horgby argues that tavern life was an important component in working-class culture until the latter part of nineteenth-century industrialization when taverns lost their previous role. The disintegration of the drinking culture facilitated the increase in efficiency at the workplaces and control of criminality, but also self-discipline and organization among the labourers.

62 A late eighteenth-century view of the role of taverns in the daily life of certain upper or middle strata is provided by Albertrandi, stating that merchants and journeymen used to mind their business in the morning, eat at noon, and then spend the rest of the day until 10 p.m. at a tavern discussing, reading newspapers, smoking, and having dinner. Dinner usually consisted of hard bread with herring. Meanwhile the wife and servants had a porridge dinner at home. Anckarsvärd, 'Stockholm 1789–90', 106.

63 The inventories of the deceased often provide glimpses into the complex network of borrowers and lenders not only in higher but also in the lower social stratum. It is not

The structure of the male labour market created a demand for exactly these services, much more so than the female labour market dominated by more long-term service employment. It could be said that information gathering was more costly for the males, given the structure of the pre-industrial labour market. These costs can be conceived not only in terms of money and time but also in terms of health.

The period following the Napoleonic Wars was characterized by agricultural depression, lowering the cost of living of the urban population. The pre-industrial habit of a real wage increase raising not savings but the short-run consumption of drink, amongst other things, may explain the worries of contemporary observers fearing the consequences among the labouring population of a reduction in foodstuff prices. 'Drink, and drunkenness, were the traditional objects of expenditure on those rare occasions in the past when cash was at hand', observes Roberts with reference to Germany in the period after the mid nineteenth century.[64]

At least during parts of the 1820s and 1850s there are comments by contemporaries suggesting that such a demand pattern was a reality in Stockholm as well. An official report of the late 1820s deplores

> this unfortunate inclination towards drunkenness, which through the increased and, it may be rightly said, exaggerated production of brännvin, has gained momentum; as was also the case during the years 1822, 1823, 1824, and 1825, when the country was blessed with rich harvests, and when the wages of one single day were sufficient for maintenance during several days, multiplying the want and misery'.[65]

The conclusion put forward that the price of brännvin must be kept artificially high in order to counteract destructive consequences, did not receive much support at this time.[66] During the renewed wave of drinking of the early 1850s, however, the demands of the temperance movement were more efficient. The temperance movement was to exercise considerable influence during the latter part of the century. A more restrictive legislation was introduced in 1855, largely as a result of growing opinion against drinking.

Demand for brännvin was stimulated by falling prices. Several factors worked in this direction. From the 1820s onwards brännvin increasingly was distilled not from grains but from the cheaper

unusual that so many debts are listed that the net value of the estate is negative. Justitiekollegiets arkiv, Stockholm City Archive.

64 J. Roberts, *Drink, Temperance, and the Working Class in Nineteenth Century Germany* (Boston, 1984), 42ff.

65 *Överståthållarämbetets underdåniga femårsberättelse 1822–1826* (Stockholm, 1829), 24.

66 *Överståthållarämbetets underdåniga femårsberättelse 1827–1832* (Stockholm, 1834), 11.

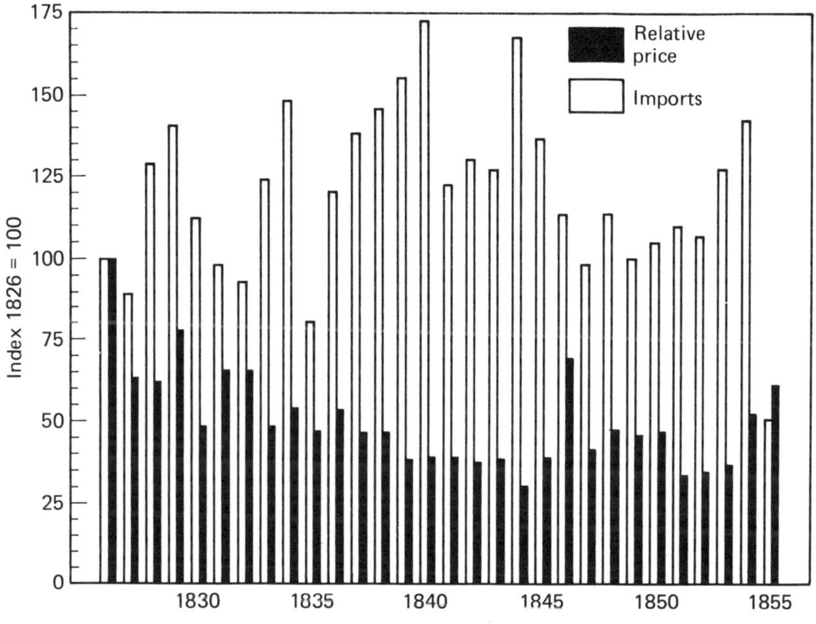

Figure 8.16 Relative price of brânnvin to rye and imports of brânnvin from other Swedish areas, 1826–55. *Sources*: Brännvin prices and imports: T. Larsson, *Reformen i brännvinslagstiftningen 1854–1855* (Stockholm, 1945), 559, 562; rye prices: Chapter 5, *Appendix 2* above, and T. Larsson, *Reformen i brännvinslagstiftningen 1854–1855*, 563.

potatoes. As a result of this profits improved, stimulating the establishment of steam distilleries with increasing returns to scale. As the processes of grain and brännvin diverged, it now for the first time was possible for basic foodstuffs to be scarce while brännvin was plentiful and cheap.[67]

The reduction in the price of brännvin, relative to the price of rye, is illustrated by figure 8.16. The relative price of brännvin to rye clearly declined in the long term up to 1850. The figure also exhibits the imports of brännvin to Stockholm from other areas in Sweden. Though there were some big distilleries in the counties surrounding Stockholm, even more was imported from the counties of Malmöhus and Kristianstad in southernmost Sweden. The period from the mid

[67] T. Larsson, *Reformen i brännvinslagstiftningen 1854–1855. Förhistorien* (Stockholm, 1945) provides a thorough treatment of the technological, economic, and political aspects of the brännvin question of the time. The opinion against unrestricted distilling was strengthened by the substantial rise in grain prices in connection with the Crimean War. On the riots and demonstrations of the mid 1850s see R. Karlbom, *Hungerupplopp och strejker 1793–1867* (Gothenburg, 1967).

1830s to the mid 1840s, in particular, is characterized by growing imports parallel with low brännvin prices. The diverging curves of imports and prices suggest that supplies of brännvin must have been plentiful. This evidence is not inconsistent with the hypothesis that low prices stimulated consumption of brännvin.

It is probably correct to characterize the decades preceding 1855 as the heyday of Swedish alcoholism, as is often done in the literature.[68] This judgement takes not only consumption of alcohol into account but also the fact that alcoholism increasingly was seen to be a form of deviant behaviour during the later nineteenth century, condemned not only by the authorities and the temperance movement but also by the labour organizations.

Before the mid nineteenth century this change in the perception of drinking had hardly begun.[69] The importance of drinking as part of social life in Stockholm during the stagnation, contributing to a more general irregularity of life, should have been reinforced by the demographic tendencies involving a growing proportion of unmarried men.

However, we do not think that the sex mortality differential in general and for tuberculosis and dropsy in particular can be explained by referring to alcoholism alone. If it had been determined by that factor only, we should have had some indications of a similar phenomenon in other European cities as well. Male alcoholism was not confined to Stockholm exclusively.

In the General Registrar's 1840 report, cause-specific death rates for a number of cities with different characteristics were presented, unfortunately crude rates only. The English pattern was far from uniform. London and Birmingham had a significant male disadvantage in tuberculosis mortality. In cities dominated by the textile industry, such as Manchester or Leeds, the differential was either insignificant or to the disadvantage of women (table 8.9).

68 See Horgby, *Den disciplinerade arbetaren*, chapter 4, for references to the literature.

69 The dissolution of the pre-industrial pattern of drinking in Stockholm during the latter part of the nineteenth century is discussed by S. Sperlings, 'Violent criminality and social control during Stockholm's industrialization', *Scandinavian Studies in Criminology* 7 (1980).

The traditional attitude saw liquor as a healthy beverage providing the strength necessary for heavy outdoor work. During the 1870s the sale of alcohol was reorganized, partly as a response to the industrial employers' complaints about heavy drinking among the labourers. The number of pubs was limited and business hours restricted. The aim of the authorities to transfer the sale of alcohol from the taverns to retail trade was largely successful, and at the same time overall consumption was reduced. Patterns of consumption also changed from brännvin to beer. Yet, due to stricter police supervision (and better resources in terms of personnel), the number of persons sentenced for drunkenness grew markedly during the second half of the century.

Table 8.9 *Mortality from respiratory tuberculosis in London, Birmingham, Liverpool, Manchester, and Leeds, 1838 and Stockholm, 1821/30 (Deaths per 10,000).*

	Men	Women	Difference
London	45.1	37.7	7.4
Birmingham	52.6	41.0	11.6
Liverpool	59.5	57.1	2.4
Manchester	54.9	54.8	0.1
Leeds	44.0	47.7	−3.7
Stockholm	116.7	73.0	43.7

Sources: *Second Report of the Registrar General* (1840); G. Sundbärg, 'Dödligheten i lungtuberkulos i Sverige åren 1751/1830', *Statistisk Tidskrift*, 1905.

In the English example it seems as if the structure of the local labour market was a more important factor behind the mortality differential than possible differences in ways of life. Obviously, it is not possible to attribute the extreme male rate in general and for tuberculosis in particular to a single factor. Nonetheless, we think it is in the interplay between the economic and social context and the factors at the individual level that we ought to look for possible explanations. The more unstable conditions in the male labour market may have served to maintain a more destructive life-style than we find among females. The growing barriers to family formation, expressed in a secularly declining nuptiality, are likely to have hurt males in active ages more than females (at old age, on the other hand, poverty data presented in chapters 4 and 6 rather suggest that the females were the most disadvantaged). There are indications that male mortality was lower among married (controlling for age), while the reverse is sometimes true for women. In terms of health (linked to a less destructive life style?), males probably were those gaining most from marriage. Declining nuptiality then should have had greater detrimental effects on males than on females.[70]

[70] For the later part of the nineteenth century, data for Stockholm by marital status very clearly show the lower mortality among married males as among unmarried in the same age groups, whereas mortality among females was little affected by marriage. The earliest published statistics are for the period 1871–80, when mortality in the age group 35–40 was as follows (per 1,000):

	Males	Females
Unmarried	41.1	13.8
Married	21.3	12.8
Widows/widowers	31.9	16.2

Source: *Statistisk årsbok för Stockholms stad* 38 (Stockholm, 1905), 86.

Mortality among married males thus was only half as high than among unmarried males, while the differential with regard to the females was rather insignificant. In terms of mortality, the males were gaining most from marriage.

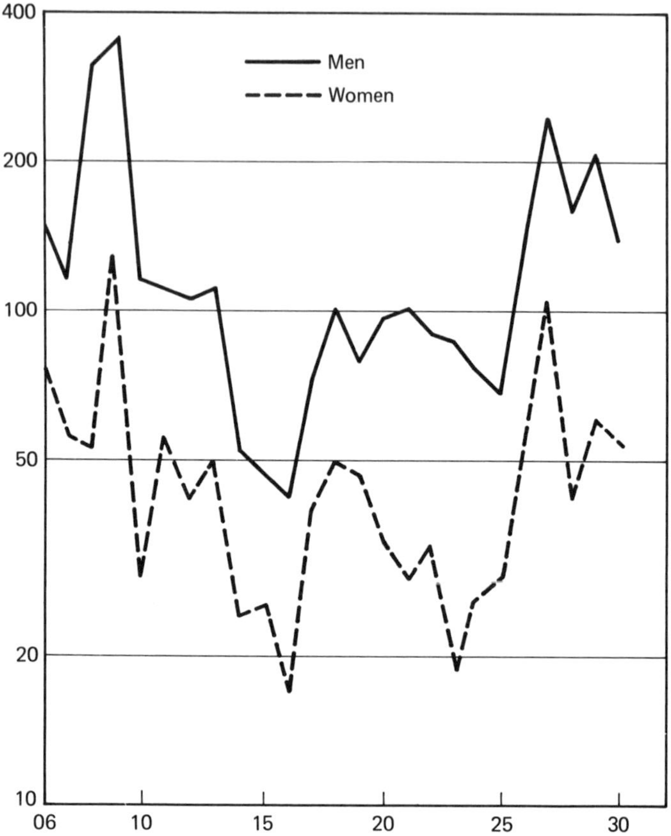

Figure 8.17 Mortality from fevers in Stockholm 1806/30 in the age group 25–49. Deaths per 10,000. *Source*: See *figure 8.14*.

The third big cause of death, fevers of all kinds, can be used as an additional indicator of the vulnerable position of adult men in nineteenth-century Stockholm. Under this vague headline both epidemic and endemic diseases were hidden. The differential was almost the same in years of heavy epidemics as under more normal conditions. Epidemics did hit men harder. When conditions improved, male mortality decreased at a slower rate than female (figure 8.17). Males

The figures for widows and widowers once more indicate the female disadvantage at old age suggested above. In all the active age groups, mortality among widows exceeded that of unmarried and married women. Mortality among widowers on the other hand was substantially lower than among unmarried men, but higher than among the married. It is tempting to link the large male mortality differences by civil status to the greater regularity of life imposed by marriage.

thus must have been more exposed to infections. Probably their resistance was weaker. A factor that can be explained by a way of life more injurious to their health than that of women. However, the exposure to infections was also to a large extent a function of economic and social forces outside the command of the individual.

The specificities of the mortality pattern in eighteenth- and nineteenth century Stockholm

In spite of Mols' pioneering works on European cities from the fourteenth to eighteenth centuries and recent impressive progress, urban demography has been a rather underdeveloped field compared with what has been accomplished on rural societies.[71] Wrigley and Schofield's *The Population History of England 1541–1841*, for example, is essentially a history of rural England. Of course there are completely rational reasons for this state of affairs. The sources normally available to the prospective urban demographer are exceptionally time consuming. This is perhaps an important reason why urban demographic studies often have the form of monographs. When comparisons are made, they mostly have been concerned with urban/rural differentials on the national level. As we have noticed earlier the same kind of explanations have frequently been used for different cities with highly different rates of mortality to account for this urban/rural mortality gap. To a certain extent the monographers of specific cities do not seem to be aware of how much urban death rates diverged in nineteenth-century Europe.

In particular the first part of the nineteenth century constitutes a privileged period for comparative studies in European urban demography. From that epoch we have acceptable and rather easily accessible data for a fairly large number of European towns. On the other hand, to a large extent most European town dwellers faced the same kind of overcrowding, inadequate sanitary conditions, etc. On the whole this was a pre-sanitary reform era. Hence, in a number of strategic dimensions the citizens of urban Europe were struggling against the same problems, those threatening their health and condemning them to an early death. Still, the cities were not equally unsuccessful. By comparing them we can at least get a rough idea of what was to be considered as a common urban disadvantage and what were the specific traits of each city.

Many towns fit into the picture of Allan Sharlin in his polemic

71 R. J. S. Mols, *Introduction à la démographie historique des villes d'Europe du XIVe au XIXe siècle*, 1–3 (Louvain, 1954–56).

against the conventional view of early modern cities as places of extraordinary mortality. Sharlin maintains the hypothesis that mortality was usually higher in towns, though not so much higher as to justify the image of the city as an inordinately unhealthy environment that acted as a brake on population growth.[72] On the whole, Sharlin's view is confirmed in my sample of English cities, and country districts 1838/44. Adult men in the English cities, both industrial and non-industrial, had a moderately higher mortality than their rural counterparts until the age of 44. Women in non-industrial cities in ages 25–34 in fact had a lower death rate than their rural sisters. In the age group 45–54 urban male mortality exceeded the rural one by more than 50 per cent. In the ages 25 to 54 the sex-specific mortality differential was as shown in table 8.10.

In this rather idyllic picture of nineteenth-century cities, Stockholm and Vienna did constitute really deviant cases. In Vienna a larger share of total mortality can be attributed to infant and child mortality than in Stockholm, at least in the period 1810–60.[73] As we have shown, the most specific trait of the mortality pattern in Stockholm is the extremely high male mortality in the age group 25–49. Hence, the kind of explanations used to account for the urban/rural mortality gap in a number of monographic studies on different European cities are clearly insufficient in the case of Stockholm. A more complex approach stressing combinations of a broader spectrum of different factors is needed.

Concluding comments

The thrust of the discussion has been to play down the importance of economic influences on the demographic system of Stockholm. As far as short-run relationships are concerned, such links are certainly weaker in Stockholm than in Sweden and in the other investigated countries (with the exception of fertility in France). Stockholm exhibits a situation in which economic and demographic systems are comparatively independent. Moreover, relationships between various demographic variables are less close than in Sweden as a whole. Medium-term economic-demographic cycles probably exist but are unlikely to account for a major part of the vital rates behaviour.

With regard to long-term demographic change in Stockholm, estab-

72 A. Sharlin, 'Natural decrease in early modern cities: a reconsideration', *Past and Present* 79 (1978).

73 The share of persons under the age of 10 of total deaths in Vienna in the period 1810–59 was 46.1 per cent versus 37.5 per cent in Stockholm.

Table 8.10 *Sex-specific mortality differentials in non-industrial cities, industrial cities, and country districts, England 1838/44.*

Age group		Non-industrial cities	Industrial cities	Country districts
25/34	men	11.5	10.5	9.1
	women	9.5	11.2	11.4
35/44	men	15.5	13.6	10.4
	women	12.5	14.6	12.4
45/55	men	21.8	21.3	14.1
	women	14.4	18.6	14.1

lishing close links with economic change is not an easy matter. It is tempting to connect the secular decline in nuptiality and the rise in bastardy, dramatic during the last decades of the eighteenth century, with de-industrialization, employment problems, and falling real wages. While there probably is something in this interpretation, there are strong reasons to believe that much of the demographic change is not attributable to measurable economic change. The analysis of short-term variation provides little support for the hypothesis of a strong economic impact on nuptiality and bastardy. The very different response in bastardy between Stockholm and the country as a whole during the second half of the eighteenth century, although the real wage decline was about the same, rather suggests that the flexibility of social norms of sexual and family behaviour was critical.

For Geneva, Perrenoud observes a similar negligible short-term relationship between prices and mortality ($r_{xy} = 0.14$ for the period 1750–87)[74] as for Stockholm. Perhaps the loosely coupled economic-demographic system of Stockholm is compatible with a view of the pre-industrial urban economy which emphasizes the precariousness of large segments of the urban population (certainly larger than the wage-labouring groups), producing a life-style with short planning horizons and an apparent unresponsiveness to changing economic circumstances, at least in the short run.

The strengthening of the informal sector in the Stockholm economy during the latter part of the eighteenth century may well have modified and weakened the extent to which the lower stratum behaved according to the ideal type of the low-pressure system, e.g., postpon-

[74] A. Perrenoud, *La population de Genève du seizième au début du dix-neuvième siècle* (Geneva, 1977), 421.

ing marriages when the formal economy experienced a downswing. The relative unpredictability of demographic behaviour, differing from contemporary Sweden, Finland, England, and France, could well be seen as an expression of such a situation.

Regarding Malthusian mechanisms, we believe hypotheses of low-pressure or high-pressure systems benefit from being discussed in a comparative perspective and in more continuous terms than by reference to simple dichotomies only. Economic-demographic systems were not simply either high-pressure or low-pressure. As has been demonstrated above, they were low-pressure or high-pressure to quite varying degrees. Finland thus displays more of low-pressure characteristics than do Sweden and England. France constitutes more of a high-pressure system although being far from the ideal type exhibiting a mortality very sensitive to economic fluctuations.

Stockholm, finally, is the case that fits least well into either of these categories. It was less of a low-pressure system than the others while simultaneously being less of a high-pressure one, too. The classification into low- or high-pressure types should thus be supplemented by another dimension referring to the overall strength of relationships between economic and demographic fluctuations. In this latter dimension, Stockholm ranks lowest among the systems explored above, although there may be some reasons to expect that other pre-industrial urban economies will turn out not to be very dissimilar in this respect.

9

A stagnating capital

The previous chapters have analysed several aspects of the long stagnation that Stockholm experienced between the mid eighteenth and the mid nineteenth centuries. It is time to summarize the main conclusions.

The comparative perspective has highlighted the processes where Stockholm is very much a part of a wider European world economy, as well as phenomena which are unusual or unique to the Swedish capital. One of the most fundamental aspects in which Stockholm follows the broader European patterns is with regard to the long eighteenth-century inflation, the rise in agricultural prices, and the corresponding real wage decline. Although Stockholm was economically stagnating, the extent of the depression in real wages was not much stronger than in rural Sweden, and in the comparative European perspective the capital is rather in the middle of the scale. The real wage decline of the eighteenth century is thus not to be seen as generated by economic stagnation.

Unlike several other European towns, however, there does not appear to have been any marked rise in inequality in eighteenth-century Stockholm. On the contrary, the tendency towards levelling was predominant among owners of real estate. The regression of the economic position of the nobility is the main factor. No urban bourgeoisie was accumulating sufficient resources so as to advance to an equally prominent position enjoyed by the old nobility.

There are also indications of an eighteenth-century levelling in income distribution in the sense that the salaries of civil and military functionaries in Stockholm deteriorated more than did the daily wages of unskilled and skilled labourers. The labourers thus were approaching the functionaries during a great part of the eighteenth century (continuing up to about 1810). Even though the labourers suffered from the downward pressure on real wages, the functionaries lost even more.

In other words, there were tendencies towards levelling in the distribution of real estate as well as in the distribution of earnings (narrowing gaps between labourers and functionaries) in the capital during the eighteenth century. These egalitarian tendencies, rather than the real wage decline, should probably to some extent be seen as an expression of the stagnation of the capital, limiting possibilities of accumulation at the same time as investments in other regions and branches (e.g., from the iron-producing districts) appeared more attractive.

During the period from about 1810 to mid century, on the other hand, there are several indications that inequality widened. After lagging behind for a long time, the day of the functionaries had come. Skill rewards were rising, the pay gaps increasing between functionaries and labourers (and between skilled and unskilled labour). The inegalitarian trend was further strengthened as the real estate market of the capital (as well as of rural Sweden) successively grew more exclusive, a decreasing proportion being able to acquire real property.

One of the intriguing but elusive consequences of the long stagnation is that it implied an informalization of the urban economy. This probably involved a growing proportion of people ekeing out their livings in a wide range of activities outside the guilds and the regular service sector, often on the borderline of legality. Another side of the informalization is the decreasing size of factories. The manufacturing sector failed to develop into a basis for the subsequent industrialization in the latter part of the nineteenth century.

The eighteenth-century deterioration of labourers' wages as well as of salaries in the public sector also must have stimulated various forms of combinations of employments and side activities. The labour markets facing males and females were different, the males to a higher degree being affected by seasonal unemployment.

Stockholm possessed a peculiar demographic structure in which the extremely high mortality is a key phenomenon. There are two intriguing and interrelated phenomena here. One is the high mortality rate, the other is its age- and sex-specific structure involving a marked excess mortality among males in active ages. In the active ages 25–50 years, male mortality often was twice as high as in other European cities, whereas female mortality in the same age span differed far less from a more general international pattern.

Poor sanitary conditions is one of the classical explanations often mentioned in the Stockholm literature, widespread drinking is another. The first could in principle help in explaining the high level of mortality but hardly the sex-specific structure of mortality. The unsatisfactory habitations, the foul drinking water, the uncleaned gutters, and the lakes of filth, the 'endless dirt' of which contemporaries complained, should have affected females as much as males.[1] The stress of alcoholism is on the other hand better suited towards explaining excess male mortality. Sometimes the high mortality is linked to the poverty of the population.

In a comparative perspective, however, important objections can be raised against all of these hypotheses. It is by no means clear that sanitary conditions were worse in Stockholm than in many other urban centres exhibiting a substantially lower mortality. In Stockholm as well as in most other Western European towns, the great sanitarian reforms (e.g., the construction of a sewage system) were not carried out until the decades following the mid nineteenth century. Unusually unhealthy sanitary conditions also should have augmented infant mortality, but this was not at a remarkably high level in Stockholm.[2] Similarly, it cannot easily be demonstrated that drinking should have been more of a hazard to health in the Swedish capital than in many other places which do not exhibit the same adverse mortality pattern.

Neither does a focus on poverty or standards of living among the majority of the population seem very fruitful. Though Stockholm appears to have been a relatively poor place by national standards in the mid nineteenth century, at least one of the dominating causes of death among the adult population, tuberculosis, was not a simple effect of low nutritional standards. Short-term mortality fluctuations also are, as was shown in chapter 8, practically unrelated to real wage change. The lowest real wage level among labourers as well as among functionaries was around 1800, when there are strong indications that real wages and salaries had declined substantially for several decades. Yet, mortality levels were fairly stable in the long term from the mid eighteenth century up to 1860 (chapters 5 and 8 above). While death rates were highest in the poor parish of Katarina, and clearly lower in the more well-to-do districts, the connection between living standards and mortality can hardly have been a very direct one.

1 For one small example of the lack of hygienic measures see the complaint of a female silver polisher in July, 1800 that bread she had bought from the baker Wennberg contained a rat baked into it, 'from which an evil taste arose'. The baker had to pay a fine to the woman. Överståthållarämbetets arkiv. Äldre poliskammaren, diarier, Stockholm City Archive.

2 Infant mortality in Stockholm, as was shown in chapter 8 above, reduced from about 1750 to 1810, and remained approximately constant during the next half-century. There is little to support an argument that sanitarian conditions should have worsened during the century after 1750.

The real wage trends do not capture the changing structure of earnings that can be expected to have accompanied the expansion of the informal sector.[3] As noted in the previous chapters, the legal restrictions pertaining to informal activities probably were less of a hindrance to various odd jobs among the females than among males. Industrialization, primarily a matter of the decline of the dominating textile factories, should have affected females more than males. We may assume that female involvement in small-scale, labour-intensive informal sector activities was growing, perhaps culminating in the 1840s.

Two consequences are likely to have followed, as was argued in chapters 4 and 8. First, those females who could provide for themselves were less dependent and interested in formal marriage. The 'Stockholm marriage' as a form of extralegal cohabitation became more common, but sexual relations without cohabitation may also have seemed more attractive than previously. Illegitimacy rose substantially from the later decades of the eighteenth century, exhibiting an inverted U curve with a maximum in the 1840s when more than 40 per cent of the children were born out of wedlock (see figure 4.4).

Second, the women paid a price for their heavier work-load in terms of their physical health as well as of their children. One of the measurable indicators is an increase in the proportion of still-born children, reaching its highest level in the 1840s. Maternal mortality was also high at this period, and unlike Sweden as a whole the proportion of deceased in childbirth in the capital did not decline during the first half of the nineteenth century. The differential in infant mortality between legitimate and illegitimate children was large and tended to widen in the 1830s and 1840s.

Still, the changes in maternal and infant mortality do not address the problem of the basic characteristics of Stockholm mortality, the overall high level and the excess male mortality.

Other, less discussed hypotheses have to be considered. Regarding the level of mortality, chapter 2 above pointed to the high rates of

[3] Real wage measurements refer to the formal sector only but, as was pointed out in chapter 5 above, employment levels and trends are unknown (though some seasonal patterns can be established as in figure 4.1). We do not have any systematic information on informal sector incomes or employment. If we assume that the informal sector expanded from the later eighteenth to the mid-nineteenth century while no income data can be obtained for this sector, the consequence is that inference from real wages to standards of living will be successively more problematic during the course of this phase. Stockholm poverty levels are strikingly high by the mid nineteenth century in comparison with other Swedish regions (chapter 6 above), but poverty data are not suited towards establishing long-term trends. This problem is basically one of scarce information, and no real solution seems feasible.

population turnover which served to maintain mortality at a high level in a self-reinforcing way. The incidence of one of the most common causes of death, tuberculosis, was sensitive to exposure. Exposure to disease, which must have been related to the intensity of migration, appears to have been more important than nutritional standards in explaining the spatial variation of tuberculosis.

No doubt, the high mortality was only the tip of an iceberg of widespread poor health among the population, lowering the capacity to work. We should expect the relative disadvantage of the capital with respect to general state of health to have been most prominent among the adults, making it more difficult to achieve economic growth and to meet the competition from more dynamic Swedish regions who adapted more successfully to the changing conditions of the culmination phase of pre-industrial society.

Short-term demographic movements were relatively insensitive to short-term economic fluctuations, suggesting short planning horizons (chapter 8 above). Mortality fluctuations were practically independent of real wage changes, and nuptiality and fertility were only weakly linked to economic swings. To a lesser degree than in rural areas, marriages were postponed as there was a downswing in real wages (largely in connection with bad harvests).

Stockholm thus is very far from Heckscher's picture of the Malthusian demographic system in which economic downturn inevitably multiplied the number of dead. Neither the high level of mortality nor its fluctuations render themselves to a straightforward economic interpretation, at least not in terms of the high-pressure economic-demographic system, with mortality closely linked to economic oscillations, of which Heckscher thought.[4] Neither is the ideal type of the low-pressure system, in which economic swings affect nuptiality and fertility, a good characteristic of the Stockholm case. Though marriages were depressed as part of the stagnation, fertility remained at a fairly constant level during most of the century after 1750. As legitimate births dropped, illegitimate ones rose.

One of the observations that would be difficult to resolve if the economic and demographic systems were not fairly independent of each other is the lack of parallelism between real wages and certain demographic indicators. While real wage data suggest very low levels around 1800, and rising although highly fluctuating levels during the

[4] To a certain extent, though, economic stagnation may be seen as having affected mortality in the long run indirectly through establishing growing barriers to marriage. It can be argued that declining nuptiality was conducive to adult male mortality through permitting more irregular ways of life. This is, however, a far more indirect influence than Heckscher had in mind.

former part of the nineteenth century, the demographic data on the other hand indicate more severe problems shortly before the mid nineteenth century. At least this seems to apply to the situation of the females. It is during this later period, particularly in the 1840s, that marriage rates are at their lowest while illegitimacy and the number of stillborn peak (chapters 4 and 8 above).

The demography of the capital brings mind what Arthur E. Imhof calls a 'system of wastage' as contrasted to a 'system of conservation' of human life, existing side by side.[5] He suggests certain striking German variations in mortality are linked not so much to economic conditions directly as to different mental structures, in turn being shaped by historical events such as the devastating wars of the seventeenth century. Attitudes to life and death have differed, involving the attitudes of parents towards the life and death of their children, the care of which often was neglected in high-mortality regions, but also collective attitudes among the adult population towards themselves as well as others. Though Imhof deals here primarily with infant and maternal mortality, a reasoning along these lines may be fruitful when applied to the characteristic traits of Stockholm's pre-industrial demography as well.

The Stockholm demographic system was wasteful of human life, health, and resources for reasons that cannot be found directly in the economy. In this case, it is not possible to provide a very specific alternative explanation. Mentalities and behaviours were possibly influenced by the irregularity of life and lack of positive prospects, one component of which was a low valuation of life.

The eighteenth-century inflation meant a redistribution of resources from the urban to the rural sector, and within the rural sector from the large-scale agriculture or estate economy to peasant farming. Agrarian growth during the century after 1750 took place primarily within the peasant farming sector. If one single cause of the stagnation is to be singled out as more decisive than any other in the long term, it is the dynamism of the peasant economy. Both the urban-rural and the landed estate-peasant redistribution were disadvantageous to Stockholm's growth, the capital finding itself in the midst of a manorial economy which developed little. One effect of this is the decentralization of economic activity, pointed out by Heckscher, a

5 A. E. Imhof, 'The amazing simultaneousness of the big differences and the boom in the 19th century', in *Pre-Industrial Population Change*, ed. T. Bengtsson *et al.* (Stockholm, 1984). See also Imhof, 'Unterschiedliche Einstellung zu Leib und Leben in der Neuzeit', in *Der Mensch und sein Körper von der Antike bis heute*, hrsg. A. E. Imhof (Munich, 1983).

number of smaller Swedish and Finnish towns expanding and enlarging their shares of domestic and foreign trade.

The lagging behind of Stockholm's economic growth relative to that of agrarian Sweden can be thought of to some extent as having generated an informal sector in the capital. Even though the burghers, strongly anti-liberal in their conception of economic policy, tried to protect themselves by means of monopoly rights, they could not prevent numerous infringements on their spheres. The bitter complaints of the small merchants sometimes amount to, as it were, a catalogue of those areas in which they were unable to provide the inhabitants of the capital with goods and services in an efficient way.

In 1774 and 1779, for instance, the merchants requested that there must be an end to the actions of pedlars and tradesmen from Västergötland and peasants from Hälsingland, dealing in linen and other textile produce from the cottage industry.[6] Likewise, the garrison soldiers (working with handicrafts without belonging to the guilds) and female small-scale vendors should be stopped. All these were underbidding the Stockholm burghers, and the merchants also pointed out that the low prices of their competitors depended upon their cheating with the quality of the goods. 'Disloyal' competition must be done away with. After having observed that their market suffered from a lack of natural growth, the merchants reached the conclusion that the number of merchants must be legally restricted (*numerus clausus*).[7]

There is certainly no reason to doubt that many Stockholm craftsmen and other burghers were in difficulties (see chapter 5 above on the

[6] On the peasant trade in linen see K. Ullenhag, *Sörkörare; bönder med lärft på lassen från norra Ångermanland 1750–1850* (Bjästa 1982). The peasants, producing linen as a labour-intensive, domestic industry, were supposed to sell their goods to the Stockholm linen merchants. In practice, however, the merchants often were bypassed as the peasants sold directly to the consumer. Stockholm merchants repeatedly demanded that linen be sold only in certain places in the capital and not as free street vending. Restrictions remained until the 1850s. The peasant linen trade probably culminated during the 1830s and 1840s. See also G. Utterström, *Jordbrukets arbetare II* (Stockholm, 1957), 60ff.

[7] Boëthius, *Magistraten och borgerskapeti Stockholm 1719–1815* (Stockholm, 1943), 447ff. Another source of dissatisfaction among the Stockholm burghers was the Finnish peasants and small burghers who sailed to Stockholm in small vessels selling agricultural products, firewood, and tar. The peasants had legal rights (extended in 1766) to go to Sweden in order to exchange or market 'their own produce', but not more. In practice, however, this trade assumed larger proportions, the peasants exporting more or less anything they could get their hands on, bringing back to Finland those goods which were cheaper in Stockholm than in the Finnish towns. This rural-urban trade had been well established since medieval times, and was an important activity for the Finnish coastal provinces. See K. Samuelsson, 'Den ekonomiska betydelsen för Stockholm av Finlands förlust', *Forum navale* 6 (1945).

growth problems of the handicrafts of the capital). This fact was generally acknowledged in government circles, making it much easier for the burghers of the capital to maintain their plea for protective regulation. Nevertheless, the animated defence of mercantilist policies underlines the reality of the changing and sharpening interregional competition. County merchants and county craftsmen were constantly perceived as a disorganizing menace to the established order. Far from wishing to compete on equal terms, the merchants advocated the contrary policy of strengthening the mercantilistic division between town and country. Their vision of economic life as divided into stable, closed categories, protected from possible external disturbances, has solidly medieval qualities. Urban economic stagnation, accompanied by relative regional retrogression, within the framework of mercantilist policies was bound to lead to black-market-type problems.

A long-term stagnation over nearly a century, without any abrupt economic or demographic crisis, is unusual in the European perspective. Unlike the dramatic crises that several French cities experienced, for instance, Stockholm's difficulties were largely unconnected with war or revolution. None of the three wars that Sweden was engaged in during our period of investigation (the Prussian war 1756–63, the Russian wars of 1788–90 and 1808–9) affected Stockholm directly. Neither did the loss of Finland in 1809 lead to any marked decline in the Finnish trade. Throughout this volume, focus has been on more long-term processes. The long-term evolution of the wider Swedish regional framework is one of the processes that must be kept in mind.

The fact that Stockholm's demographic growth was weak does not mean that the capital played a minor part in the wider regional economic or demographic development. On the contrary, the high mortality made it possible for Stockholm to absorb very large numbers of migrants, primarily from the neighbouring counties of the lake Mälaren valley.[8]

The migratory movements to Stockholm at the same time enabled the agricultural system of the lake Mälaren plains to continue to exist in stable form, even though agrarian growth there was comparatively slow. Because of migration to Stockholm there arose no strong pressures on the manorial economy of the surrounding counties to provide institutional arrangements to absorb their growing populations. Few marginal farming units could emerge of the type common

[8] U. Jonsson, 'Population growth and agrarian economic and social structures: some Swedish examples', in *Pre-Industrial Population Change*, ed. T. Bengtsson *et al.* (Stockholm, 1984).

in other parts of the country dominated by small peasants. The paternalistic ideology and the traditional forms of labour rent, with a prominent place for service tenants in the organization of work, could continue to exist well into the second half of the nineteenth century. Large-scale operations based on wage labour were not the ordinary pattern. Out-migration thus played an important part in the solution to the classical dilemma of the large landed estate: 'to extract as large as possible an economic surplus from the property while maintaining social stability'.[9]

In terms of industrialization, Stockholm's adaptation to economic realities was late but successful. During the latter part of the nineteenth century, the comparative advantages of the capital were increasingly exploited. Relatively capital- and skill-intensive sectors such as mechanical engineering and printing grew in importance, in contrast to the previous dominance of textile manufacturing. In the industrial upswing, the enterprises establishing themselves had to face rising urban prices of sites and real property, or move somewhere else. This stimulated industries with a relatively high value added per worker. The gains from being at the centre of communications grew, the new Stockholm industries being comparatively technologically advanced. The introduction of steam and later electricity favoured a capital lacking water power.[10] The poorest districts of the city gained most from the improving conditions, at least in terms of mortality which was reduced most drastically in parishes such as Katarina.[11]

The informal sector is likely to have been reduced in importance. One of the major gains of industrialization was not only the growth in real wages, which was sustained after about 1860 (real wages of unskilled labourers approximately trebled from 1860 to 1914), but also the creation of more stable conditions of employment.[12] Stockholm emerged as a centre of industrial innovation. It cannot be said, however, that Stockholm was leading the upturn that is noticeable from the mid nineteenth century. One factor contributing to the upswing is the changing regional pattern of agrarian economic growth, in which the lake Mälaren valley, after a long period of stagnation at a relatively high level, became more dynamic after the mid nineteenth century.

[9] Quoted from U. Jonsson, *Jordmagnater, landbönder och torpare i sydöstra Södermanland 1800–1880* (Stockholm, 1980), 221.

[10] I. Hammarström, *Stockholm i svensk ekonomi 1850–1914* (Stockholm, 1970).

[11] Mortality data by parish are reported annually in *Statistisk årsbok för Stockholms stad*.

[12] On the growth in real wages 1860–1930 in Sweden as well as in Stockholm see G. Bagge *et al.*, *Wages in Sweden 1860–1930* (London, 1933), and *Kommunalarbetarnas löner i Sverige 1865–1930* (Stockholm, 1933).

Similarly, as during the stagnation period, several intertwined processes were at work, but now they served to generate rather than hamper growth and development. While a set of mutually interlocking and reinforcing mechanisms (changing relative prices detrimental to the urban economy, de-industrialization, high mortality and poor health, mercantilist economic policies) prolonged the stagnation, another set of interrelated forces worked in a positive direction after the mid nineteenth century. In both phases, the major processes influencing the course of development are to be found not in the urban economy itself but outside it.

Bibliography

UNPUBLISHED SOURCES

Riksarkivet (RA)

Ekonomisk-historiska institutionens deposition
  Eli F. Heckscher's collection
Kommerskollegii arkiv
  Fabriksberättelser
  Städernas priskuranter
Överståthållarens skrivelser till Kungl. Maj:t

Statistiska Centralbyråns (SCB) arkiv

Äldre tabellkommissionens arkiv
  Folkmängdstabeller
  Mortalitetstabeller

Stockholm City Archive (SSA)

Brandvaktskasseadministrationens arkiv
  Taxeringslängder
  Trakt- och kvarterslistor
Byggnadskontorets arkiv
  Huvudböcker med verifikationer
Börs-, bro- och hamnbyggnadskommitterades arkiv
  Huvudböcker med verifikationer
Grosshandelssocietetens arkiv
  Handlingar rörande spannmålspriser 1784–96
Hall- och manufakturrättens arkiv
  Fabriksberättelser
Handelskollegiets arkiv
  Protokoll
Justitiekollegiets arkiv
  Bouppteckningar
Karl XII:s kontributionsarkiv
  Skattningslängder
Katarina församlings kyrkoarkiv
  Avflyttningslängder
Magistraten och rådhusrätten
  Ingående konkursdiarier

Politi-, ämbets- och byggningskollegii arkiv
Protokoll angående hyrkusk- och åkaretaxor samt taxor å bröd, kött mm
Stadskamrerarens arkiv
Stockholms stads verifikationer
Ämbets- och byggningskollegii arkiv
Taxor m fl handlingar rörande prissättning
Överståthållarämbetet (ÖÄ) för uppbördsärenden
Huvudböcker med verifikationer
Kronotaxeringslängder
Mantalslängder
Överståthållarämbetets arkiv
Äldre poliskammaren, diarier

PUBLICATIONS

Abel, W., *Geschichte der deutschen Landwirtschaft vom frühen Mittelalter bis zum 19. Jahrhundert*. Stuttgart, 1962.
Massenarmut und Hungerkrisen im vorindustriellen Europa. Hamburg, 1974.
Agricultural Fluctuations in Europe from the Thirteenth to the Twentieth Century, 3rd edn. London, 1980.
Abrams, P., 'Towns and economic growth: some theories and problems', in *Towns in Societies*, eds. P. Abrams and E. A. Wrigley. Cambridge, 1979.
Acerbi, G., *Travels Through Sweden, Finland, and Lapland, to the North Cape*. London, 1802.
Adamson, R., *Järnavsättning och bruksfinansiering 1800–1860*. Gothenburg, 1966.
Adolfsson, R., 'Arbetsmarknad och geografisk rörlighet', in *Ett militärt stadsproletariat*, ed. G. Artéus. Stockholm, 1988.
Adolfsson, R., Brick, O. and Dahlström, J., 'Garnisonen, staden och källmaterialet', in *Ett militärt stadsproletariat*, ed. G. Artéus. Stockholm, 1988.
Ahlberg, G., *Stockholms befolkningsutveckling efter 1850*. Stockholm, 1958.
Alexander, J. K., 'The city of brotherly fear; the poor in late eighteenth-century Philadelphia', in *Cities in American History*, ed. K. T. Jackson and S. K. Schultz. New York, 1972.
Almquist, J. E., 'Om kontributionsränteriet', *Karolinska förbundets årsbok* 1917.
Almquist, J. A., 'Kommerskollegium och riksens ständers manufakturkontor samt konsulsstaten', *Meddelanden från svenska Riksarkivet, N.F.*, 4. Stockholm, 1912–15.
Alsne, S., *Från prästtionden till reglerad lön; pastoraliekonventionerna i Uppsala ärkestift 1810–1862*. Uppsala, 1966.
Anckarsvärd, D., 'Stockholm 1789–90 skildrat av en polsk kanik', *Sankt Eriks årsbok* 1933.
Anderson, M., *Family Structure in Nineteenth-Century Lancashire*. Cambridge, 1971.
Anderson, P., *Lineages of the Absolutist State*. London, 1974.
Annual Report of the Registrar General IV–IX. London, 1841–1848.
Armstrong, A., *Stability and Change in an English County Town; A Social Study of York, 1801–51*. Cambridge, 1974.
Artéus, G., *Krigsmakt och samhälle i frihetstidens Sverige*. Stockholm, 1982.
Austin, P. B., *The Life and Songs of Carl Michael Bellman*. Malmö, 1967.

Ayçoberry, P., 'Probleme der Sozialschichtung in Köln im Zeitalter der Frühindustrialisierung', in *Wirtschafts- und Sozialgeschichte der frühen Industrialisierung.*
L'histoire sociale de la ville de Cologne, 1. Lille, 1980.
Ågren, K., 'The Reduktion', in *Sweden's Age of Greatness*, ed. M. Roberts. London, 1973.
Baar, L., *Die Berliner Industrie in der Industriellen Revolution.* Berlin, 1966.
'Probleme der Industriellen Revolution in grosstädtischen Industriezentern: das Berliner Beispiel', in *Wirtschafts- und Sozialgeschichtliche Probleme der frühen Industrialisierung*, ed. W. Fischer. Berlin, 1968.
Baars, C., 'Boukhoudingen van landbouwbedrijven in de Koeksewaard mit de zeventidende en achttiende eeuw', *A. A. G. Bijdragen* 19 (1975).
Baehrel, R., *Une croissance: La Basse-Provence rurale (fin du XVIe siècle-1789).* Paris, 1961.
Bagge, G., Lundberg, E., and Svennilsson, I., *Wages in Sweden 1860–1930.* London, 1933.
Bardet, J.-P., *Rouen aux XVIIe et XVIIIe siècles*, 1. Paris, 1983.
Baulant, M., 'Le prix des grains à Paris de 1431 à 1788', *Annales E. S. C.* 23 (1968).
Befolkningsforholdene i Danmark i det 19. aarhundrede. Copenhagen, 1905.
Behre, G., Larsson, L.-O., and Österberg, E., *Sveriges historia 1521–1809.* Stockholm, 1985.
Bengtsson, T. and Ohlsson, R., 'Population and economic fluctuations in Sweden 1749–1914', in *Pre-industrial Population Change. The Mortality Decline and Short-term Population Movements*, ed. T. Bengtsson, G. Fridlizius and R. Ohlsson. Lund, 1984.
Berg, F. T., 'Om folkräkningen i Stockholm vid utgången av året 1860', *Statistisk tidskrift* 1 (1862).
'Statistiska minnesblad öfver Stockholm', *Statistisk tidskrift* 3 (1869).
Berg, G., 'Boskapsskötsel och jordbruk i det gamla Stockholm', *Sankt Eriks årsbok*, 1932.
Berg, L. O., 'Hall- och manufakturrätten i Stockholm', *Stockholms stads arkivnämnd och stadsarkiv. Årsberättelse*, 1967.
Bergh, S., 'Svenska Riksarkivet 1618–1837', *Meddelanden från svenska Riksarkivet, N.F., II:5.* Stockholm, 1916.
Bezucha, R., *The Lyon Uprising of 1834.* Cambridge, Mass., 1974.
Bidrag till Sveriges officiella statistik A) Befolkningsstatistik 1851–1855, andra afdelningen. Stockholm, 1859.
Bidrag till Sveriges officiella statistik A) Befolkningsstatistik 1856–1860. Stockholm, 1863–5.
Birbeck, C., 'Self-employed proletarians in an informal factory: the case of Cali's garbage dump', *World Development* 6 (1978).
Björkman, J. O., *Bonde och tjänstehjon; om social stratifiering i äldre svensk agrarbygd.* Uppsala, 1974.
Blayo, Y., 'Mouvement naturel de la population française de 1740 a 1829', *Population* 30 (1975).
Bloomberg, S. E., Fox, M. F., Warner, R. M., and Warner Jr., S. B., 'A census probe into nineteenth-century family history: Southern Michigan, 1850–1880', *Journal of Social History* 5 (1971).

Blumin, S., 'Mobility and change in ante-bellum Philadelphia', in *Nineteenth-century cities*, ed. S. Thernstrom and R. Sennett. New Haven and London, 1969.

Boëthius, B., *Magistraten och borgerskapet i Stockholm 1719–1815*. Stockholm, 1943.

'New light on eighteenth century Sweden', *Scandinavian Economic History Review* 1 (1953).

Bowley, A. L., 'The statistics of wages in the United Kingdom during the last hundred years, Part VIII. Wages in the building trades – London', *Journal of the Royal Statistical Society* 64 (1901).

Braudel, F., *Les structures du quotidien: le possible et l'impossible*. Paris, 1979.

Brick, O., 'Familjebildning och dödlighet', in *Ett militärt stadsproletariat*, ed. G. Artéus. Stockholm, 1988.

Brolin, P.-E., *Hattar och mössor i borgarståndet 1760–1766*. Uppsala, 1953.

Broomé, B., 'Om register och andra hjälpmedel för forskare i Stockholms stadsarkiv', *Stockholms stads arkivnämnd och stadsarkiv. Årsberättelse*, 1942.

Brown, E. H. Phelps and Hopkins, S. V., *A Perspective of Wages and Prices*. London, 1981.

Calhoun, C., *The Question of Class Struggle; Social Foundations of Popular Radicalism during the Industrial Revolution*. Oxford, 1982.

Campbell, Å., *Det svenska brödet; en jämförande etnologisk-historisk undersökning*. Stockholm, 1950.

Carlsson, S., *Ståndssamhälle och ståndspersoner 1700–1865*. Lund, 1973.

'Flyttningsintensiteten i det svenska agrarsamhället', *Turun historiallinen arkisto* 28 (1973).

Fröknar, mamseller, jungfrur och pigor; ogifta kvinnor i det svenska ståndssamhället. Uppsala, 1977.

Cayez, P., 'Une proto-industrialisation decalée: le ruralisation de la soierie lyonnaise dans la première moitié du XIXe siècle', *Revue du Nord* 63 (1981).

Cederquist, J., *Arbetare i strejk*. Stockholm, 1980.

Census of Scotland, 1861, vol 1. Edinburgh 1862.

Census of Great Britain, 1851. Population tables I. London, 1852.

Chandler, T., and Fox, G., *3000 Years of Urban Growth*. New York, 1974.

Chevalier, L., *La formation de la population parisienne au XIXe siècle*. Paris, 1950.

Laboring Classes and Dangerous Classes in Paris during the First Half of the Nineteenth Century. Princeton, N.J., 1973.

Chorley, P., *Oil, Silk and Enlightenment; Economic Problems in Eighteenth Century Naples*. Naples, 1965.

Cochrane, E., *Florence in the Forgotten Centuries 1527–1800*. Chicago and London, 1973.

Confora-Argadona, E., and Guerrand, T. H., *La repartition de la population et les conditions de logement des classes ouvrières à Paris au 19e siècle*. Paris, 1976.

Conzen, C. N., *Immigrant Milwaukee 1836–1860*. Cambridge, Mass., 1976.

Cosemans, A., *Bijdrage tot de demografische en sociale geschiedenis van de stad Brussel 1796–1846*. Liège, 1966.

Crafts, N. F. R., 'British economic growth, 1700–1831: a review of the evidence', *Economic History Review*, 36 (1983).

Dagligt Allehanda. Stockholm, 1770–1850.

Dardel, P., *Commerce, industrie et navigation à Rouen et au Havre au XVIIIe siècle*. Rouen, 1966.

Navires et marchandises dans les ports de Rouen et du Havre au XVIIIe siècle. Paris, 1963.

Daunton, M. J., 'Towns and economic growth in eighteenth-century England', in *Towns and Societies*, eds. P. Abrams and E. A. Wrigley. Cambridge, 1979.

Davidoff, L. and Hall, C., *Family Fortunes. Men and Women of the English Middle Class, 1780–1850*. Chicago, 1987.

Derouet, B., 'Clés pour un système auto-regulateur des populations d'Ancien Régime', *Annales E. S. C.* 35 (1980).

de Vries, J., *The Dutch Rural Economy in the Golden Age*. New Haven and London, 1974.

The Economy of Europe in an Age of Crisis. Cambridge, 1976.

European Urbanisation 1500–1800. London, 1984.

Deyon, P., 'Les registres de capitation d'Amiens au XVIIIe siècle', *Revue du Nord* 1960.

Dhondt, J., 'The cotton industry at Ghent during the French régime', in *Essays in European Economic History 1789–1914*, eds. F. Crouzet, W. H. Chaloner and W. M. Stern. London, 1969.

Dijk, H. van, *Rotterdam 1810–1880*. Schiedam, 1976.

Dokumenten voor de geschiedenis van prijzen en lonen in Vlaanderen 1–2, ed. C. Verlinden. Bruges, 1959–65.

Dreyfus, F. G., *La societé en Rhénanie et particulièrement à Mayence dans la seconde moitié du XVIIIe siècle 1740–1792*. Paris, 1968.

Dupuis, A., 'Bâtiments construits par les Etats', *Cahiers d'histoire des prix* 3 (1958).

Durand, Y., 'Recherches sur les salaires des maçons à Paris au XVIIIe siècle', *Revue d'histoire économique et sociale* 44 (1966).

Economic History of Britain since 1700, vol. 1, eds. R. Floud and D. McCloskey. Cambridge, 1981.

Ehmer, J., 'Produktion und Reproduktion in der Wiener Manufakturperiode', in *Wien im Vormärz*, eds. Banik-Schweitzer, A. Baryli, J. Ehmer, P. Feldbauer, W. Häusler and G. Meissl. Vienna, 1980.

Familienstruktur und Arbeitsorganisation im frühindustriellen Wien. Munich, 1980.

Elmroth, I., *Nyrekryteringen till de högre ämbetena 1720–1809*. Lund, 1962.

För kung och fosterland. Lund, 1981.

Elsas, M. J., *Umriss einer Geschichte der Preise und Löhne in Deutschland, vol. 2A*. Leiden, 1940.

Enequist, G., *Nedre Luledalens byar*. Uppsala, 1937.

Ergebnisse der Volkszählung . . . 1861. Preussische Statistik, 5. Berlin, 1864.

Eriksson, I. and Rogers, J., *Rural Labor and Population Change*. Uppsala, 1978.

Ett militärt stadsproletariat. Studier av garnisonsmanskapets levnadsförhållanden i 1800-talets Stockholm, ed. G. Artéus. Stockholm, 1988. (Meddelanden från Militärhistoriska avdelningen vid Militärhögskolan 4.)

Fällström, A.-M., 'Göteborgs fattigvård från 1800 till 1840', *Göteborg förr och nu* 9, (1974).

'Befolkningens sociala och ekonomiska struktur i Göteborg 1800–1840', *Historisk tidskrift* 94 (1974).

Feinstein, C. H., 'The rise and fall of the Williamson curve', *Journal of Economic History* 48 (1988).

Felloni, G., 'Italy', in *Introduction to the Sources of European Economic History 1500–1800*, eds. C. Wilson and G. Parker, London, 1977.
Fisher, F. J., 'London as an "Engine of Economic Growth"', in *Britain and the Netherlands*, ed. J. S. Bromley. The Hague, 1971.
Forster, R., *The Nobility of Toulouse in the Eighteenth Century*. Baltimore, 1960.
'The noble wine producers of the Bordelais in the eighteenth century', *Economic History Review* 14 (1961).
Foster, J., *Class Struggle and the Industrial Revolution*. London, 1974.
François, E., 'Unterschichten und Armut in rheinischen Residenzstädten des 18. Jahrhunderts', *Vierteljahrschrift für Sozial- und Wirtschaftsgeschichte* 62 (1975).
Frêche, G., *Toulouse et la région Midi-Pyrenées au siècle des lumières (vers 1670–1789)*. Paris, 1974.
Fridholm, M., Isacson, M. and Magnusson, L., *Industrialismens rötter*. Stockholm, 1976.
Fridlizius, G., *Swedish Corn Exports in the Free Trade Era*. Lund, 1957.
The Demographic Transition of Sweden 1750–1930. Lund, 1976 (mimeo).
'The mortality decline in the first phase of the demographic transition: Swedish experiences', in *Pre-Industrial Population Change*, eds. T. Bengtsson, G. Fridlizius and R. Ohlsson. Stockholm, 1984.
Friis, A. and Glamann, K., *A History of Prices and Wages in Denmark, vol. 1*. Copenhagen, 1958.
Fritz, S., *Studier i svenskt bankväsen 1772–1789*. Stockholm, 1967.
Fuller, W. A., *Introduction to Statistical Time Series*. New York, 1976.
Furtak, T., *Ceny w Gdansku w latach 1701–1815*. Lwow, 1935.
Gadd, C.-J., *Järn och potatis; jordbruk, teknik och social omvandling i Skaraborgs län 1750–1860*. Gothenburg, 1983.
Garden, M., *Lyon et les lyonnais au XVIIIe siècle*. Paris, 1970.
Georgelin, J., *Venise au siècle des lumières*. Paris, 1978.
Gerentz, S., *Kommerskollegium och näringslivet 1651–1951*. Stockholm, 1951.
Gilbert, A. and Gugler, J., *Cities, Poverty and Development; Urbanization in the Third World*. Oxford, 1982.
Gilboy, E. W., *Wages in Eighteenth Century England*. Cambridge, Mass., 1934.
Godechot, J. and Moncassin, S., 'Structures et rélations sociales à Toulouse en 1749 et en 1785', *Annales historiques de la Révolution française*. 1965.
Gorkiewicz, M., *Ceny w Krakowie w latach 1796–1914*. Poznan, 1950.
Goubert, P., 'Sociétés rurales françaises du XVIIIe siècle: vingt paysanneries contrastées', in *Conjoncture économique, structure sociale. Hommage à Ernest Labrousse*. Paris, 1974.
Greenfield, K. R., 'Commerce and new enterprise at Venice, 1830–48', *Journal of Modern History* 11 (1939).
Gustafson, U., *Industrialismens storstad*. Stockholm, 1976.
Hägg, S. A., *Mina levnadsminnen*. Stockholm, 1950.
Hamilton, E. J., 'Profit inflation and the Industrial Revolution, 1751–1800', *Quarterly Journal of Economics* 56 (1941–2).
War and Prices in Spain, 1651–1800. Cambridge, Mass., 1947.
'Prices as a factor in business growth', *Journal of Economic History* 12 (1952).
Hammarström, I., *Stockholm i svensk ekonomi 1850–1914*. Stockholm, 1970.
Hansen, S. A., *Økonomisk vækst i Danmark, vol, 1*. Copenhagen, 1974.

Hansen, V. Falbe, *Hvilke forandringer er der siden Amerikas opdagelse foregaaet i priserna paa Danmarks væsentligste frembringelser*. Copenhagen, 1869.

Harrison, J., *An Economic History of Modern Spain*. Manchester, 1978.

Häusler, W., 'Von der Manufaktur zum Maschinensturm', in *Wien im Vormärz*, eds. R. Banik-Schweitzer, A. Baryli, J. Ehmer, P. Feldbauer, W. Häusler and G. Meissl. Vienna, 1980.

Heckscher, E. F., *Sveriges ekonomiska historia från Gustav Vasa* I:2. Stockholm, 1936.

'De svenska manufakturerna under 1700–talet', *Ekonomisk Tidskrift* 39 (1937).

'Städernas plats i Sveriges samhällshistoria', *Ekonomisk Tidskrift* 40 (1938).

Sveriges ekonomiska historia från Gustav Vasa II:2. Stockholm, 1949.

An Economic History of Sweden. Cambridge, Mass., 1954.

Svenskt arbete och liv. Stockholm, 1968.

Hedlund-Nyström, T., *Svenska kriser och internationella konjunkturer*. Lund, 1970.

Hélin, E., 'Les capitations liègoises', *Anciens pays et assemblées d'états* 21 (1961).

Hellberg, V., 'Turist i Stockholm 1799', *Sankt Eriks årsbok* 1946.

Herlitz, L., *Jordegendom och ränta*. Gothenburg, 1974.

Hildebrand, K.-G., *Fagerstabrukens historia, vol. 1*, Uppsala, 1957.

Hildebrandsson, H. H. 'Sur le prétendu changement du climat européen en temps historiques', *Nova Acta Regiae Societatis Scientiarium Upsaliensis*, 4th Series, vol. 4:5. Uppsala, 1915.

Hirdman, Y., *Magfrågan; mat som mål och medel. Stockholm 1870–1920*. Kristianstad, 1983.

Historisk statistik för Sverige 1. Befolkning 1720–1950. Stockholm, 1955.

Historisk statistik för Sverige 3. Utrikeshandel 1732–1970. Stockholm, 1972.

Hobsbawm, E. J., 'The general crisis of the European economy in the seventeenth century', in *Crisis in Europe, 1560–1660*, ed. T. Aston, London, 1965.

Hofsten, E. and Lundström, H., *Swedish Population History*. Stockholm, 1976.

Högberg, S., *Utrikeshandel och sjöfart på 1700–talet*. Stockholm, 1969.

Stockholms historia 1 2. Stockholm, 1981.

Höjer, T., *Stockholms stads drätselkommission 1814–1864*. Stockholm, 1953.

Sockenstämmor och kommunalförvaltning i Stockholm fram till 1864. Stockholm, 1967.

Horgby, B., *Den disciplinerade arbetaren; brottslighet och social förändring i Norrköping 1850–1910*. Stockholm, 1986.

Hoselitz, B., 'Generative and parasitic cities', *Economic Development and Cultural Change* 3 (1954/5).

Hubbard, W. H., 'Forschungen zur städtischen Haushaltsstruktur am Ende des 19. Jh.:das GRAZHAUS-Projekt', in *Sozialgeschichte der Familie in der Neuzeit Europas*, ed. W. Conze. Stuttgart, 1976.

'Städtische Haushaltsstruktur um die Mitte des 19. Jahrhunderts', in *Moderne Stadtgeschichte*, ed. W. H. Schröder. Stuttgart, 1979.

Hugins, W., *Jacksonian Democracy and the Working Class; a Study of the New York Workingmen's Movement 1829–1837*. Stanford, 1960.

Hunt, E. W. and Botham, F. W., 'Wages in Britain during the industrial revolution', *Economic History Review* 40 (1987).

Hyde, F. E., *Liverpool and the Mersey*. Newton Abbot, 1971.

Imhof, A. E., 'Mortalität im Berlin vom 18. bis 20. Jahrhundert', *Berliner Statistik*, 8 (1977), No. 8.

'Unterschiedliche Einstellung zu Leib und Leben in der Neuzeit', in *Der Mensch und sein Körper von der Antike bis heute*, hrsg. A. E. Imhof. Munich, 1983.

'The amazing simultaneousness of the big differences and the boom in the 19th century', in *Pre-Industrial Population Change*, eds. T. Bengtsson, G. Fridlizius and R. Ohlsson. Stockholm, 1984.

Imhof, A. E., and Lindskog, B., 'Dödsorsakerna i Sydsverige 1749–1773', *Sydsvenska medicinhistoriska sällskapets årsskrift*, 1973.

Isacson, M., *Ekonomisk tillväxt och social differentiering 1680–1860*. Uppsala, 1979.

Jackson, R. V., 'The structure of pay in nineteenth-century Britain', *Economic History Review* 40 (1987).

Jansen, P., 'Poverty in Amsterdam at the close of the eighteenth century', *Acta Historiae Neerlandica* 10 (1978).

Johanson, U., *Fattiga och tiggare i Stockholms stad och län under 1700-talet*. Stockholm, 1984.

Johanson, V. F., 'Markegångspris i Finland åren 1731–1870', *Statistiska översikter* 3 (1926), No. 8.

Johnsen, G., *Folket i Oslo 1801*. Oslo, 1950.

Jonsson, U., *Jordmagnater, landbönder och torpare i sydöstra Södermanland 1800–1880*. Stockholm, 1980.

'Population growth and agrarian economic and social structures: some Swedish examples', in *Pre-Industrial Population Change*, eds. T. Bengtsson, G. Fridlizius and R. Ohlsson. Stockholm, 1984.

'Godsens förändring under 1800-talet; omvandlingsmönster och effekter på befolkningsutvecklingen', *Bebyggelsehistorisk tidskrift* 9 (1985).

Jonsson, U., Köll, A.-M., and Pettersson, R., 'Eine Agrargesellschaft im Wandel', *Zeitschrift für Agrargeschichte und Agrarsoziologie* 28 (1980).

Jörberg, L., *A History of Prices in Sweden, I–II*. Lund, 1972.

Julius, A., *Sverige sett med främlingsögon*. Stockholm, 1930.

Kaplow, J., *The Names of Kings; the Parisian Laboring Poor in the Eighteenth Century*. New York, 1972.

Karlbom, R., *Hungerupplopp och strejker 1793–1867*. Gothenburg, 1967.

Katz, M. B., *The People of Hamilton, Canada West*. Cambridge, Mass., 1975.

Köll, A.-M., *Tradition och reform i västra Södermanlands jordbruk 1810–1890*. Stockholm, 1983.

Kommunalarbetarnas löner i Sverige 1865–1930. Stockholm, 1933.

Krantz, O., 'Production and labour in the Swedish manufactories during the 18th century', *Economy and History* 19 (1976).

Kraus, A., *Die Unterschichten Hamburgs in der erste Hälfte des 19. Jahrhunderts*. Stuttgart, 1965.

Krüger, H., *Zur Geschichte der Manufakturen und der Manufakturarbeiter in Preussen*. Berlin, 1958.

Kruithof, J., De sociale samenstelling van de bevolking te Antwerpen, Brussel, Gent en Luik in 1846–1847. *Handelingen der maatschappij voor Geschiedenis en Oudheidkunde te Gent* 11 (1957).

Kulikoff, A., 'The progress of inequality in Revolutionary Boston', *William and Mary Quarterly* 28 (1971).

Kuznets, S., *Economic Growth and Structure*. London, 1966.
Labrousse, E., 'Les bons prix agricoles du XVIIIe siècle', in *Histoire économique et sociale de la France*, dir. F. Braudel and E. Labrousse. Paris, 1970.
Le prix de froment en France au temps de la monnaie stable. Paris, 1970.
Lager, B., *Stockholms befolkning på Johan III:s tid*. Stockholm, 1962.
Lane, F. C., *Venice; a Maritime Republic*. Baltimore and London, 1973.
Larsson, M., *Arbete och lön vid Bredsjö bruk: en studie av löneprinciper och lönenivåer för olika yrkeskategorier vid Bredsjö bruk 1828–1905*. Uppsala, 1986.
Larsson, T., *Reformen i brännvinslagstiftningen 1854–1855. Förhistorien*. Stockholm, 1945.
Laslett, B., 'Social change and the family: Los Angeles, California, 1850–1870', *American Sociological Review* 42 (1977).
Law, C. M., 'Some notes on the urban population of England and Wales in the eighteenth century', *Local Historian* 10 (1972).
Laxton, P. 'Liverpool in 1801: a manuscript return for the First National Census of Population', *Transactions of the Historical Society of Lancashire and Cheshire* 130 (1981).
Le Roy Ladurie, E., 'Pour un modèle de l'économie rurale française au XVIIIe siècle', *Cahiers d'histoire* 19 (1974).
Le Roy Ladurie, E. and Goy, J., *Tithe and Agrarian History from the Fourteenth to the Nineteenth Centuries*. Cambridge, 1982.
Lévy-Leboyer, M., *Les banques européennes et l'industrialisation internationale dans la première moitié du XIXe siècle*. Paris, 1964.
Lewis, O., *La Vida; A Puerto Rican Family in the Culture of Poverty - San Juan & New York*. New York, 1966.
A Death in the Sánchez Family. New York, 1969.
Liebchen, G., 'Zu den Lebensbedingungen der unteren Schichten im Berlin des Vormärz', in *Untersuchungen zur Geschichte der frühen Industrialisierung vornehmlich im Wirtschaftsraum Berlin/Brandenburg*, hrsg. O. Büsch. Berlin, 1971.
Lindberg, F., 'Stockholm vid tiden för den stora kommunalreformen', *Samfundet Sankt Eriks årsbok*, 1963.
Lindegren, J., 'Den svenska militärstaten 1560–1720', in *Magtstaten i Norden i 1600-tallet og de sociala konsekvenser*, ed. E. Ladewig Pedersen. Odense, 1984.
Lindert, P., *Lucrens Angliae: The Distribution of English Private Wealth since 1670*. Working Paper Series, No. 18–19 (February, 1985). Agricultural History Center, University of California, Davis.
'Unequal English wealth since 1670', *Journal of Political Economy* 94 (1986).
Lindert, P. H., and Williamson, J. G., 'English workers' living standards during the Industrial Revolution: a new look', *Economic History Review* 36 (1983).
Lindgren, H., *Spannmålshandel and spannmålspriser vid Uppsala akademi 1720–1789*. Uppsala, 1971.
Linn, J. F., *Cities in the Developing World*. New York, 1983.
Lis, C., 'Proletarian Networks in Antwerp during the First Half of the Nineteenth Century'. Paper presented at the conference 'Methodological Problems in Urban History', Stockholm, 1984.
Lis, C., and Soly, H., 'Food consumption in Antwerp between 1807 and 1859: a contribution to the standard of living debate', *Economic History Review* 30 (1977).

Poverty and Capitalism in Pre-Industrial Europe. Hassocks, 1979.
Lomnitz, L., *Networks and Marginality: Life in a Mexican Shanty Town*. New York, 1982.
Lundsjö, O., *Fattigdomen på den svenska landsbygden under 1800–talet*. Stockholm, 1975.
Maddalena, A. de, *Prezzi e mercedi a Milano dal 1701 al 1860*. Milan, 1974.
Magnusson, L., *Ty som ingenting angelägnare är än mina bönders conservation*. Uppsala, 1980.
Reduktionen under 1600-talet: debatt och forskning. Malmö, 1985.
'Drinking and the Verlag System 1820–1850: the significance of taverns and drink in Eskilstuna before industrialization', *Scandinavian Economic History Review* 34 (1986).
Martinius, S., *Agrar kapitalbildning och finansiering 1833–1892*. Gothenburg, 1970.
Jordbruk och ekonomisk tillväxt i Sverige 1830–1870. Gothenburg, 1970.
Peasant Destinies; the History of 552 Swedes born 1810–12. Stockholm, 1977.
Jordbrukets omvandling på 1700– och 1800-talen. Lund, 1982.
Marx, K., *Capital*, vol. 1. Aylesbury, 1976.
Matović, M., *Stockholmsäktenskap; familjebildning och partnerval i Stockholm 1850–1890*. Stockholm, 1984.
Maynard, G., *Economic Development and the Price Level*. London, 1962.
Miller, R. and Gerger, T., *Social Change in 19th-Century Swedish Agrarian Society*. Stockholm, 1985.
Minchinton, W. E., 'Bristol – metropolis of the west in the eighteenth century', *Transactions of the Royal Historical Society*, Fifth Series, 4 (1954).
Minnesskrift med anledning av den svenska befolkningsstatistikens 200-åriga bestånd. Stockholm, 1949.
Mitchell, B. R., and Deane, P., *Abstract of British Historical Statistics*. Cambridge, 1962.
Mitchell, B. R., *European Historical Statistics 1750–1970*. London, 1975.
Mitterauer, M., 'Auswirkungen von Urbanisierung und Frühindustrialisierung auf die Familienverfassung an Beispielen des österreichischen Raums', in *Sozialgeschichte der Familie in Neuzeit Europas*, ed. W. Conze. Stuttgart, 1976.
Modée, R. G., *Utdrag utur alla ifrån än 1718 utkomne publique handlingar*, 14. Stockholm, 1804.
Mohl, R. A., *Poverty in New York, 1783–1825*. New York, 1971.
Mokyr, J., *Industrialization in the Low Countries, 1795–1850*. New Haven, 1976.
'The Industrial Revolution and the New Economic History', in *The Economics of the Industrial Revolution*, ed. J. Mokyr. London, 1985.
Mols, R. J. S., *Introduction à la démographie historique des villes d'Europe du XIV*e *au XIX*e *siècle*, 1–3. Louvain, 1954–6.
Morell, M., 'On the stratification of the Swedish peasant class', *Scandinavian Economic History Review* 28 (1980).
Morgan, V., 'Agricultural wage rates in late eighteenth-century Scotland', *Economic History Review* 24 (1971).
Moser, C., 'Informal sector or petty commodity production: dualism or dependence in urban development', *World Development* 6 (1978).
Müller, J., *Fattigvården i Stockholm från äldre till nyare tid*. Stockholm, 1906.
Myrdal, G., *The Cost of Living in Sweden 1830–1930*. London, 1933.

Näsström, G., 'Med gubben Gjörwell i det gustavianska Stockholm', *Sankt Eriks årsbok*, 1972/3.
Nerman, T., *Crusenstolpes kravaller*. Stockholm, 1938.
Nicolas, J., *La Savoie au XVIIIe siècle*. Paris, 1978.
Niephaus, H.-T., *Genuas Seehandel von 1746–1848*. Cologne and Vienna, 1975.
Nisbeth, Å., 'Kungsholms glasbruk', *Sankt Eriks årsbok* 1963.
Nun, J., 'Superpoblación relativa, ejérjito industrial y masa marginal', *Revista Latinoamericana de sociología* 2 (1969).
Nygård, F., and Sandström, A., *Measuring Income Inequality*. Stockholm, 1981.
Nyström, J. F., *Bidrag till svenska handelns och näringarnas historia*, 1. Stockholm, 1884.
Nyström, P., *Stadsindustriens arbetare före 1800-talet*. Stockholm, 1955, reprinted 1983.
Obermann, K., 'Du rôle et du caractère des migrations internes vers Berlin de 1815 à 1875', *Annales de démographie historique* 1971.
Odén, B., 'Socialhistoria i blickpunkten', *Historisk tidskrift* 83 (1963).
Ohlsson, R., and Bengtsson, T., 'Population and economic fluctuations in Sweden 1749–1914', in *Pre-Industrial Population Change*, eds. T. Bengtsson, G. Fridlizius and R. Ohlsson. Stockholm, 1984.
Överståthållarämbetets underdåniga femårsberättelse 1822–1826. Stockholm, 1829.
Överståthållarämbetets underdåniga femårsberättelse 1827–1832. Stockholm, 1834.
Palmer, J. L., *Inflation, Unemployment, and Poverty*. Lexington, Mass., 1973.
Perrenoud, A., *La population de Genève du seizième au début du dix-neuvième siècle*. Geneva, 1977.
'Mortality decline in its secular setting', in *Pre-Industrial Population Change*, eds. T. Bengtsson, G. Fridlizius and R. Ohlsson. Stockholm, 1984.
Perrot, J.-C., *Genèse d'une ville moderne: Caen au XVIIIe siècle, vol. 2*. Paris, 1975.
Pessen, E., *Riches, Class, and Power before the Civil War*. Lexington, Mass 1973.
Phillips, A. D. M. and Walton, J. R., 'The distribution of personal wealth in English towns in mid-nineteenth century', *Transactions. Institute of British Geographers*, 1975.
Poitrineau, A., *La vie rurale en Basse-Auvergne au XVIIIe siècle (1726–1789)*. Paris, 1965.
Pollard, S., *Peaceful Conquest*. Oxford, 1981.
Population. Récensement général 1846. Brussels, 1849.
Population. Récensement général 1856. Brussels, 1861.
Portes, A., and Walton, J., *Labor, Class, and the International System*. New York, 1981.
Posthumus, N. W., *Nederlandische prijsgeschiedenis, vol. 1*. Leiden, 1943.
Poussou, J.-P., *Bordeaux et le Sud-Ouest au XVIIIe siècle*. Paris, 1983.
Preston, S. H., *Mortality Patterns in National Populations. With Special Reference to Recorded Causes of Death*. New York, 1976.
Preston, S. H., and van de Walle, E., 'Urban French mortality in the nineteenth century', *Population Studies*, 32 (1978).
Pribram, A., *Materialien zur Geschichte der Preise und Löhne in Österreich*. Vienna, 1938.
Prix de froment en France au temps de la monnaie stable (1726–1913), ed. E. Labrousse. Paris, 1970.
Puranen, B.-I., *Tuberkulos; en sjukdoms förekomst och dess orsaker. Sverige 1750–1980*. Umeå, 1984.

Quellen zur Bevölkerungs-, Sozial- und Wirtschaftsstatistik Deutschlands, 1815–1875, 1, ed. W. Köllman. Boppard am Rhein, 1980.

Recherches statistiques sur la ville de Paris, I-IV. Paris, 1821–29.

Reenstierna, M. H., *Årstadagboken 1–3. Journaler från åren 1793–1839 utgivna genom S. Erixon, A. Stålhane och S. Wallin*. Stockholm, 1985.

Report on the Sanitary Conditions of the Labouring Population of Great Britain, ed. M. Flinn. Edinburgh, 1965.

Roberts, B., *Cities of Peasants; the Political Economy of Urbanization in the Third World*. London, 1978.

Roberts, M., *Drink, Temperance, and the Working Class in Nineteenth Century Germany*. Boston, 1984.

Romano, R., *Prezzi, salari e servizi a Napoli nel secolo XVIII (1734–1806)*. Milan, 1965.

Rosen, G., 'Debility and disease', in *Victorian cities*, eds. H. J. Dyos and M. Wolf. London, 1973.

Rouel, F., (K. A. af Kullberg), *Minnen från en vistelse i Stockholm åren 1844–45* (Norrköping, 1845).

Rougerie, J., 'Remarques sur l'histoire des salaires à Paris au XIXe siècle', *Mouvement social* 1968.

Rudé, G., 'Prices, wages, and popular movements in Paris during the French Revolution', *Economic History Review* 6 (1954).

Paris and London in the Eighteenth Century. London, 1970.

Rystad, G., 'Till frågan om tjänster och löner inom kansliet under frihetstiden', *Historisk tidskrift* 86 (1966).

Samuelsson, K., 'Den ekonomiska betydelsen för Stockholm av Finlands förlust', *Forum navale* 6 (1945).

De stora köpmanshusen i Stockholm 1730–1815. Stockholm, 1951.

Sandgruber, R., *Die Anfänge der Konsumgesellschaft*. Munich, 1982.

Schellenberg, W., *Die Bevölkerung der stadt Zürich um 1780*. Affoltern am Albis, 1951.

Scholliers, E., 'De materiele verschijningvormen van de armoede voor de industriele revolutie', *Tijdschrift voor geschiedenis* 88 (1975).

Schön, L., *Från hantverk till fabriksindustri; svensk textiltillverkning 1820–1870*. Lund, 1979.

Industrialismens förutsättningar. Lund, 1982.

Schwarz, K., *Die Lage der Handwerksgesellen in Bremen während des 18. Jahrhunderts*. Bremen, 1975.

Schwarz, L. D., 'Income distribution and social structure in London in the late eighteenth century', *Economic History Review* 32 (1979).

'The standard of living in the long run: London, 1700–1860', *Economic History Review* 38 (1985).

Scottish Population History, ed. M. Flinn. Cambridge, 1977.

Seventh Census of the United States: 1850. Washington, 1853.

Sewell, W. H. Jr., 'Social change and the rise of working-class politics in nineteenth-century Marseille', *Past and Present* 65 (1974).

Structure and Mobility. The Men and Women of Marseille, 1820–1870. Cambridge, 1985.

Sharlin, A., 'Natural decrease in early modern cities: a reconsideration', *Past and Present* 79 (1978).

Shorter, E., 'Female emancipation. Birth control and fertility in European history', *American Historical Review* 78 (1973).

The Making of the Modern Family. New York, 1975.
Siegel, S., *Ceny w Warszawie w latach 1816–1914*. Poznan, 1949.
Simonsson, I., 'Fredmansdiktens verklighet', *Bellmansstudier* 2 (1926).
Singer-Kérel, J., *Le coût de la vie à Paris de 1840 à 1954*. Paris, 1961.
Slicher van Bath, B. H., *The Agrarian History of Western Europe A.D. 500–1850*. London, 1963.
'Les problèmes fondamentaux de la société pré-industrielle en Europe occidentale', *A. A. G. Bijdragen* 12 (1965).
Smith, C. R., *The People's Health 1830–1914*. London, 1978.
Snell, K. D. M., Annals of the Labouring Poor. Social Change and Agrarian England 1660–1900. Cambridge, 1985.
Söderberg, J., *Agrar fattigdom i Sydsverige under 1800-talet*. Stockholm, 1978.
'Causes of poverty in Sweden during the nineteenth century', *Journal of European Economic History* 11 (1982).
'A long-term perspective on regional economic growth in Sweden', *Scandinavian Economic History Review* 32 (1984).
'Stockholm på 1700–talet: metropol i stagnation', *Folkets Historia* 13 (1985).
'Trends in inequality in Sweden, 1700–1914', *Historisch-Sozialwissenschaftliche Forschungen* 21 (1987).
'Wage differentials in Sweden, 1725–1950', in *Income Distribution in Historical Perspective*, ed. Y. S. Brenner, H. Kaelble and M. Thomas. In press.
Söderberg, J., and Jansson, A., 'Corn-price rises and equalisation: real wages in Stockholm 1650–1719', *Scandinavian Economic History Review* 36:2 (1988).
Söderberg, J., and Lundgren, N.-G., *Ekonomisk och geografisk koncentration i Sverige 1850–1914*. Lund, 1982.
Söderberg, T., *Den namnlösa medelklassen*. Stockholm, 1956.
Söderlund, E., *Stockholms hantverkarklass 1720–1772*. Stockholm, 1943.
Hantverkarna II. Stockholm, 1949.
Soltow, L., 'The Swedish census of wealth at the beginning of the 19th century', *Scandinavian Economic History Review* 33 (1985).
Soubeyroux, J., *Paupérisme et rapports sociaux à Madrid au XVIIIe siècle, vol. 1*. Paris, 1978.
Sperlings, S., 'Violent criminality and social control during Stockholm's industrialization', *Scandinavian Studies in Criminology* 7 (1980).
Stadin, K., *Småstäder, småborgare och stora samhällsförändringar*. Uppsala, 1979.
'Skattepolitiken och de kapitalistiska företagen 1719–1812', *Historisk tidskrift* 102 (1982).
Staf, N., 'Mantals- och taxeringslängder i Stadsarkivet', *Stockholms stads arkivnämnd och stadsarkiv. Årsberättelse*, 1932.
Polisväsendet i Stockholm 1776–1850. Uppsala, 1950.
Statistik der Stadt Wien, 2. Vienna, 1861.
Statistique de la France, S. 2, Tome 2. Paris, 1855.
Statistische Tableus über die Bewegung der Bevölkerung. Vienna, 1869.
Statistisk årsbok för Stockholms stad 38. Stockholm, 1905.
Statistisk årsbok för Stockholms stad 84. Stockholm, 1953.
Statistisk tidskrift 1 (1860). Stockholm.
Statistisk tabelværk, N.R., 12. Copenhagen, 1856.
Stearns, P. N., *The Revolutions of 1848*. London, 1974.
Stockholms stads pris-courant. Stockholm, 1740–76.
Stockholms wecko-blad. Stockholm, 1745–79.
Stolnitz, G. A., 'A century of mortality trends II', *Population Studies* 10 (1956).

Strindberg, A., *Arbetare och radikaler i 1700–talets Sverige*. Stockholm, 1935.

Sundbärg, G., 'Dödligheten i lungtuberkulos i Sverige åren 1791/1830', *Statistisk Tidskrift*, 1905.

Sundbärg, G., *Bevölkerungsstatistik Schwedens 1750–1900*. Stockholm, 1907, reprinted 1970.

Svenskt biografiskt lexikon 16. Stockholm, 1964.

The History of Working-Class Housing, ed. S. Chapman. London, 1971.

Thestrup, P., *The Standard of Living in Copenhagen 1730–1800*. Copenhagen, 1971.

Thienel, I., *Städtewachstum in Industrialisierungsprozess des 19. Jahrhunderts*. Berlin, 1973.

Titmuss, R. M., *Poverty and Wealth: A Study of Infant Mortality*. London, 1943.

Tomaszewski, E., *Ceny w Krakowie w latach 1601–1795*. Lwow, 1934.

Uitkomsten der derde tienjarige volkstelling in het Koningrijk der Nederlanden ... 1849. The Hague, 1852.

Ullenhag, K., *Sörkörare; bönder med lärft på lassen från norra Ångermanland 1750–1850*. Bjästa, 1982.

Underdånigt betänkande afgifvet af de för uppgörande af förslag till ny tulltaxa ... komiterade. Stockholm, 1863.

Underdånigt betänkande angående Sveriges ekonomiska och finansiella utveckling under åren 1834–1860. Stockholm, 1863.

Uselding, P., 'Wage and consumptions levels in England and on the Continent in the 1830s', *Journal of European Economic History* 4 (1975).

Utterström, G., 'Stockholms folkmängd 1663–1763', in *Historiska studier tillägnade Nils Ahnlund*. Stockholm, 1949.

'Befolkningsutveckling och näringsliv efter mitten av 1700-talet', in: *En bok om Mälardalen*. Stockholm, 1953.

'Some population problems in pre-industrial Sweden', *Scandinavian Economic History Review* 2 (1954).

Jordbrukets arbetare II. Stockholm, 1957.

Valentine, C. A., *Culture and Poverty; Critique and Counter-Proposals*. Chicago, 1968.

Vandenbroeke, C., 'L'alimentation à Gand pendant la première moitié du XIXe siècle', *Annales E. S. C.* 30 (1975).

'Mutations économiques et sociales en Flandre au cours de la phase proto-industrielle, 1650–1850', *Revue du Nord* 63 (1981).

Verhaegen, A., 'Note sur le travail et les salaires en Belgique au XVIIIe siècle', *Bulletin de l'Institut de recherches économiques et sociales* 19 (1953).

Viennot, J.-P., 'La population de Dijon après le récensement de 1851', *Annales de démographie historique* 1969.

Vigo, G., 'Real wages of the working class in Italy: building workers' wages (14th to 18th century)', *Journal of European Economic History* 3 (1974).

Vilar, P., 'Elan urbain et mouvement des salaires dans le bâtiment: le cas de Barcelone au XVIIIe siècle', *Revue d'histoire économique et sociale* 28 (1950).

'La Catalogne industrielle', in *L'industrialisation en Europe au XIXe siècle'*, eds. P. Léon, F. Crouzet and R. Gascon. Paris, 1972.

Wallgren, H., *Sveriges bageriidkarförening och Stockholms bageriidkarförening. Minnesskrift*. Stockholm, 1924.

Ward, D., 'Environs and neighbours in the "two nations": residential differentiation in mid-nineteenth-century Leeds', *Journal of Historical Geography* 6 (1980).
William-Olsson, W., *Huvuddragen av Stockholms geografiska utveckling 1850–1930*. Stockholm, 1937.
Williamson, J. G., *Did British Capitalism Breed Inequality?* Boston, 1985.
Williamson, J. G. and Lindert, P. H., *American Inequality*. New York, 1980.
Winberg, C., *Folkökning och proletarisering*. Gothenburg, 1975.
'Giftas på stockholmska', *Historisk tidskrift* 106 (1986).
Wohl, A. S., 'Unfit for human habitation', in *Victorian cities*, ed. H. J. Dyos and M. Wolf. London, 1973.
The Eternal Slum. London, 1977.
Wollin, N. G., *Industrierna vid Hargs ström under fyra sekler*. Stockholm, 1943.
Wretlind, W., *Undersökningar rörande Stockholms mortalitet*. Stockholm, 1866. (*Medicinskt arkiv*, III).
Wrigley, E. A. and Schofield, R. S., *The Population History of England, 1541–1871*. London, 1981.
Zacke, B., *Koleraepidemin i Stockholm 1834*. Stockholm, 1971.
Zethelius, G., 'Stockholms-varven under 1700-talet', *Sjöhistorisk årsbok* 1955/6.

Index

Cambridge Studies in Population, Economy and Society in Past Time

1 *Land, kinship and life-cycle* edited by RICHARD M. SMITH.
2 *Annals of the labouring poor: social change and agrarian England 1660–1900* K. D. M. SNELL*
3 *Migration in a mature economy: emigration and internal migration in England and Wales 1861–1900* DUDLEY BAINES
4 *Scottish literacy and the Scottish identity: illiteracy and society in Scotland and northern England 1600–1800* R. A. HOUSTON
5 *Neighbourhood and society: a London suburb in the seventeenth century* JEREMY BOULTON
6 *Demographic behavior in the past: a study of fourteen German village populations in the nineteenth century* JOHN E. KNODEL
7 *Worlds within worlds: structures of life in sixteenth-century London* STEVE RAPPAPORT
8 *Upland communities: environment, population and social structure in the Alps since the sixteenth century* PIER PAOLO VIAZZO
9 *Height, health and history: nutritional status in the United Kingdom 1750–1980* RODERICK FLOUD, KENNETH WACHTER and ANNABEL GREGORY
10 *Famine, disease and the social order in early modern society* edited by JOHN WALTER and ROGER SCHOFIELD
11 *A general view of the rural economy of England, 1538–1840* ANN KUSSMAUL
12 *Town and country in pre-industrial Spain: Cuenca 1540–1870* DAVID REHER
13 *A stagnating metropolis: the economy and demography of Stockholm 1750–1850* JOHAN SÖDERBERG, ULF JONSSON and CHRISTER PERSSON

Titles available in paperback are marked with an asterisk.